Nickelodeon Nation

Nickelodeon Nation

The History, Politics, and Economics of America's Only TV Channel for Kids

EDITED BY

Heather Hendershot

NEW YORK UNIVERSITY PRESS

New York and London

NEW YORK UNIVERSITY PRESS
New York and London
www.nyupress.org

Library of Congress Cataloging-in-Publication Data
Nickelodeon nation : the history, politics, and economics of
America's only TV channel for kids / edited by Heather Hendershot.
p. cm.
Includes bibliographical references and index.
ISBN 0–8147–3651–3 (alk. paper) —
ISBN 0–8147–3652–1 (pbk : alk. paper)
1. Nickelodeon (Television network). 2. Television programs
for children—United States. I. Hendershot, Heather.
PN1992.92.N55N53 2001
384.55'23'0973—dc22 2003020601

New York University Press books are printed on acid-free paper,
and their binding materials are chosen for strength and durability.

Manufactured in the United States of America

c 10 9 8 7 6 5 4 3 2 1
p 10 9 8 7 6 5 4 3 2 1

Contents

III Programs and Politics

IV Viewers

Introduction

Nickelodeon and the Business of Fun

Heather Hendershot

How big a deal is Nickelodeon? Well, everyone knows that America's most popular cartoon characters are cross-promoted with fast-food restaurants. Characters from summer blockbusters inevitably end up festooned on Taco Bell drink cups, and cheap plastic action figures are a common prize included in MacDonald's Happy Meals. For many years, Disney has excelled at promoting its family movies via product tie-ins with fast-food companies. Looking to switch partners, in 1998 Disney terminated its contract with Burger King, ending an arrangement that for ten years had well served both companies. One would think this would be a major loss for Burger King. Undaunted, though, the fast-food chain quickly signed a contract with children's television producer Nickelodeon, and soon thereafter sales of Burger King's Rugrats wristwatches exceeded the volume of previous promotional tie-ins for both *The Lion King* and *Pocahontas*. *The Rugrats Movie,* in fact, quickly grossed over $100 million, officially qualifying the film as a blockbuster. That Nickelodeon was able to take over when Disney jumped ship is a testament to the company's strength in the children's media marketplace.

In just twenty years, Nickelodeon has established itself as a powerful competitor for Disney's audience. Unlike Disney, of course, Nickelodeon is best known not as a film producer but as a television channel—and a very successful one. Since 1996, Nick has ranked *number one* in daytime ratings. As the networks have lost their grip on the child audience, Nickelodeon has only gotten stronger. In fact, when CBS sought to bolster its sagging Saturday morning ratings in 2000, it turned to Nick for programming. CBS's overall ratings for Saturday morning kids' shows immediately shot up 250 percent, and ratings for its preschool shows increased by 550 percent. In terms of dollars and cents, Nick is clearly a big deal.

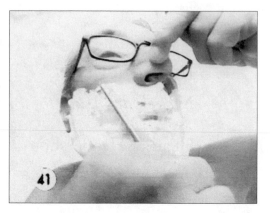

Unlike children, adults must shave . . .
Frame grab from *How to Nickelodeon* video. © 1992 MTV Networks.

Nickelodeon's impact, however, far exceeds its status as a successful operator in the children's media marketplace. Nick is also an important cultural phenomenon. Like Disney and Sesame Workshop (formerly the Children's Television Workshop), Nick is a brand that most adults consider safe and trustworthy. Nickelodeon shows won't inspire kids to kick and punch each other. They are more likely to hinge on interpersonal relationships

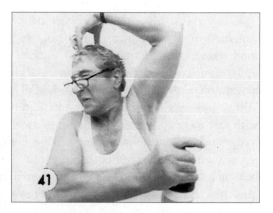

. . . use deodorant . . .
Frame grab from *How to Nickelodeon* video. © 1992 MTV Networks.

than on good versus evil morality tales, and they don't show a world in which only white boys have brains. And some shows, like *SpongeBob SquarePants*, are equally loved by both adults and kids. How has Nickelodeon found such phenomenal success?

Nickelodeon succeeds, in large part, by simultaneously satisfying both children and adults. For kids, Nick offers gross-out jokes and no-holds-barred goofiness, while for adults it offers a violence-free world, ethnic

... and go to work.
Frame grab from *How to Nickelodeon* video. © 1992 MTV Networks.

Adults are hopelessly square.
Frame grab from *How to Nickelodeon* video. © 1992 MTV Networks.

and racial diversity, and gender parity. Nick gives kids the fun they want by gently violating adult ideas of propriety, and it satisfies adults by conforming to their vision of "quality" children's programming. To put it bluntly, parents are willing to tolerate gags about burps, pee, and poopy diapers in exchange for programming that is sensitive to racism and sexism and doesn't show anyone getting pummeled with anvils. Of course, Nick's appeal to kids is not limited to gross-out humor. In particular, Nick successfully emphasizes the differences between children and adults. In a nutshell: adults are boring, kids are fun. This is made explicit in an early nineties Nick promotional spot: adults have to do terrible things like shave their faces, use deodorant, and go to work. Adults are hopelessly square. But not so square that they can't enjoy a program like *Rugrats,* which gently parodies adults and includes jokes that make more sense to adults than to kids.

Given the surge in interesting research on children's media, it is surprising that more research has not been published on Nickelodeon. More attention tends to go to the faddish, profitable hit shows—like *Pokémon*—that seize the limelight every few years. But even writing on fad shows is a recent phenomenon. Fifteen years ago, a reader looking for a critical perspective on children's television would have had limited choices: William Melody's *Children's Television: The Economics of Exploitation,* Cy Schneider's *Children's Television: The Art, the Business and How It Works,* a handful of books by the creators of *Sesame Street,* and a variety of social scientific articles published in scholarly journals.[1] Since then, the amount of scholarly work on children's media has grown dramatically, and there now exists a wide-ranging literature on the history, economics, culture, and politics of children's television.[2]

Yet in all of this work—with the exception of books about *Sesame Street*—there is a striking lack of emphasis on individual television producers or production companies like Nickelodeon. While film scholars have given us portraits of specific studios and directors, television scholars have focused less on specific "auteurs" (individual or corporate).[3] Television is even more the product of assembly-line production than film is, which makes it difficult to associate specific styles with specific creators. Yet even if the individual auteur is hard to pin down—with clear exceptions such as Stephen Bochco, David Kelley, Joss Whedon, Chris Carter, and now HBO, a sort of NC-17 version of MTM (the company which produced *The Mary Tyler Moore Show* and had a reputation for "quality" programs)—it is clear that individual networks have aggressively forged "brand identities" for themselves as a way of standing out in the increasingly diversified cable environment.[4] While individual creators may not come to mind when we think of VH1, MTV, BET, Showtime, or Lifetime, we do know what style of programs airs on each of these networks. In terms of forging a clear brand identity, Nickelodeon is exceptionally successful. As everyone knows, it is the only channel for kids. Nick devotes sixteen hours a day to children's programming and has surpassed all the other networks in terms of claiming the child audience.

In discussing the many facets of Nickelodeon, this book seeks to increase our understanding of both contemporary children's culture and the television industry. The methodologically diverse essays in *Nickelodeon Nation* are grouped into four sections. Part I focuses on economics and marketing. Norma Pecora covers the nuts-and-bolts issues: who has owned Nickelodeon (from Warner Communications to Viacom), what kinds of synergies have fueled its success, and, most centrally, how it has functioned differently under its three different heads, Cy Schneider (1980–1984), Geraldine Laybourne (1985–1995), and Herb Scannell

(1996–present). Pecora also situates the changes that Nickelodeon has undergone within the wider picture of the industrial history of children's programming in the United States. Kevin Sandler examines Nickelodeon's marketing tactics, explaining the company's promotional strategies and how it has successfully branded itself. Susan Murray discusses Nickelodeon's evening programming, Nick at Nite, and the reincarnation of this programming niche as a separate channel, TV Land. Murray argues that with Nick at Nite and TV Land, Nickelodeon sells adults a reassuring idea of childhood. Adults can nostalgically revisit their youth via baby-boomer shows such as *The Donna Reed Show,* while at the same time ironically, and pleasurably, distancing themselves from such frivolous, youthful diversions. With these ironized reruns, Nickelodeon uses the concept of "the child in all of us" to widen its audience beyond the children's market.

Part II takes us behind the scenes to examine the Nickelodeon production process. Here, the focus is not on Nickelodeon as a massive corporate entity but rather as an enterprise dependent on real people, the creative employees who actually shape the programming. Linda Simensky, who worked in the animation department at Nick from 1989 to 1995, gives a detailed account of the genesis of "Nick Toons," Nickelodeon's original animation block, which was developed through a time-consuming pilot system. The pilot process is laborious and expensive and, while common in adult programming, quite unusual in the children's television world.[5] Simensky explains how Nickelodeon undertook eight pilots (of which three made it on the air and succeeded), and why it decided to create original characters at a time when television was dominated by programs based on preexisting licensed characters. Mimi Swartz recounts the production history of Nickelodeon's first major cartoon hit, *The Rugrats,* exploring in particular the animators' disagreements over how nasty their toddler villain, Angelica, could be. Ellen Seiter and Vicki Mayer draw on interviews with children's television producers to discuss Nickelodeon's gender and race politics and its position in relationship to other children's television producers in today's postnetwork environment. Although Nickelodeon programming has broken new ground in terms of race and gender parity, other producers see this as more threatening than revolutionary. Amazingly, even after Nickelodeon has produced shows that are equally enjoyed by boys and girls, other children's television producers continue to maintain the attitude they have held for years: girls may watch boys' shows, but boys will not watch girls' shows. Finally, Henry

Jenkins interviews former Nickelodeon president Geraldine Laybourne, who explains how Nick went from being the "green vegetable" network—full of goody two-shoes shows that adults thought were good for kids—to a supercool network with some of the most successful shows on the air.

Part III of the book focuses on specific programs. Mark Langer discusses *Ren & Stimpy,* a program that also figures in both Sandler's and Simensky's essays. What was a kids' network doing producing such a naughty cartoon, and one which, to everyone's embarrassment, children really seemed to love? Since Sandler focuses on marketing, for him the show is what one might call a "branding error," a program that could not, at least under the hand of its creator John Kricfalusi, be appropriate for a network that had branded itself as a kids-only world. Simensky, focusing on Nickelodeon's creator-driven animation, notes that once Kricfalusi was fired, Nick had a creator-driven show without a creator. Langer offers a different angle, arguing that "while Nickelodeon sought to provide a product for a juvenile or juvenile-oriented audience, Kricfalusi's product was influenced by his participation in a postmodernist young adult fan culture" of what Langer calls "animatophiles." After repeatedly censoring Kricfalusi for being too masochistic, phallic, and scatological, Nickelodeon finally let him go.

My own essay charts the rise of *SpongeBob SquarePants,* currently the hottest children's show on the air. Like most popular children's shows, *SpongeBob* has spun off a plethora of licensed merchandise. In 2002, Nickelodeon grossed $700 million on SpongeBob products. In addition to examining the show's financial success, my essay dissects the program's intergenerational appeal and the ways its characters perform their age, gender, and sexuality. *SpongeBob,* I argue, brilliantly illustrates the ways in which the boundaries between children and adults can, as David Buckingham has shown, be simultaneously blurred and reinforced.[6]

Sarah Banet-Weiser writes on Nick's discourses of "citizenship," "rights," and "empowerment," looking in particular at *The Rugrats* and *Nick News.* "How does Nickelodeon respond to the tensions between politics and consumerism in definitions of citizenship?" Banet-Weiser asks. With great audacity, Nick promotes itself as "Nickelodeon Nation." One advertising spot from the early nineties even appropriated the Statue of Liberty as a kids' icon: underneath those austere robes, she's wearing sneakers! Rather than dismissing Nickelodeon's idea of the consumer-citizen as inherently tainted, Banet-Weiser examines the tension

SpongeBob SquarePants is popular with both kids and adults, and has spawned a wide variety of profitable merchandise.

inherent in the idea of the consumer-citizen and investigates exactly *how* Nickelodeon defines the child as both a free liberal subject and a consumer.

Part IV, the final section, turns to viewers. Daniel R. Anderson's essay describes his studies of the attention patterns and comprehension of child television viewers and how, as a consultant for Nickelodeon, he applied his knowledge of child development theory to the development of *Blue's Clues* and other programs. Reacting strongly against the standard "couch potato" conceptualization of young viewers, Anderson persuasively argues for the active nature of the child's viewing experience and for the positive potential of television to educate children.

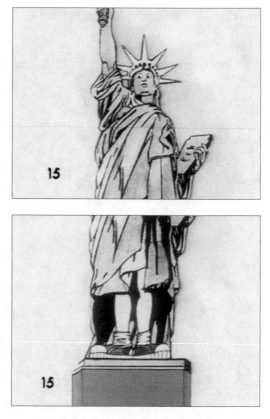

Nickelodeon's Statue of Liberty wears tennis shoes beneath her gown.
Frame grabs from *How to Nickelodeon* video. © 1992 MTV Networks.

Nickelodeon Nation is far from definitive. The section on production, for example, cannot possibly cover the history of all Nickelodeon programs, and the short section on audiences could easily be expanded into an entire volume, or even several volumes. This book, then, has a modest ambition: to take a first step toward understanding the Nickelodeon phenomenon. Hopefully, much more research will follow.

. . .

Nickelodeon will clearly play a crucial role in the future of children's TV. Yet it is also indebted to the past insofar as its roots are tangled in the regulatory history of children's television. In 1969, the FCC ruled that ABC's kids' show *Hot Wheels* was inappropriate; it was obviously a "program length commercial." Network executives might have seen children's shows as little more than the padding between ads, but shows could not actually be designed to advertise toys. In the 1980s, when the Reagan FCC deregulated television, children's television experienced a boom. Suddenly, to the despair of many activists and parents, the airwaves were flooded with toy-driven shows like *He-Man and the Masters of the Universe, The Care Bears,* and *My Little Pony.* Where was the creativity?

When Geraldine Laybourne took over Nickelodeon, she saw the same thing that activists like Action for Children's Television did: kids' shows were created in mass-produced sixty-five-program syndicated packages. If someone could take an initial loss and create better, more creative shows, it would pay off in the future. Trendy toy-driven shows tend to oversaturate the marketplace and then crash and burn. Higher quality programming would not only serve kids, but it would also have staying power. Nickelodeon would create a library of programs that could, in theory, be repeated indefinitely. The *Rugrats* would be the new Roadrunner cartoons: brilliant and timeless. (Nickelodeon has, arguably, achieved this to an even greater extent with *SpongeBob SquarePants* than it did with *Rugrats.*) Nickelodeon succeeded because the product-based shows, which owed their existence to deregulation, had drastically lowered the standards of children's TV.[7] There was a vacuum waiting to be filled.

Nickelodeon really took off with its original Nicktoons programming in 1991. "Rather than being driven by toy companies and marketing concerns and finding (at best) short-term success," as Simensky explains in her contribution to this volume, "animated shows for kid audiences can succeed in a much greater way when driven by creative forces." With Nicktoons, Nick proved that cartoons could be about more than toys. And then they started to sell toys. By the late 1990s, money spent for advertising on children's television had increased to $1 billion annually. Nickelodeon was responsible, in part, but there was also the Disney Channel, and PBS increased its children's television offerings. Not only were there more shows than ever before, but shows were even broken down by age; TV shows used to be for "two-to-eleven-year-olds," but now there was a dramatic increase in preschool shows. A 2002 article in *Newsweek* gave credit to PBS's *Barney and Friends* for creating the preschool programming boom. After PBS launched *Barney* in 1992, "kids went wild, and merchandise flew off the shelves. Until then, Nickelodeon and Disney had been content to leave pre-school shows to the do-gooders at PBS. Now they saw gold."[8] In sum, it seems that the amount of children's television has increased, and programming has improved, in large part because of the rise of cable and the competition between Nickelodeon, PBS, and the Disney Channel. One might speculate that the rise of videos and DVDs is also an important factor: if parents can pop in a tape instead of turning on a show, the shows have to improve to compete.

So where is children's television going from here, and what will Nickelodeon's role be? Conceptualized by Laybourne in opposition to the toy-driven shows of the eighties, under current president Herb Scannell Nickelodeon appears to be increasing its toy output. While *SpongeBob SquarePants* (developed under Scannell) and *Rugrats* were slowly developed, and then licensed out for toys and other merchandise, *Jimmy Neutron: Boy Genius* evolved in a way that was strangely reminiscent of the eighties cartoons. The TV show was preceded by massive advertising, a film in 2001, a video game, and toys, before the lackluster television program finally premiered in 2002. Under Laybourne, Nickelodeon achieved its Golden Age. It will certainly continue to be highly profitable, and Nick should be very proud of the brilliant *SpongeBob SquarePants*. But is *Jimmy Neutron* a model for future ventures? If so, Nickelodeon may well be a victim of its own commercial success.

NOTES

1. Cy Schneider, *Children's Television: The Art, the Business and How It Works* (Chicago: NTC Business Books, 1987); William Melody, *Children's Television: The Economics of Exploitation* (New Haven: Yale University Press, 1973); Edward L. Palmer, *Television and America's Children: A Crisis of Neglect* (New York: Oxford University Press, 1988) and *Children in the Cradle of Television* (Lexington, Mass.: Lexington Books, 1987); Gerald S. Lesser, *Children and Television: Lessons from Sesame Street* (New York: Random House, 1974); Richard M. Polsky, *Getting to Sesame Street: Origins of the Children's Television Workshop* (New York: Praeger, 1974).

2. See, for example: Ellen Seiter, *Sold Separately: Parents and Children in Consumer Culture* (New Brunswick: Rutgers University Press, 1993) and *Television and New Media Audiences* (Oxford: Oxford University Press, 1999); Marsha Kinder, *Playing with Power in Movies, Television and Video Games: From*

Muppet Babies to Teenage Mutant Ninja Turtles (Berkeley: University of California Press, 1991) and her edited collection *Kid's Media Culture* (Durham, N.C.: Duke University Press, 1999); Norma Odom Pecora, *The Business of Children's Entertainment* (New York: Guilford, 1998); Henry Jenkins, ed., *The Children's Culture Reader* (New York: NYU Press, 1988); and Jerome L. Singer and Dorothy G. Singer, eds., *Handbook of Children and the Media* (Thousand Oaks: Sage, 2001). David Buckingham is one of the most prolific, and interesting, writers on children's television. See, for example, *After the Death of Childhood: Growing Up in the Age of Electronic Media* (Cambridge: Polity Press, 2000), *Children Talking Television: The Making of Television Literacy* (London: Falmer, 1993), and *The Making of Citizens: Young People, News and Politics* (London: Routledge, 2000).

3. There are several obvious exceptions: Jane Feuer, Paul Kerr, and Tise Vahimagi, eds., *MTM: Quality Television* (London: BFI, 1984); Horace Newcomb and Robert S. Alley, eds., *The Producer's Medium: Conversations with Creators of American Television* (New York: Oxford University Press, 1983); Christopher Anderson, *Hollywood TV: The Studio System in the Fifties* (Austin: University of Texas Press, 1994); Julie D'Acci, ed., *Camera Obscura*, 33–34, special issue on Lifetime.

4. See Kevin S. Sandler, "Synergy Nirvana: Brand Equity, Television Animation, and Cartoon Network," in Carole A. Stabile and Mark Harrison, eds., *Prime Time Animation: Television Animation and American Culture* (New York: Routledge, 2003), 89–109.

5. Other producers of children's programs have learned from Nickelodeon's success with the pilot process. Allen Larson argues that a successful Hanna-Barbera short initiative undertaken by Cartoon Network in 1993 "set in motion a new animation economy in which the potential for long-term profits was seen to warrant large capital investment in an experimental 'laboratory' production environment where much of what was produced would never be further developed. . . . [T]he venture begat *Dexter's Laboratory, Cow and Chicken,* and *Johnny Bravo . . ."* (69). "Redrawing the Bottom Line" in Stabile and Harrison, 55–73. Although Larson does not credit Nickelodeon as a model for Cartoon Network, it is hard to believe that the Network was not at least partially inspired by the 1991 success of Nick's "laboratory" productions *Doug, Rugrats,* and *The Ren & Stimpy Show.*

6. Buckingham, *After the Death of Childhood.*

7. This is not to say that the product-based shows were utterly without interest. See Seiter, 1993; Kinder, 1991; and Heather Hendershot, *Saturday Morning Censors: Television Regulation before the V-Chip* (Durham, N.C.: Duke University Press, 1998). Adults insisted that the shows were nothing but ads and lacked complex characterization and aesthetic value, but many young viewers formed intense connections with programs such as *Strawberry Shortcake* and *He-Man*

and the Masters of the Universe. Still, there is no denying that these shows bear the signs of quick mass-production and that they were designed to sell licensed products. Nickelodeon is also happy to make a mint off of toy tie-ins, yet their productions are clearly more expensive and aesthetically innovative than most of the popular shows of the 1980s.

8. Daniel McGinn, "Guilt Free TV," *Newsweek* (November 11, 2002): 56.

PART I

Economics and Marketing

1

Nickelodeon Grows Up

The Economic Evolution of a Network

Norma Pecora

In 1973, William Melody and Wendy Ehrlich wrote: "As the commercial broadcasting system continues to evolve, there is no reason to believe that the process of market specialization in providing children's audiences for advertisers will not become more intense, more precise, and more persuasive."[1] Within five years, Warner Cable Company launched Nickelodeon, the first television outlet specifically for children—all kids, all the time—and Melody and Ehrlich's prophecy was on the way to fulfillment. What Melody and Ehrlich could not foresee was the structural change to the television industry, brought about by cable content providers, allowing "more intense, more precise, and more persuasive" marketing to children. The introduction of cable created precisely the kind of system they had predicted. This essay traces the corporate evolution of Nickelodeon and its contribution to the children's entertainment industry. Along the way we will pause to consider, first, Warner Communications, Inc. and later, Viacom, the corporate parents to Nickelodeon. As we will see, Nickelodeon has been more than just a venue for children's entertainment; it has also served as a Pied Piper bringing cable into the community and the home by way of the children; and, more recently, it has become a model for those in the children's entertainment industry.

Nickelodeon went on the air on April 1, 1979 with programming exclusively for children—nothing comparable existed.[2] Initially hours were filled with *Pinwheel*, a program concept that had been part of QUBE, Warner Cable Company's experimental interactive television service. Other programs were *Video Comic Books*; *Nickel Flicks*, movie cliffhangers; and *By the Way*, a live-action, informational program.[3] The

largest block of programming, *Pinwheel,* was a mix of puppets, live action, and cartoons designed to offer, "pro-social, non-stereotypical children's programming [that] became a package used in franchising . . . attractive to town fathers and state governors."[4] It served as both a lure and
a shill. According to one source: "While Nick has worked to reinforce the
'kids only' image, it's also worked to bolster its identification with
adults—particularly advertisers—and with parents, who decide whether
or not to hook up cable."[5]

Cy Schneider, then an executive with the advertising agency Ogilvy
and Mather, was hired in 1980 to build Nickelodeon's programming base
and reputation. Schneider claimed that: "Nickelodeon, for all its lofty
aims and subsequent broadcasting awards, was and is, a product born of
the demands of the marketplace. Very little quality television for children
existed. We believed there was a small market for it, and we could fill that
void. Beyond that, our customers, the cable operator universe, wanted it,
needed it, and would pay for it."[6] In other words, when Warner Cable
Company went in to negotiate a community cable franchise, it was able
to offer something not available on broadcast television or from other
cable systems operators, namely, quality programming for children. It
was, quoting a trade magazine of the time, "hearty, wholesome programming that will delight PTAs, community groups and just plain anxious parents . . . as well as the kids."[7]

Nickelodeon grew from this block of local children's programming on
QUBE to become the dominant children's television entertainment
venue.[8] Nickelodeon can now be seen 24/7, and it has branded retail
products and crossed platforms into books, movies, videos, and software.
As of 2001, the audience was reported to be 300 million children *worldwide,* reaching more than 75 percent of the U.S. audience.[9] Nickelodeon
reflects the growing market specialization of children's television, but the
channel's corporate evolution also reflects many of the changes in the
media industry. Starting out as a part of Warner Communications, one of
the first companies to enter the cable market, Nickelodeon is now a part
of Viacom with holdings across the industry. This is the story of its growth
from 1979 to the present, during which time three individuals guided
Nickelodeon: Cy Schneider, Geraldine Laybourne, and Herb Scannell.

Douglas Gomery warns us of the dangers of "great man" theorizing.
In a discussion of another children's powerhouse—Disney—he claims:
"We are fools if we ascribe all the actions and strategies of a company to
one man or woman."[10] For the most part I would agree that structural

changes within an economic system, not individual "greatness," drive decisions within the entertainment industry. However, in the case of Nickelodeon, I would argue that the "actions and strategies of a company" have been directed by those thought best able to carry out its corporate philosophy. Consequently, this essay will be organized around three people who best represent the Nickelodeon philosophy. The first will be Schneider (1980–84), a former advertising executive who gave direction to the channel in the early days when Nickelodeon was a part of Warner Communications Inc. and was the only channel exclusively for children. The second phase was the time of Laybourne (1984–95), a former schoolteacher and television producer who was a part of the shift to innovative, original programming. Among her accomplishments at Nickelodeon were the branding of Nickelodeon dayparts with Nick at Nite for the family and Nick Jr. for the preschooler; the move to children's television "with an attitude"; and the introduction of a number of award-winning creative programs. During her tenure Nickelodeon became a part of Viacom and the international market. The third is the time of Scannell (1995–present) who has made Nickelodeon a competitive force not just in the television industry but in children's entertainment in general.

The reign of each of these three has run parallel to changes in the television broadcasting industry and in children's television, and to the growing consumerization of childhood: Schneider worked to bring the nascent cable channel direction and branding at a point when cable was new; Laybourne was important in establishing a programming direction during a time when there was a tremendous increase in children's television programming, in part because children were increasingly being recognized as consumers. Finally, Scannell serves at a time when competition for children's attention is strong and corporations are increasingly looking to synergistic relationships and diversification.[11]

The Industry Climate

The story must start with the role of cable and satellite distribution, for without cable there would be no Nickelodeon. A series of events in the cable industry set the stage for Nickelodeon. The first was the introduction of satellite technology that improved cable distribution; the second was the growth of cable as a programming source and the consequent need for subscribers; and the third was the Federal Communication

Commission's (FCC) regulation of the cable industry, which both hindered and helped its evolution.[12]

Several factors came together in the late 1960s and 1970s that established cable as a signal distribution system, not just to areas where geography made reception difficult, but also as a source of programming. The cable services put in place during the early 1940s were designed to improve reception to areas where geography, either because of distance or terrain, limited the possibility of signal reception. But eventually the technology of satellite distribution gave cabled homes access to channels beyond those licensed to the broadcast stations. Cable television as a signal distribution system found a new growth area, cable television as a program provider. As reported in *Standard & Poor's,* the ability to offer programming or pay-TV "afforded cable systems operators the opportunity to materially improve profitability with a minimum of additional capital investment."[13] Once an area was wired and satellite technology could support programming distribution, it was a small leap to subscription services like Home Box Office or the Movie Channel.

By the late 1970s cable offered superstations, pay-TV, and ancillary services like weather, stock information, and news. Content providers in 1979 included Time's HBO and Viacom's Showtime, while cable system operators, who provided the signal distribution technology, included Warner Communications Inc. and Viacom International Inc. With these new services, industry revenues grew annually by about 15 to 20 percent; premium TV was the fastest-growing segment of the market with a predicted annual growth rate of 30 percent compared to 9 percent for basic cable services.[14] Clearly the industry was on to a good thing.

Initially, the FCC, with the encouragement of broadcasters, stepped in to control and regulate cable's expansion (though often these rulings were overturned by the courts), but cable grew nonetheless. For example, in 1972 an FCC ruling required that companies negotiating cable franchises with a community include channels dedicated to local government and public access. The intent was to give local entities control of the franchises and to contain the growth of cable franchises. But in fact the ruling did not accomplish this. It did, however, establish a climate where cable systems could offer public service programming, such as Nickelodeon, in return for a community's franchise.

While over-the-air broadcasters went for the widest audience, early cable providers recognized the value of special-interest audiences, and for the most part programmed accordingly. The late 1970s saw Nickelodeon competing with religious networks (Christian Broadcast Network, PTL, Trinity Broadcasting), news and information networks (C-SPAN, ESPN, the Learning Channel, and CNN), and movie outlets (the Movie Channel, Home Box Office, and Showtime).[15] MTV, the music video network and eventually the parent network for Nickelodeon, was introduced in 1981.

As the cable industry grew it quickly became "well positioned to increase profit-generating capabilities."[16] While the early years had been spent in franchise negotiations and construction, once the United States and particularly the major urban areas were wired for cable, attention turned to making the systems profitable. By 1985 the FCC had deregulated the monthly subscription rates, allowing cable providers, not community franchise holders, to set rates. With an increasing subscriber/viewer base and specialized niche audiences, cable was becoming a strong venue for advertising revenue.[17] Increased profitability drew more providers and the number of cable channels grew from nine in 1976 to twenty-three in 1985.[18]

Almost half the United States had now been wired to receive cable, and cable advertising revenue increased from $58 million in 1980 to $546 million in 1984.[19] Nickelodeon, still the only cable network for children, was clearly a part of this bounty.

The Children's Television Marketplace

When Nickelodeon was first introduced, the three broadcast networks were the only game in town. While independent stations such as Chicago's WGN and New York City's WOR programmed some weekday afternoon or lunchtime cartoons, it was ABC, CBS, and NBC that shared in the ratings for the two- to eleven-year-old audience. Initially Nickelodeon offered very little competition. However, by 1992 Nickelodeon was a serious competitor, and five other cable channels carried at least some children's programming (the Cartoon Network, the Family Channel, USA Network, Black Entertainment, and the SciFi Channel). Cable networks now had 51 percent of the two- to eleven-year-old audience, and broadcast television no longer dominated the market.[20] In fact, by fall 2002, Saturday morning programming on all three networks was controlled by cable: ABC was a part of the Disney family; NBC had arrangements for programming from the Discovery Channel; and CBS was owned by Viacom and used Nickelodeon programming for the Saturday morning block.

In any discussion of the children's television industry, we must consider the consequences of government regulation. Although the Federal Communications Commission does not regulate children's programming on cable, cable tends to be sensitive to the climate created by the FCC, Congress, advocacy groups, and parents. In 1979, the FCC released the results of almost a decade of reports and hearings about the status of children's television, which were first initiated in 1970 by Action for Children's Television. The report put broadcasters on notice—though with no punitive damages—that children were clearly underserved. Gains in children's programming achieved during the 1970s were overturned by the deregulatory climate of the 1980s, when it was argued that the marketplace with its new services like cable, satellite technology, and home video would offer an alternative to the television broadcast networks. Although the argument overlooked the public interest responsibility of broadcasters, it became "the law of the land" for the 1980s. It was under these circumstances that Nickelodeon, with its attention to children, stepped into the void.

When Nickelodeon was first introduced as a cable network in 1979, the landscape of children's television was very different from what we have today. *Sesame Street* and *Mister Rogers' Neighborhood* were on PBS, but most children's programs could be found on one of the three commercial broadcast networks. Programming on Saturday morning on these networks was overwhelmingly animation. (See Table 1.1)

TABLE 1.1

Saturday Morning Network Programming, October 1979

ABC	CBS	NBC
World's Greatest Superfriends	New Adventures of Mighty Mouse	Daffy Duck
Plastic Man	Bugs Bunny/Road Runner	Casper
Spider Woman	Popeye	Fred and Barney Meet the Thing
Scooby and Scrappy Doo	Fat Albert	Super Globetrotters
Weekend Special [Movie]	Jason of Star Command	Flash Gordon
		Godzilla

Source: New York metropolitan market *TV Guide*, October 20, 1979; 8:00 A.M.–1:00 P.M.

If you lived in a large city such as New York or Chicago, you might see syndicated programs like *Big Blue Marble, Davey and Goliath,* or *Gigglesnort Hotel* on independent stations. But mostly there were the Big Three networks, and they offered mostly cartoons. While the networks argued that the programs were now more educational and less violent and sexist, with "blacks and Hispanics . . . showing up in authority positions,"[21] live-action, prosocial programs like *Captain Kangaroo* and *The CBS Library* were the exception. A landscape of animated products dominated the network channels.

In those days pajamas only occasionally came with licensed characters; there were no VCRs or DVDs; books were about fairy tales, the Pokey Pup, the Little Engine That Could, or, of course, Disney characters; and video games were something called Pong. But now children, and parents, could turn on Nickelodeon at any time of the day and know that they would find something especially for children. Advertisers and merchandisers would eventually also take note of Nickelodeon. However, when Nickelodeon was introduced in 1979, there were very few homes wired for cable and little programming available to view. The growth of Nickelodeon is thus strongly bound up with the growth of cable in the home.

The Corporate Family

Warner Communications Inc. (WCI), original parent company to Nickelodeon, has been a part of the cable industry since the early 1970s with the acquisition of cable distribution systems that eventually became Warner Cable Corporation (WCC). As cable grew, to offset the cost of wiring new communities WCI turned to American Express for an infusion of capital, forming Warner Amex. In addition to capital, American Express brought marketing skills, computer systems technology, and consumer credit experience to the table,[22] all of which were essential as WCI moved into cable as a content provider. Schneider observed that the fifty-fifty partnership between Warner Communications Inc. and American Express perhaps came about because American Express wanted to move into the communications industry. But as he remarked: "Undoubtedly they also had visions of consumers participating in electronic home shopping with their American Express Cards."[23] Indeed, a major part of the experimental QUBE was its potential for home shopping.

At the time Nickelodeon was introduced, WCI owned a range of entertainment and leisure outlets, including Warner Bros. Studios; WCI Home Video; Warner Publishing, which included DC Comics and Warner Books; Warner Music Label; Knickerbocker Toys and Atari games; the Malibu Grand Prix outdoor amusement centers; the New York Cosmos Soccer Team; Licensing Corporation of America; and Warner Fragrances. A commonality among these divisions in WCI was their business strategy "based on an understanding of the things people like to do with their leisure time and discretionary income, the things that provide style, variety, and excitement in daily life."[24]

The Schneider Years: 1980–84

Cy Schneider was brought in to head Nickelodeon in early 1980. As he tells the story, while visiting clients as an advertising executive for Ogilvy & Mather, he was asked to "pay a call on one of the . . . clients in the cable business who was trying to start a new cable network for kids and was sorely in need of some counsel."[25] That client was the newly formed Warner-Amex Satellite Entertainment Company (WASEC), the cable programming division of Warner Communications Inc. Schneider soon found himself "charge[d] to pioneer [Nickelodeon] and build it into a significant and profitable business—a bright and shining new light in children's television."[26] During this time original, live-action programming was added to *Pinwheel*, including *Reggie Jackson's World of Sports, Kid's Writes, Livewire, Mr. Wizard, Standby: Lights! Camera! Action!, Against the Odds,* and *You Can't Do That on Television.* These programs were often by (*Kid's Writes*) or about (*Livewire* and *Against the Odds*) children and teens. *Standby: Lights! Camera! Action!* was, perhaps, one of the first television programs grounded in the concepts of media literacy. Hosted by Leonard Nimoy of *Star Trek* fame, the show took children behind the scenes to see how movies were made. This was novel at a time when the Saturday morning broadcast networks only offered children *Plastic Man, Popeye, Bugs Bunny,* and *Jonny Quest.*

The economics of program production are important to note here. Game shows and talk shows are low-budget productions, but they have little shelf life and age quickly. Live drama and animation are, conversely, very costly to produce but they are more easily exportable and can be shown to succeeding generations. Low-budget programs dominated

Nickelodeon's 1980 schedule. For example, *Kid's Writes* had a mime acting out letters children sent in—the ultimate in a low-budget production.

Building a cable network of quality children's programming, even using mimes to read letters, was costly and could not be sustained on the revenue from cable subscriber fees.[27] Consequently, advertising was introduced in 1983. For the first few months, advertising followed the model of public broadcasting with corporate underwriting by Quaker Oats and M&M Mars.[28] Although organizations like Action for Children's Television protested the company's move to make Nickelodeon an advertising-driven channel, commercial spots were added in early 1984. That year, advertising dollars helped Nickelodeon turn a profit for the first time in its short history and allowed for the development and acquisition of more original programming.

While many of the early programs were successful with critics,[29] the channel gained a reputation for being the "green vegetable" of children's programming. Winning a prestigious Peabody Award for overall quality in 1982, it was good programming by adult standards but not necessarily what children wanted to watch. According to Schneider: "Here was a product that grew . . . because adults perceived the need for better quality television for their kids—not necessarily because children demanded it."[30] Nevertheless, parents subscribed to Nickelodeon and Warner Cable, with the number of subscribers increasing from 630,000 in 1979 to more than 13 million in 1983.[31] Nielsen data, reported in Warner's 1983 Annual Report, indicated that Nickelodeon grew from 10 million households at the end of 1982 to 17.5 million households at the end of 1983. By 1984 when Schneider left Nickelodeon, the cable channel had established a full range of programming, a Nielsen audience, and advertising.

The Growth Years: Gerry Laybourne, 1985–95

When Gerry Laybourne took over Schneider's role at Nickelodeon, the cable channel was well on its way as a branded network for children. In January 1985 Nickelodeon introduced a "new" Nickelodeon, throwing off the old green vegetable image. This positioned the cable network as kids' television with an attitude.[32] About the same time, the channel came under new ownership when WCI sold Warner Amex Satellite Entertainment Corporation (now renamed MTV Network) to Viacom.

Children's television was beginning to reflect the changes brought on by a rising investment in advertising dollars, a growing number of new independent television stations, and a recognition that children were a part of, and contributed to, the consumer economy.[33] As in 1980 when Schneider was head of Nickelodeon, when Laybourne took over Nickelodeon the networks were programming primarily on Saturday morning and were primarily programming animation. So the landscape of children's television in 1985 looked much like that of 1980; animation dominated the broadcast spectrum. (See Table 1.2)

One difference, though, was that now independent stations were programming for children, and the Disney Channel, launched in 1983, offered commercial-free children's entertainment (though as a premium channel and at a price). Also, as changes in technology brought about changes in cable distribution, the development of low-cost home video technology allowed for a new market distribution for children's products. One short-sighted executive said he didn't see "[home video] as representing a terribly meaningful opportunity."[34]

Another significant change between 1980 (Schneider) and 1985 (Laybourne) was the success of product-based programming and character licensing. Generic characters like the teddy bears and trucks of the 1970s gave way to the Smurfs, Strawberry Shortcake, and the multiple

TABLE 1.2

Saturday Morning Network Programming, October 1985

ABC	CBS	NBC
Bugs Bunny/LooneyTunes	Berenstein Bears	Snorks
Ewoks	Wuzzles	Disney's Adventures of the Gummi Bears
The Droids	Jim Henson's Muppet Babies and Monsters	Smurfs
Adventures of R2D2 and C3PO	Hulk Hogan's Rock 'n Wrestling	Punky Brewster
Super Powers Team	Storybreak [Cartoons]	Alvin and the Chipmunks
13 Ghosts of Scooby Doo	Dungeon and Dragons	Kid Video
The Littles	Land of the Lost	Mr. T
Weekend Special [Cartoons]	Charlie Brown and Snoopy	Spider-Man and His Amazing Friends

Source: New York metropolitan market *TV Guide*, October 12, 1985; 8:00 A.M.–1:00 P.M.

characters of *He-Man.* Hardly a toy, t-shirt, or lunch box could be found without one of these new media characters. Unlike the networks and syndicated programmers, whose program characters promoted a licensing character concept, Nickelodeon created a concept around the cable channel. With the slick orange NICK symbol on products like green slime shampoo (named after the consequences of losing on the *Double Dare* game show), Nickelodeon became a part of the licensing phenomenon.

While children have been seen as consumers since the early days of radio and television, for the most part their purchasing power was seen as limited to snacks and cereals, clothing, and other minor items. However, by the 1980s children were increasingly being seen as consumers in their own right and, with an expendable income in the billions, they were heavily sought after by advertisers and retailers.[35] Nickelodeon, in particular, became an attractive advertising buy with rates at one-third to one-half what one would pay to advertise on the networks. Plus, advertisers were guaranteed a young audience all day long.[36] A study commissioned by Nickelodeon in 1987 showed that, in addition to influencing the purchase of apparel and pet food, 21 percent of the nine- to fifteen-year-olds who participated in the study helped purchase televisions and 19 percent influenced the purchase of the family car.[37] (This survey, the Youth Monitor, has been conducted by Nickelodeon/USA Today/Yankelovich every year since, and was the first nationwide, comprehensive study of six- to fifteen-year-olds.)[38] The same study found that children "spend $15.8 billion annually of which $13.2 is discretionary."[39] With its lower than average advertising costs and its status as a niche market for children, Nickelodeon had become an economic and cultural force in children's television. This success led Nickelodeon toward new marketing adventures. Long-term agreements were signed with Epic Records and Sony Music to manufacture and distribute home video, and among the first shows to be distributed on video were Nickelodeon's new animated shows, *The Ren & Stimpy Show, Rugrats,* and *Doug,* and the new preschool program *Eureeka's Castle.* Nick Club helped the channel build a database of more than 50 million names. Among the premiums was a membership card that served as a credit card with select businesses using the motto "Don't grow up without it," thereby reinforcing consumption and consumerism. In addition, a Consumer Products Group was formed in 1992 to further promote Nick-inspired merchandise. By 1994, there were more than four hundred licensed toys and products.[40]

The Corporate Family

Meanwhile, back at the ranch, to build on the name recognition of the tremendously successful MTV cable channel, in 1984 the Warner Amex satellite entertainment division was renamed MTV Networks. The 1984 Annual Report for Warner's reported,

> MTVN's basic strengths are three-fold: its expertise in providing quality entertainment to targeted audiences; its ability to deliver entertainment to targeted audiences; its ability to deliver desirable demographics, which makes it attractive to advertisers; and its appeal with cable operators, who find MTVN's programming services uniquely effective in attracting and retaining new subscribers.[41]

In response to an economic downturn, Warner Communications Inc. consolidated, reorganized, and sold off several properties, so that in 1984 WCI included a film entertainment division (Warner Bros., Warner Bros. Television, Warner Home Video, and Licensing Company of America); recorded music and music publishing (Warner Bros. Records, Atlantic Records, and Elektra/Asylum/Nonesuch Records); publishing companies (Warner Books, DC Comics, *Mad Magazine,* and Warner Publishing); and broadcast and cable holdings (sharing ownership of Warner Amex Cable Company and MTV Network with American Express, and sharing ownership of Showtime/the Movie Channel Inc. with Viacom); and Hasbro Toys. Gone were Warner Cosmetics, Atari, Panavision, and Franklin Mint, as Warner Communications Inc. restructured to create a "synergy" that would build on the company's holdings in the entertainment industry.[42] This synergy was demonstrated by a 1984 "event" by the Warner Bros. recording artist, Prince, that was held up as an example of what could be done. In May a single was released from his forthcoming movie *Purple Rain,* produced by Warner Bros. studios. The single quickly moved to the top of the charts; the movie was released in theaters in July; the sound track album received heavy exposure on MTV; and in November (just in time for Christmas) the movie was released on videocassette. From single record to motion picture to album to music video to videocassette—all brought to you by WCI. This was the adult version of the character-licensing phenomenon in children's television.

WCI continued restructuring into the fiscal year 1985 when Warner Communications sold off MTV Networks, Showtime/the Movie Channel, and its interest in Hasbro Toy Company. The subtext of the Annual Reports for 1983–85 clearly revealed a company in financial trouble. By selling off marginal properties and restructuring, the company was able to stave off the wolves until Time Inc. came along in 1984. But that's another story. As of January 1985, Nickelodeon was a part of the Viacom family.

Viacom's major holdings have, historically, been in the television industry. The company began as a wholly owned cable production and distribution subsidiary of CBS in 1970. In response to an FCC ruling that required networks to divest themselves of production holdings, CBS transferred the company to its stockholders, forming Viacom International Inc. In 1985 Viacom's holdings included cable networks (MTV, Nickelodeon, VH1, and equity in Lifetime, Showtime/the Movie Channel, and Viewer's Choice); cable television systems; satellite services; and television and radio stations. In addition to serving the U.S. market, Viacom distributed programming internationally through Viacom World-Wide. Unlike WCI, with its roots in feature film production, Viacom was strictly about television.

Sumner Redstone became the primary shareholder of Viacom during a 1987 fight for control of the company. Redstone bought a majority of the company holdings, and the company was restructured as Viacom Inc., with Redstone as the primary shareholder. This event is important to the discussion here because Nickelodeon had been a marginal part of first WCI and later Viacom International Inc. until Redstone came along. According to insider accounts, Laybourne supported Redstone during his takeover bid, and consequently he looked favorably upon her requests when he became director of the company.[43] Once he was director, his door was always open to her. He explained, "She was one of the first people to come to me eight years ago to say Nick was going nowhere."[44] His investment and belief in Nickelodeon helped the network build a presence and develop programming that eventually became competitive with the broadcast networks.

Over the years, Laybourne and her staff found ways to leverage the links with parent company Viacom. Perhaps the most successful has been a television production studio built near Orlando, Florida, in 1990. While Laybourne was president, 85 percent of Nickelodeon's programming was produced there, and tourists served (and continue to serve) as audience, game show participants, and research subjects. The studio is reported to be the largest children's program production studio,[45] and by

1994 more than a thousand hours of new programming had been taped at the studio.[46]

Laybourne's Programming

When Laybourne became head of Nickelodeon in 1985, the network was beginning to see gains from commercial advertising dollars. This infusion of capital allowed Nickelodeon to develop its own in-house productions like *Double Dare*. However, there were other events occurring that had an impact on Nickelodeon's programming. In 1984, space was available on the satellite transponder used to distribute the cable channel, and it fell to Laybourne to program the resulting prime-time hours available.[47] Thus was born Nick at Nite. Using 1960s sitcoms, Nickelodeon created a programming block in the evening to attract adults and family viewing with old favorites like *The Donna Reed Show* and *Route 66*.

The Saturday and Monday programming schedules for Laybourne's first year as head of Nickelodeon reflect both the old and the new. *Pinwheel* had been on since the first transmission, and *Mr. Wizard*, *Livewire*, and *Lights, Camera, Action* were from Schneider's programming days. *You Can't Do That on Television* and *Dangermouse*, on the other hand, bore Laybourne's signature. (See Table 1.3)

Two new animated programs, *Mysterious Cities of Gold* and *Spartakus*, were introduced in 1986 along with Nick's first off-network program, the animated *Star Trek*. However, one new program was introduced in 1986 that went a long way toward defining the "new" Nickelodeon, branding the network as television with an attitude. *Double Dare*, produced in the Florida studios, was a game show that doused the losers (and those nearby) with green slime—Nick's first licensed product.

Minor changes in programming also occurred in 1987, but the general tenor of the network remained the same, heavy on studio productions and imported animation. Minor changes were made to *Pinwheel*, a few new preschool programs were added to the lineup, and new old programs were acquired for Nick at Nite. However, dramatic changes came about in 1989 when the channel phased out *Pinwheel* and put in place *Eureeka's Castle*, a Nickelodeon-commissioned program, and *Fred Penner's Place* and *The Elephant Show*, both Canadian imports.[48] These programs served as the backbone of Nick Jr., launched in 1989.

The tenth anniversary of Nickelodeon in 1989 saw a channel very different from what it had been in 1979. Programming was more sophisticated, retail products featured the Nick brand, advertising dollars supported the channel, and, now no longer the "green vegetable" channel, Nickelodeon was strongly entrenched as *the* kids' channel. Programs maintained the prosocial and educational mission first established by Schneider and reinforced by Laybourne, but with an edge. The years from 1990 to 1995 under Laybourne saw a continued branding of the network as dayparts were identified and labeled with unique characteristics. The success of branding lies in predictability—children, parents, and advertisers know what to expect when they tune into Nickelodeon, and by branding dayparts by age, children, parents, and advertisers know what target audience is being served.

TABLE 1.3

Nickelodeon Programming Schedule, October 1985

	Saturday	Monday
8:00 A.M.	*Pinwheel*	*Belle and Sebastian*
8:30		*Today's Special*
9:00	*Out of Control*	*Pinwheel* [5 hrs]
9:30	*Mr. Wizard's World*	
10:00	*Lassie*	
10:30	*Little Prince*	
11:00	*Nick Rocks*	
11:30		
12:00	*You Can't Do That on Television*	
12:30	*Dangermouse*	
1:00	*Belle and Sebastian*	
1:30	*Lassie*	
2:00	*Witch's Sister* [drama]	*Today's Special*
2:30		*Belle and Sebastian*
3:00		*Adventures of Black Beauty*
3:30	*Who Spooked Rodney*	*Lassie*
4:00	*Lights, Camera, Action*	*You Can't Do That on Television*
4:30		*Turkey Television*
5:00	*Livewire* [a discussion on nuclear disarmament]	
5:30		*Dennis the Menace*
6:00	*Out of Control*	*Mr. Wizard's World*
6:30	*Nick Rocks*	*Nick Rocks*
7:00	*You Can't Do That on Television*	*You Can't Do That on Television*
7:30	*Dangermouse*	*Dangermouse*
8:00	*National Geographic* [3 hrs]	*Nick at Nite block*

Source: New York metropolitan market *TV Guide*, October 1985. Saturday and Monday were selected as representative of scheduling patterns.

Nickelodeon slimes kids . . .
and celebrities like Stephen Spielberg.
Frame grabs from *How to Nickelodeon* video. © 1992
MTV Networks.

Laybourne's support of Redstone paid off when he approved $40 mil-
lion for program development.[49] The consequence was three new programs that were launched in 1991: *Rugrats, The Ren & Stimpy Show,*
and *Doug.* Clearly, animation was becoming the programming of choice
and Redstone was willing to invest heavily in the future of Nickelodeon.
Nick Jr. was revamped in 1994 with a $30 million commitment as
preschoolers were increasingly acknowledged as a consumer audience
recognizing brand icons at a very early age. Laybourne explained: "We
recognize that if we start getting kids to watch us at this age, we have
them for life."[50]

Whereas the network Laybourne inherited had been limited in both audience and programming, by 1995 the schedule reflected a commitment from Viacom/Redstone for quality animation and a branded cable network that was well recognized by its primary audience of children. Schneider's influence was nowhere to be seen in the 1995 schedule, as live-action programs were in the minority and programs were now likely to be more costly drama and puppet shows than the low-budget game shows and talk shows of the early 1980s. The 1995 schedule included original animation, new preschool programming, and the results of Viacom's purchase of the library of Warner Bros. animation. (See Table 1.4)

An interesting shift was occurring. Increasingly, the programming found on Nickelodeon was animated. Only 3.5 hours of animation (*Little Prince, Dangermouse, Belle and Sebastian*) were on Nick when Laybourne took over in 1985; by 1995 that number had increased to 15.5

TABLE 1.4

Nickelodeon Programming Schedule, October 1995

	Saturday	Monday
8:00	Doug	Looney Tunes
8:30	Rugrats	
9:00	Muppet Babies	Rugrats
9:30		Richard Scarry
10:00	Tiny Toon Adventures	Muppet Babies
10:30		Muppet Show*
11:00	Beetlejuice	Allegra's Window*
11:30	Salute Your Shorts*	Gullah Gullah Island*
12:00	Hey Dude*	Rupert
12:30	My Brothers and Me*	Richard Scarry
1:00	Looney Tunes	Eureeka's Castle
1:30		Papa Beaver's Stories
2:00	What Would You Do?*	Muppet Babies
2:30	Wild and Crazy Kids?*	Alvin and the Chipmunks
3:00	Weinerville*	Rocko's Modern Life
3:30		Aaahh, Real Monsters
4:00	Welcome Freshmen*	All That
4:30	Global Guts*	Ren and Stimpy
5:00	Land of the Lost*	Tiny Toons
5:30	Clarissa Explains It All*	
6:00	Doug	Legends of the Hidden Temple
6:30	Rocko's Modern Life	Rugrats
7:00	Aaahh, Real Monsters	Doug
7:30	Rugrats	Clarissa Explains It All*
8:00	SNICK	Nick at Nite

* Live action, puppets, or game show

Source: New York metropolitan market *TV Guide*, October 1995.

hours of animation. Since expansion into the international market depends on the possession of easily dubbed material, this shift toward animation would have long-lasting consequences.

Indeed, during Laybourne's time at Nickelodeon the channel entered the global market. While Nickelodeon had licensed individual programs and programming blocks in other countries before 1993, this was the first aggressive move into that market. Animation, with its easily dubbed format, crosses international boundaries more readily than more culturally bound game shows or talk shows. Three other factors influenced Nick's move into international distribution. The first was the success of MTV.[51] The second was the increasingly commercial nature and changes in advertising policy in the European market.[52] Finally, the third factor was simply—because it was there: fundamental to capitalism is expansion. So, the factors contributing to a global Nick include: cable networks that had already established international models to build on; a more receptive European market; and the "natural" evolution of capitalism that calls for expansion. Nick UK was the first formal agreement between Nickelodeon and an international market. When asked how they had decided which Nick shows should be exported, Laybourne said: "We learn from the kids. It's the thing that's made us what we are. . . . There are some guiding principles that will anchor us, and there are worldwide themes that all kids are interested in."[53]

Cable was relatively well established by now with most of the country wired, or at least those areas that were seen as financially viable. And Nickelodeon was beginning to be seen as a smart buy for advertisers. During her ten years as the head of Nickelodeon, Laybourne saw the channel grow in audience and stature. In addition to Nick at Nite, which pulled in the more profitable adult audience, niche programming was developed for preschoolers (Nick Jr.) and tweens (Snick). Nickelodeon went international and was poised to go onto the web. When asked in 1994 to identify the next challenge facing those in children's television, Laybourne responded that it was "interactivity." That's where Nickelodeon headed next.[54]

The Sovereign Years: Scannell, 1996 to the present

Herb Scannell was appointed president of Nickelodeon in February 1996, taking over Laybourne's responsibilities for Nickelodeon's daytime programming, Nick at Nite, and the new network that was a spin-off of Nick at Nite, TV Land.[55] He had joined Nickelodeon in 1989 and had been involved in the development of *The Ren & Stimpy Show, Rugrats,* and *Doug*[56] and the move toward girl-programs with *Clarissa Explains It All* and *The Secret World of Alex Mack.*[57] As the network vice president of programming he had worked closely with Laybourne. Where Laybourne was the education president, Scannell has become the marketer. He came to Nickelodeon with a background in marketing and promotions, having worked as promotions coordinator at a radio station before moving up with increasing responsibility to the Movie Channel, Showtime, and eventually Nick at Nite.[58] He moved into Nickelodeon through Nick at Nite, working his way up to executive vice president to Laybourne.[59]

When Laybourne took over Nickelodeon there had been little competition. The three networks had limited Saturday morning programming and virtually no weekday or Sunday programming. Under Scannell, ten years later, there were new cable and broadcast outlets that competed for the youth audience. In addition to programming on PBS and the three networks, broadcast channels such as Fox, UPN, and WB, and cable channels like the Discovery Channel, USA Network, the Family Channel, Comedy Central, the Learning Channel, and Cartoon Network were programming for children. Aside from the premium channel Disney, Nickelodeon was still the only channel that programmed "all-kids, all the time," but the competition was strong. Over the eight years that Scannell has been president, children's television has seen a remarkable growth in programs and availability.

Saturday morning has been the traditional "children's hour" for television and serves as a useful benchmark for the status of children's television. Although there have been exceptions such as *Captain Kangaroo,* local programming, and public broadcasting, for the most part (like it or not) children's television has been defined by these two things: Saturday morning and animation.[60] By 1995, things were changing as the broadcast networks were now joined by Fox, UPN, and WB stations that programmed for the youth audience. So, where there were three broadcast networks for Laybourne and Schneider to contend with, Scannell now had six, plus new cable channels. (See Table 1.5)

As can be seen, in 1996 Saturday morning was almost exclusively animation. By this time there were also cable channels that programmed for children in a more limited way, and Sunday morning, once the domain of

TABLE 1.5

Saturday Morning Network Programming, October 1996

ABC	CBS	NBC	Fox	WB
Adventures of Madeline	Hyperman	NBA Inside Stuff*	Where on Earth Is Carmen San Diego?	Animaniacs
Free Willy	Timon and Pumbaa	Hang Ten*	Power Rangers*	Sylvester & Tweety
Bump in the Night	Aladdin		Masked Rider	Pinky and the Brain
Fudge*	Ninja Turtles		Eekstravaganza	Freakazoid
Reboot	The Mask		Spiderman	Earthworm Jim
Bugs Bunny	Santo Bugito		The Tick	Soul Train*
	Felix the Cat		X-Men	Saved by the Bell*
	Ninja Turtles		Life with Louie	
	Beakman			

* Live action

Source: New York metropolitan market *TV Guide*, October 1996; 8:00 A.M.–1:00 P.M.

religious broadcasting, had become a competitive arena for the child viewer. On Sundays UPN programmed *SkySurfer Strikeforce, Ultraforce, Street Sharks, Space Strikers, Teknoman, Action Man, The Hardy Boys,* and *Nancy Drew.* WB filled Sunday morning with *Sonic the Hedgehog, Mega Man, Iron Man, Fantastic Four, Saved by the Bell, California Dreams, Blossom,* and *Sweet Valley High.* The Family Channel programmed *Popeye and Son, Madeline, Wish Kid, Masters of the Maze, Wild Animal Games,* and *Family Change.*[61]

The next five years (1995–2001) were interesting, as a series of mergers changed the face of television, especially Saturday morning television. While the FCC and Congress were debating the Children's Television Act and the resultant Three-Hour Rule that established guidelines for children's programming on broadcast television, the lines between broadcast television and cable were blurring and production and distribution had become part of the same family. From 1995 to 1996 there was a flurry of mergers as Disney bought ABC/Cap Cities, luring Laybourne to leave Nickelodeon to work for Disney as it attempted to revamp ABC's Saturday morning. Time Warner acquired Turner's Cartoon Network and the Hanna Barbera library, and an outlet for the Warner Bros. library of animation. News Corp first bought into the Family Channel and then merged Family Channel and Fox Kids Network with Saban Entertainment Inc., marrying Fox's television stations for distribution with Saban's production house.

In an attempt to improve programming economics, several other arrangements were made as Nelvana, a Canadian animation house, took the charge to supply CBS's Saturday morning programming, and the cable channel Discovery did the same for NBC. These mergers and economic arrangements continued as Viacom bought CBS in 1999 and Disney acquired Fox Family Worldwide in 2001. The Viacom-CBS merger created the second largest media corporation, combining broadcast and cable television with motion pictures and book publishing. As a result, cable was now supplying programming for broadcast networks, and companies that had formerly competed for the two to eleven audience now found themselves partners.

The corporate landscape was, on the one hand, very different from that of Warner Communications Inc. when Nickelodeon was first introduced, but on the other hand, it was not so different. The distinction was one of magnitude. Both Warner and Viacom owned a range of entertainment and leisure companies. However, Viacom is now the second largest media conglomerate, far overshadowing the Warner of the 1970s. Viacom's corporate holdings translate into the ability to control all points in the promotion, production, and distribution process including television, film, the Internet, and print. (See Table 1.6)

During the 1996 season, when Scannell became president of Nickelodeon, there was a general decline in kids' viewing with only Nickelodeon's ratings on the increase. For ABC, CBS, and NBC viewing was down 20 percent from 1995 and down 60 percent from 1986. WB and Fox had lost 26 percent and 9 percent respectively over the year, while NBC had dropped children's television, for the most part, in the early 1990s. Programmers justified the decline by reasoning that children were turning to the web or by blaming warmer weather and the unpredictable nature of Nielsen data. But the fact was that CBS ratings went from 3.2 in 1995 to 1.4 in 1996.

On the other hand, Nickelodeon's Saturday morning ratings grew by 23.5 percent in that same time, and by late that year, Nickelodeon had become the number one network on cable and the highest rated children's network. The cable network had reached 70 percent penetration, with a 3.7 rating on Saturday morning (Fox Kids Network had a 3.5 rating;

TABLE 1.6

Viacom Holdings in the Entertainment Industries, Summer 2002

Paramount Stations Group [21 broadcast stations]
    UPN
    The Paramount Channel
    Nickelodeon
    VH1
    Comedy Central (joint with Time-Warner)
    Showtime Network
    BET, Black Entertainment Television
    TNN, The National Network
    CMT, Country Music Television
    Viacom Interactive Services
Film and Television Production/Distribution
    Paramount Pictures
    Paramount Television
    Paramount Home Video
    Viacom Productions
    MTV Films, MTV Productions
    Nickelodeon Studios
    Nickelodeon Movies
    Spelling Entertainment Group, Spelling Films, Spelling Television
    Republic Entertainment
    Big Ticket Television
    Worldvision Enterprises
Video and Music/Parks
    Retail
        Blockbuster Video
        Blockbuster Music
        Viacom Entertainment Stores
    Paramount Parks
    Other
    Viacom Consumer Products
        Famous Music
        Star Trek Franchise
Publishing
    Archway Paperbacks and Mistrel Books
    The Free Press
    MTV Books
    Nickelodeon Books
    Simon and Schuster Consumer Group, Audio Books, Children's Publishing
    Pocket Books
    Scribner
    Star Trek
    Touchstone
Theaters and Film Distribution
    Paramount Theatres
    Paramount (Europe)
    United International Pictures
CBS Television [15 stations]
    Group W Network Services
New Media—Online
    CBS.com, CBSNews.com
CBS Radio—Infinity Broadcasting
Production
    CBS Production
    EYEMARK
    King World Productions
    World Wresting Entertainment[a]

[a] www.cjr.org (retrieved August 2002).

ABC was 1.8; and CBS was 1.5 for that same time period). Nickelodeon programmed 103.5 hours each week for children; the Cartoon Network and syndication accounted for about 20 hours; and the networks contributed less than 5 hours. Those numbers held a year later when Nickelodeon reported its September 1996 to July 1997 ratings with the two to eleven market at 3.2; Fox Kids ratings were 2.9; ABC ratings were 2.7; Disney's syndicated programming ratings were 1.8; UPN ratings were 1.5; Kids WB! and CBS ratings were 1.3; and the Cartoon Network ratings with the two to eleven group for that year were 0.7. Nickelodeon has maintained the number one ratings overall for the two to eleven demographic group since then.[62]

Meanwhile the channel continued to expand the Nick at Nite block of programming, and in August 1998 the 8:00 P.M.–9:00 P.M. Sunday-through-Friday slot was branded the Nickel-O-Zone. It featured three new series, *The Wild Thornberrys, Cousin Skeeter,* and *Animorphs,* and returning shows, *The Mystery Files of Shelby Woo, Nick News,* and *The Journey of Allen Strange.*[63] Broadening the audience to teens, in 2001 the Sunday evening block was branded TEENick and brought new advertisers to Nickelodeon such as Coca-Cola and Sega.

Despite the poor showing of the networks during the 1995–96 season, children's television was still seen as a gold mine. As Scannell said, when discussing the success of *Rugrats* and *Blue's Clues* toys: "TV is the centerpiece of our business, but with it comes a lot of opportunities."[64] Merchandising, product licensing, and international revenue were all a part of the return on the investment when it came to children's television. Children's television, and particularly animation, also has a repeatability that is not a feature of adult programming. Children will watch a program multiple times without losing interest. Consequently, a single episode of *Rugrats* can be shown multiple times in the week and across the year. New generations of children can be entertained by the same program two years later. This has become important to Nick's programming strategy.[65]

Launched in 1997, *Blue's Clues* was another program built on the support of Redstone and reflecting the new model for children's programming. The cornerstone of Nick Jr., the educational program is designed for preschoolers. Because children are willing to watch the same program multiple times and because they learn from repetition, the same program was aired for five consecutive days in a week. Not only was this sound educational thinking, but it was also economically clever; Nick could fill 2.5

hours with one program over five days. Like *Rugrats,* the program generated tie-in merchandise, videos, books, CD-ROMs, and a live-performance show. And, because parents are encouraged to watch these preschool-aged programs with their children, adults are included in the marketing strategy. Ford automotive and Gateway computers both heavily advertise specially designed products that feature *Blue's Clues.*[66]

Jimmy Neutron is symbolic of both the changes at Nickelodeon under Scannell's reign and the future of children's marketing. In the spirit of the synergy created by the release of Prince's motion picture *Purple Rain,* for Warner Bros., Jimmy Neutron represents current trends that now include not only the traditional media platforms like sound and film, and music video and videocassette that were unique with *Purple Rain* but also digital media platforms not available in the past. This gives us video games and websites, not to mention that Jimmy himself is a computer-generated image. Perhaps most importantly, interactive sites like chat rooms can now be used to generate a "buzz" about a new product. Nickelodeon took full advantage of these technologies when introducing Jimmy Neutron in 2001. The character first appeared on the Nickelodeon channel as a short interstitial. He was then introduced on Nick.com and soon had his own website, www.jimmyneutron.com. The film, *Jimmy Neutron: Boy Genius,* was released for the Christmas season in 2001. The week before the film was released it had an 80 percent awareness score among its target audience.[67] Introducing Jimmy Neutron across platforms—video games, publishing, DVD, the Internet, and television—established name recognition and product demand while minimizing risk. According to Stephen Youngwood, vice president of media products at Nickelodeon: "We're using the video game arena to introduce properties that we think have potential in other media because we can connect with kids where they're already spending a good deal of their time"[68]—that is, on the Internet and with video games. Not content to market through television and other traditional licensing arrangements, resource guides were sent to teachers, reinforcing the educational component of Jimmy Neutron, and regional invention contests and radio promotional events were held across the United States.[69]

Whereas *Rugrats* and *Blue's Clues* began life on television, with *Jimmy Neutron: Boy Genius* Nickelodeon moved children's entertainment out of the television arena and into the digital world of video games, computer software, and DVDs. By the time Jimmy debuted on television in the fall of 2002 he was a well-established character and *The Adventures of*

Jimmy Neutron: Boy Genius was Nickelodeon's highest rated premiere, reaching "one-third of all kids 2–11 watching cable that night."[70]

The release of *Jimmy Neutron: Boy Genius* as a feature film is exemplary of the structural conditions that can drive corporate decisions. In an effort to control costs after Viacom took over Paramount Pictures and Blockbuster Entertainment in 1994, Redstone announced that Paramount would look to external sources for funding and "make cheaper movies under the Viacom brand names like . . . Nickelodeon films for children."[71] The first film under this partnership was released in 1995. *Harriet the Spy,* based on a young girl's adventures, had only moderate theatrical success but demonstrated that there was an audience for family films beyond those produced by Disney. While the animation studio, built in 1997 as a result of the $420 million investment, allowed the company to produce, and therefore maintain control over, in-house animation such as *Kablam!* and *SpongeBob SquarePants,* Nickelodeon Films has allowed the company to move into feature films. The partnership between Viacom, Paramount, and Blockbuster creates a synergy beyond anything Warner thought of when producing *Purple Rain.*

In the youth market, one of the major markets for video and DVD rentals, corporate synergy creates an ideal environment for the production and distribution of feature films and direct-to-video productions as well as CD-ROMs and electronic software.[72] *Jimmy Neutron: Boy Genius* is certainly an example of this relationship. Upcoming Nickelodeon films include *Hey Arnold!, The Wild Thornberrys,* and a third *Rugrats.* Building on the success of the Harry Potter books, Nickelodeon Films is developing *Lemony Snicket's A Series of Unfortunate Events,* a book series being translated into a series of live-action films.[73] While these films are spin-offs of successful Nickelodeon properties (or in the case of *Lemony Snicket* of a well-received series of books) with different origins than the well-orchestrated development of Jimmy Neutron, they will nonetheless come with software, video games, and other accoutrements. As spending on video games and software ($9.4 billion) surpasses feature film ticket sales ($8.35 billion),[74] it is likely that more Nickelodeon films will resemble *Jimmy Neutron.* According to one industry account, Nickelodeon has been working with THQ, developers of video games, to "co-create games and potentially develop them into TV shows and films. [This] has broken new—and possibly less risky—ground in the realm of studio-gameco relationships."[75] Two ideas currently in development are *Tak and the Power of JuJu* and *Interstellar P.I.G.*

Because of the high rate of failure in the capricious youth market, it is essential to minimize risk. Until recently licensing partnerships have been between the toy and television industries. It would appear that, for the near future, these relationships will develop across platforms and rely heavily on digital technology for creativity, distribution, and production.

Conclusion

The Nickelodeon of today is very different from the Nickelodeon Scannell took over in 1996. One observer has pointed out that Scannell "has taken Nickelodeon into animated feature films, high-volume licensing and merchandising, digital cable channels, and educational television partnership, Web sites and overseas expansion, all the while reaping more than half of all advertising dollars spent on children's television."[76] While Nick Jr., SNICK, and Nick at Nite were in place under Laybourne, under Scannell MTV Networks now has TV Land, Noggin, and GAS as new cable networks to showcase the Nickelodeon brand. In addition, each network has a strong presence on the web. A recent ad on CBS (an arm of Viacom) prime time showed a mother and her daughter playing a game with the alphabet. The ad was for the Nick Jr. website, where a parent could go to find help in getting a child ready for school—once again, Nick was using the parent to bring the child to the brand, or the child to bring the parent to the brand. And so it goes.

While Melody and Ehrlich could not have foreseen the structural changes to the media industries in 1973, their prediction that "the process of market specialization in providing children's audiences for advertisers" would "become more intense, more precise, and more persuasive"[77] has certainly come true. Their world was one of three networks, motion pictures, maybe a little radio, and some comic books and adventure novels. The world of children today is one of six networks, multiple cable outlets, motion pictures, videocassettes, DVDs, CDs, CD-ROMS, the Internet, websites, video games, some radio, comic books, and paperbacks. From its humble beginnings as a commercial-free cable channel with imported cartoons and game shows and talk shows, Nickelodeon has become an integral part of children's entertainment. Now with animated characters that cross platforms and national boundaries, it is the single most important venue of children's entertainment propagating marketing to children.

NOTES

1. William Melody and Wendy Ehrlich, *Children's Television: The Economics of Exploitation* (New Haven: Yale University Press, 1973), 118.

2. Warner Communications Inc., Annual Report: 1979, 53.

3. "The TV Networks: At the Center of the Storm," *Broadcasting* (1979 Oct 29, 39).

4. "Nickelodeon's Corporate Past Full of Twists and Turns," *Variety* (1989 April 5–11, 59).

5. "Vigorous Tubthumping Pays Dividends for Nickelodeon & Nick at Nite," *Variety* (1989 April 5–11, 64).

6. Cy Schneider, *Children's Television* (Lincolnwood, IL: NTC Business Books, 1987), 193.

7. Hal Erickson, *Television Cartoon Shows* (Jefferson, NC: McFarland & Company Inc., 1995), 37.

8. While the Disney Channel and PBS also offer prosocial, age-appropriate programming, until recently Nickelodeon was the only commercially supported channel. Nick is, in many ways, comparable to Disney in its branding of children's entertainment, and Nick competes heavily with public broadcasting, but for the most part PBS and Disney are not a part of this story.

9. Viacom, Annual Report: 2001, n.p.

10. Douglas Gomery, "Disney's Business History: A Reinterpretation," in Eric Smoodin, *Disney Discourse* (NY: Routledge, 1994), 86.

11. Certainly dates never work out so clearly. As we will see, Laybourne was involved in many decisions made during Schneider's tenure as Scannell was when he took over from Laybourne. Nonetheless, we will use these dates as markers for the progress of Nickelodeon.

12. There are a number of histories that explain the introduction of cable, but for this discussion it is important to know that in 1979, the first year of Nickelodeon, only about 16 percent of the country was wired for cable and then primarily in areas that could not receive broadcast signals.

13. Standard & Poor's: Industry Surveys (January 1978, C69).

14. Standard & Poor's: Industry Surveys (January 1979, C68).

15. From *Broadcasting* as reported in Standard & Poor's: Industry Surveys (1987 Oct 15, M23).

16. Standard & Poor's: Industry Surveys (1985 Aug 29, M25).

17. Standard & Poor's: Industry Surveys (1986 Oct 2, M22).

18. Standard & Poor's: Industry Surveys (1979 Nov 29, C66 and 1985 Aug 29, M27).

19. Standard & Poor's: Industry Surveys (1985 Aug 29, M27).

20. Rich Brown, "Cable Eager to Attract Small Audiences," *Broadcasting* (1992 Aug 31, 46).

21. "The TV Networks: At the Center of the Storm," *Broadcasting* (1979 Oct 29, 44).

22. Warner Communications Inc., Annual Report: 1979, 48.

23. Schneider, *Children's Television*, 192.

24. Warner Communications Inc., Annual Report: 1979, 17.

25. Schneider, *Children's Television*, 193.

26. Ibid.

27. Aljean Harmetz, "Action Group Aroused by Nickelodeon Ad Plan," *New York Times* (1984 Feb 14, C17).

28. "Warner Amex to Charge for MTV, Put Spots on Nickelodeon," *Broadcasting* (1983 May 23, 34).

29. Peter Kerr, "Cable TV Notes: Is Children's Fare Paying Its Way?" *New York Times* (1983 Nov 20, Section 2: 36).

30. Schneider, *Children's Television*, 102.

31. Standard & Poor's: Industry Survey (1980 Jan); Warner Communications Inc., Annual Report: 1983, 29.

32. "Gerry Laybourne: Architect of Children's Television," *Broadcasting* (1990 Oct 8, 95); Geraldine Laybourne, "The Nickelodeon Experience," in Gordon L. Berry and Joy Keiko Asamen, *Children & Television* (Newbury Park, CA: Sage Publications, 1993, 303–307); "Kid Vid," *Forbes* (1993 June 7, 124).

33. Norma Odom Pecora, *The Business of Children's Entertainment* (New York: Guilford Press, 1998).

34. "Program Sales Activity Starts Developing in Cable, Home Video," *Television/Radio Age* (1983 Aug 15, 88).

35. Pecora, *The Business of Children's Entertainment*.

36. "Big Advertisers Find Nickelodeon a Darn Good Deal for the Money," *Variety* (1989 April 5–11, 66).

37. Rich Zahradnick, "Kids R Them," *Marketing & Media Decisions* (1987 July, 26).

38. Ibid.; Patricia Brennan, "The Kids' Channel That 'Double Dares' to Be Different," *Washington Post* (1988 Sept 25, Y8); "Nickelodeon/Nick at Nite Chronology," *Variety* (1989 April 5–11, 70).

39. Brennan, "The Kids' Channel," Y8.

40. Gary W. Wojtas, "Consumer Kids: A New Marketing Frontier," *Direct Marketing* (1990 Aug, 49); Deborah Russell, "Nickelodeon, Epic Ink Deal for Audio, Video Releases," *Billboard* (1993 May 22, 10); Alison Fahey, "Cable Net Pushes Brand Strategy," *Brandweek* (1992 Sept 7, 1); Bill Carter, "A Cable Challenger for PBS as King of the Preschool Hill," *New York Times* (1994 March 21, 1).

41. Warner Communications Inc., Annual Report: 1984, 25.

42. Warner Communications Inc., Annual Report: 1984, letter from the chairman.

43. Brennan, "The Kids' Channel," Y8.

44. Sallie Hofmeister, "Kids' TV—She Walks the Walk," *Los Angeles Times Magazine* (1996 Sept 8, 10).

45. Larry Leventhal, "Studio Puts Out Welcome Mat," *Variety* (1993 Dec 20, 50).

46. Rich Brown, "Cable Boosts Original Programming Slate," *Broadcasting* (1994 July 25, 60).

47. Kevin Zimmerman, "Nick's Kiddie Empire Turns 15," *Variety* (1993 Dec 20, 41).

48. Kari Granville, "Nickelodeon Flexing Muscles," *Los Angeles Times* (1989 Aug 8, Part 6, 1). In a letter responding to this story on the growing success of Nickelodeon, Bob Pittman, then president of MTV Networks wrote: "Regarding [your story] . . . as a result of my quotes and the anecdotes chosen by the writer, I feel that an impression was created that I was the guiding force behind Nickelodeon. I was not. My putting Gerry Laybourne in charge of Nickelodeon and giving her the support to execute her vision was one of my greatest accomplishments in my tenure at MTVN." Robert W. Pittman, "Credit Where It's Due," *Los Angeles Times* (1989 Sept 30, Part 5, 2). Unfortunately, while affirming the value of Laybourne at Nickelodeon, this quote points to the dangers of relying on news accounts. Where possible, information in this essay has been verified and supported by other sources.

49. Sallie Hofmeister, "Viacom, CBS to Merge in Record $37-Billion Deal," *Los Angeles Times* (1999 Sept 8, 1A).

50. Carter, "A Cable Challenger," 1.

51. "Viacom to Take Nickelodeon Abroad," *Broadcasting* (1992 Dec 14, 51).

52. Standard & Poor's: Industry Report (1993 Feb 11, M16+).

53. "Nick Topper Laybourne Talks TV for Tots & Teens," *Variety* (1994 Sept 26–Oct 2, 38).

54. "Programmers: Issues and Answers," *Broadcasting & Cable* (1994 July 25, 44).

55. "Nickelodeon Names a New President," *New York Times* (1996 Feb 14, D4); Tom Lowry, "Programing Ace Picked for New Nick President," *Daily News (New York)* (1996 Feb 14, 24).

56. Lowry, "Programing Ace," 24.

57. N. F. Mendoza, "Nick Prexy Scannell Helps Make Nick No. 1," Zap2it.com, http://tv.zap2it.com/shows.features/tvbiz/p/a/96/09/28scannell.html (retrieved 9/01/02).

58. Mendoza, "Nick Prexy Scannell."

59. Lowry, "Programing Ace," 24.

60. Pecora, *The Business of Children's Entertainment*.

61. From *TV Guide: New York Metro Area* (1996 Oct 22).

62. Gina Bellafante, "Trouble in Toontown," *Time* (1996 Nov 25, n.p.); Gary Levin, "Webs Lose Their Place at the Kiddies' Table," *Variety* (1996 Oct 10–14, 1); "Nickelodeon First in Third," *Broadcasting & Cable* (1996 Sept 30, 74).

63. Mike Reynolds, "Kids Flee Broadcast for Cable," *Cable World* (1998 Dec 7, 44).

64. Eric Schmuckler, "Up in the Air," *Mediaweek* (1999 Feb 1, 58).

65. While several of Nickelodeon's programming decisions have built on traditional arrangements of children's programming and licensing merchandise, the three here are perhaps most noteworthy. *Rugrats* because it is ubiquitous; *Blue's Clues* because of the commitment to educational programming; and Jimmy Neutron because of its use of digital technology. *SpongeBob* is a pop culture phenomenon whose popularity is its claim to fame; in one week (May 13–19, 2002) it was listed as five of the top ten cable programs for the week.

66. Marci McDonald and Marianne Lavelle, "Call It Kid-Fluence," *U.S. News & World Report* (2001 July 30, 32).

67. Simon Ashdown, "Nick and THQ Try on a Next-Gen Studio-Gameco Relationship for Size," *Kidscreen* (2002 May 1, 37).

68. Ibid.

69. Moira McCormick, "Nickelodeon/Paramount Release Promotes Science," *Billboard* (2002 June 22, 60).

70. Andrew Grossman, "'Neutron' Is Positino at Nick," *Hollywood Reporter* (2002 Sept 11, n.p.).

71. Robert Marich, "Redstone Reinvents Par Finance," *Hollywood Reporter* (1994 Oct 3, n.p.).

72. Diane Mermigas, "Paramount-Viacom: A New Era Begins," *Electronic Media* (1994 Feb 21, 39).

73. Claudia Puig, "Nick Gets Sweet on 'Lemony Snicket,'" *USA Today* (2002 June 11, 1D).

74. Ashdown, "Nick and THQ," 37.

75. Ibid.

76. Laurie Mifflin, "Following a Tough Act," *New York Times* (1999 June 17, C1).

77. Melody and Ehrlich, *Children's Television*, 118.

2

"A Kid's Gotta Do What a Kid's Gotta Do"

Branding the Nickelodeon Experience

Kevin S. Sandler

Otherwise stereotyped, marginalized, or ignored by broadcast television, specific demographic groups like women (Lifetime, Oxygen) or African Americans (BET, Black Starz!) and psychographic groups like animal lovers (Animal Planet) or gastronomes (Food Network) now have a wider variety of choices thanks to cable television. To attract what is now a more discriminating and selective viewer and to compete in this crowded media arena, cable networks and their corporate parents have reconfigured their channels as brands, commodities that embrace a particular lifestyle, attitude, or experience. Children, in particular, have been one of the prime recipients of this branded mediascape. Long an underserved group of television viewers relegated to the Saturday morning ghetto, children have more options than anyone could have imagined in the 1980s, twenty-four-hour programming on a variety of networks for viewers from infancy to teenhood. Viacom's Nickelodeon network, thus, represents a notable example of the positive dimensions of corporate branding on cable television.

Even though most people would equate Nickelodeon with "fun"—which indeed it is—the network's brand personality can more succinctly be regarded as "prosocial." Promoting specific prosocial elements such as diversity, nonviolent action, appropriate levels of humor, and guidelines for success—all without ever talking down to kids—characterizes the brand attitude of Nickelodeon.[1] The network's programs, partnerships, and events teach interpersonal skills such as negotiation, cooperation, and tolerance as well as personal values such as perseverance, pride, and self-esteem. Nickelodeon's brand image is not only tailored to cater to the demands of the American market; the network adapts various media platforms in the areas of education and entertainment to meet the needs of local and regional tastes and cultures around the world. The essence of the kid-first, parent-friendly brand attitude of Nickelodeon is perfectly captured by a 1998 branding campaign in which both kids and parents sing and dance the repetitive "Thank you Nickelodeon" verse while maintaining that "A kid's gotta do what a kid's gotta do." This essay provides a history and analysis of the branding strategy of Nickelodeon, describing the means by which it became the number one children's network.

Nickelodeon: The Early Years

Television warfare over children's eyeballs and network brand recognition is currently fiercer than it has ever been before. Whereas once young viewers were all lumped together—to the dismay of activists, educators, and developmental psychologists—as "two- to eleven-year-olds," today News Corp., AOL Time Warner, Disney, and Viacom have an assortment of branded cable networks, broadcast channels, and syndication packages trying to attract three youth demographic groups: two to five, six to eleven, and nine to fourteen. When Nickelodeon premiered on April 1, 1979, under its original name Pinwheel, its competition was much smaller, its target audience was different, and its brand identity was practically nonexistent. The 1980s was a period of audience growth and cable expansion, and in fact, Nickelodeon would not fully develop into a brand until the creation of Nicktoons in 1991.

When Pinwheel became Nickelodeon in 1981, the broadcasters dominated the children's television market, a position they would hold until the mid-1990s. CBS, NBC, and ABC (and later Fox) programmed Saturday mornings while syndicators supplied independent local stations with material for the weekday morning and after-schools hours. Network hits in the 1970s and 1980s included *The Smurfs, The Bugs Bunny/Road Runner Show, Muppet Babies,* and of course, *Scooby Doo* in all its variations. Syndicated successes included *He-Man and the Masters of the Universe, G.I. Joe, Teenage Mutant Ninja Turtles,* and in the 1990s, *Mighty Morphin Power Rangers.* Aside from the Emmy-award winning *Muppet Babies*, Saturday morning continued its 1970s legacy as a haven of mostly insipid sitcom spin-offs, unadventurous adventure, and hapless reruns. Syndication featured more original offerings, yet many of these shows were no more than "program length commercials," product-based programs (mostly for boys) created by toy companies in the wake of FCC deregulation. The majority of these shows, as Heather Hendershot explains in *Saturday Morning Censors*, featured protagonists as "muscled superheroes" or "mechanical transformers" whose conflicts, weaponry, and characterizations were shaped by the demands of merchandising and licensing.[2] Toy companies also created a few "nurturing caretakers" shows for girls such as *Strawberry Shortcake, Care Bears,* and *My Little Pony*. The imperative to sell toys to young collectors for the first time made the inclusion of minorities in these shows an economic necessity. But "cartoon tokenism," as Hendershot describes it, rarely acknowledged cultural or ethnic differences in their story lines, instead relying on a merely perfunctory idea of diversity.[3]

In the midst of what was principally a male-dominated landscape of toy-based cartoons that kids loved and adults found violent and mindless, emerged Nickelodeon. The network's mission clearly was one of counterprogramming: a channel for kids without the violence of broadcast television. However, with only a small production budget for original programming, at first Nickelodeon had to rely primarily on a melting pot of nonbranded overseas productions for its schedule in the 1980s. Unlike their American broadcast brethren, these foreign-produced programs were intelligent, educational, and prosocial. From Canada, Nickelodeon aired live-action programs like *Today's Special* and *Sharon, Lois, and Bram's Elephant Show* which featured life lessons through song. From Great Britain came animated shows like *Dangermouse* and *Count Duckula,* full of the dry wit and political satire that was missing from their action-packed American counterparts. French animated imports like *Adventures of the Little Prince* and Japanese fare like *Adventures of the Little Koala* were also of a kindler and gentler vein. Alongside these international programs were off-network, live-action reruns like *Lassie, Dennis the Menace,* and *The Monkees*; cartoons like *Heathcliff* and *Inspector Gadget*; and original first runs which included *Mister Wizard's World* (kids and science), *Livewire* (a talk show with a live kids' audience), *Kid's Court* (a fake court run by kids) and the long-running *Pinwheel* (a *Sesame Street* clone).

With this mixture of domestic and foreign productions aimed at a wide range of age demographics, these shows managed to suggest Nickelodeon's commitment to non-gender-specific, empowering, and sophisticated kids' entertainment. Nowhere was this more obvious than in the Canadian import *You Can't Do That on Television,* Nickelodeon's first breakthrough hit; in 1984 it aired five times a week. Each show revolved around a theme (music, business, or technology, for example) and was comprised of comedy sketches about typical preteen experiences (such as arguing with parents, sitting in detention, or playing at the arcade).[4] According to Herb Scannell, current president of Nickelodeon, "It was kids laughing at kids lampooning authority figures," and it helped to transform the network into "a truly creative playground of kids programming" by embracing an "on-air look."[5] Defining the on-air look of *You Can't Do That on Television* was the ever-present danger of getting "slimed" by green goop.[6] Slime, together with buckets of water, and other messy approaches to entertainment soon became the brand trademark of Nickelodeon. Slime was often splashed upon the network's newly created brand logo—white letters and orange background, which displaced the old, hard, unfun silver logo.[7]

Thus it was no surprise when *Double Dare*, Nickelodeon's first original game show, became an immediate success in 1986. Repackaging *You Can't Do That on Television* as a gooey kids' competition, the network clearly grasped the brand experience desired by its viewers. Hosted by Marc Summers, *Double Dare* pitted two boy-girl teams against one another for a chance to win a family adventure to such places as Walt Disney World or Space Camp. Dollars were won either by answering trivia questions or by performing messy physical challenges within a specific time limit. The big prize could be won in the final round obstacle course—eight individual challenges each with its own reward and orange flag—to be completed in sixty seconds. On any given show, the kids might encounter the Sundae Slide (racing up a ramp coated with chocolate syrup), the Slime Canal (diving under a bar in a kiddie pool filled with green goo), or the Icy Trike (pedaling a tricycle across a slippery surface). Such antics created large amounts of excitement and humor, all performed or initiated by the kids themselves.[8] New game shows soon followed to reinforce Nickelodeon's goofy brand identity: *Finders Keepers* (kids trashing rooms to find hidden objects), *Make the Grade* (*Jeopardy* for kids), *Get the Picture* (*Concentration* for kids), *What Would You Do?* (kids and their parents performing messy acts for prizes), *Guts* (obstacle

Nickelodeon's early logo, a cold, hard, metallic sphere.
Frame grab from *How to Nickelodeon* video. © 1992 MTV
Networks.

course competition for kids), and various *Double Dare* incarnations like
Family Double Dare and *Super Sloppy Double Dare.*

Nickelodeon's sketch comedies and game shows never talked down to
kids. This approach was then extended to the network's original series at
the end of the 1980s and early 1990s. *Hey Dude* chronicled the adventures of a bumbling owner and his teenage staff on the Bar None Dude
Ranch. *Fifteen* was a high school soap opera dealing with the struggles of
high school like alcohol and dating. *Who's Afraid of the Dark?* featured
a group of teens and preteens telling scary stories around a campfire.
Nickelodeon's brand not only crossed over into three different genres
(comedy, melodrama, and horror), but it also expressed multiculturalism:
African Americans, Asian Americans, and Native Americans played
significant roles in these series. Even though one of the network's greatest
successes, *Clarissa Explains It All,* contained no central minority characters, the show still captured the Nickelodeon attitude by dramatizing the
vicissitudes of teen life in novel ways. Most notably, Clarissa talks directly
to the camera about her school, family, and friends. The mature handling
of teenage issues in all these shows further solidified the components that
made up Nickelodeon's brand essence. Nickelodeon could be goofy and
messy, and at the same time sensitive and relevant.

When Nickelodeon finally tried its hand at original animation in August 1991, it had already established itself as a network willing to use live

action to build brand consciousness and brand preference. Once again, the network set out to do something completely different from broadcast television, what Nickelodeon executive vice president Cyma Zarghami has called telling stories "about real life in animation, rather than action and fantasy."[9] The result was Nicktoons—*Rugrats, Doug,* and *Ren & Stimpy*—which first aired on Sunday morning and instantly became hits. However, only two, *Rugrats* and *Doug,* clearly captured the "kidcentric" mission of Nickelodeon. *Rugrats,* Nickelodeon's most popular franchise, presents a baby's-eye view of the world. Led by the boundless curiosity and mischief of Tommy Pickles, the show follows his adventures with his partners in crime, Chuckie, Angelica, Phil and Lil, and Spike the Dog. *Doug* is an old-fashioned *Peanuts*-like series about a self-conscious and diffident boy and his dog, Porkchop. Doug has a hyperactive best friend Skeeter and an unrequited secret love, Patty Mayonnaise. Both shows feature characters succeeding in typical life situations with a gentle moral attached at the end. *Rugrats* and *Doug* have an individual stylized look all their own while still retaining Nickelodeon's commitment to kid empowerment.

However, the third Nicktoon, *Ren & Stimpy,* violated the network's brand image. Described as a post-nuclear-holocaust Rocky and Bullwinkle,[10] the show's bizarre and grotesque gags, scenes, characters, and sometimes entire episodes were inappropriate for the network. *Ren & Stimpy* was cynical rather than endearingly moral, in bad taste rather than gross, excessively violent rather than playfully spirited. Ren, the demented Chihuahua, and Stimpy, the blithering cat, reinforced their friendship in really odd ways such as playing in kitty litter. And they certainly were not "kids" like Tommy Pickles; they were more like adults perpetually stuck in adolescence. *Ren & Stimpy* even drew half its audience share from what Mark Langer describes as animatophiles—devoted adult fans and obsessive consumers of animation.[11] Accordingly, *Ren & Stimpy* reached neither the target audience nor articulated the brand essence that a Nickelodeon environment promised to its regular audience.

The case of *Ren & Stimpy* points to the importance of consistency between brand and content for cable networks and testifies to Naomi Klein's argument that today's media primarily produce brands as opposed to products. In her scathing indictment of multinational corporatism and consumerism, *No Logo: Taking Aim at the Brand Bullies,* Klein suggests that soft drink manufacturers, coffee houses, running shoe manufacturers, media outlets, and *even cartoon characters* are all more or less in the same business: "the business of marketing their brands."[12] The brand, she suggests, has become the "core meaning of the modern corporation," as "manufacturers no longer produce products and advertise them, but rather buy products and 'brand' them."[13] Coca-Cola, Nike, and Starbucks see themselves as "meaning brokers" rather than product producers, marketing a lifestyle to consumers as opposed to manufacturing a product to be sold.[14] However, these companies, Klein suggests, all infuse their products with the same brand attitude: coolness.[15] Resonating with and specifically targeting only the eager-to-consume teens and twenty-somethings with disposable income, branding effectively decreases consumer choice since anything not reeking of the youth zeitgeist is disregarded and abandoned.

I believe that Klein's misgivings about the branding phenomenon, while applicable to many industries, do not wholly apply to cable television. Immense channel capacity enables an array of brand attitudes and values to coexist alongside one another without directly competing for the same consumer base. *Ren & Stimpy* just happened to be the right product on the wrong network. Despite critical praise and high ratings for the show, in 1991 it was believed that *Ren & Stimpy* could adversely affect the long-term prospects of the Nickelodeon brand, and the program was canceled as a result of this incongruity. Clearly, for niche networks like Nickelodeon, the brand itself is the real commodity, not the individual show, and *Ren & Stimpy* suffered for it. *Ren & Stimpy* aired in reruns on two more brand-compatible networks—on MTV until 1995 and on VH1 in 2002—and then resurfaced with six new half-hours on the rebranded TNN and its new adult animation block in June 2003.[16] That all these networks are Viacom-owned properties is significant. The rise and fall of *Ren & Stimpy,* while clearly illustrating the precariousness of the branding process, suggests that finding brand counterparts in cable television after a brand mismatch may be easy, especially in a time of media conglomeration and concentration.

Live-action and animated original programming turned Nickelodeon into a powerful brand within the U.S cable universe in the early 1990s. But not until the network took advantage of the opportunities afforded by being a subsidiary of a media conglomerate did Nickelodeon become an international brand phenomenon. As Robert McChesney explains in *Rich Media, Poor Democracy,* in the 1990s media giants such as Viacom were no longer content with having only branded media properties; these media behemoths were increasingly relying on more internally coordinated cross-promotion and cross-selling of their media properties—a process known as synergy.[17] Hence, if a media conglomerate has a hit film, it can be promoted and subsequently turned into a series on its television network, and be spun off into comic books, magazines, and other consumer products made by subsidiaries of its vast media empire. Branding thus becomes an incredibly efficient and potentially highly lucrative practice for media conglomerates.

As a brand that "puts kids first," Nickelodeon delivers original, humorous, and zany entertainment that simultaneously appeals to both boys and girls. At the same time, it offers parents a nonviolent, multicultural, prosocial environment. By the early 1990s, the "Nick" experience, a family-friendly wholesomeness once the sole province of Disney, rivaled the Mousehouse as a worldwide brand that kids loved and parents trusted. And it followed the Disney model to the letter, succeeding through cross-promotion, merchandise licensing, strategic partnerships, and globalization.

Nickelodeon: Present Day

By 2002, Nickelodeon had become the number one rated broadcast or cable network for kids aged two to eleven and the number one rated cable network in total viewers. *SpongeBob SquarePants* had supplanted five-year ratings champ *Rugrats* as the most-watched children's program,[18] and for the week of May 13–19, 2002, *SpongeBob* held the top slot for most-watched cable program of all, topping wrestling and NBA games.[19] Nickelodeon's success in building brand equity—that is, solidifying the value of the brand experience for the child and adult consumer—is partly the result of a market replenished and renewed every year by new children. Nick's success can also be attributed to the growing market awareness of children's control over the pocketbooks of their parents. More products are now being pitched to children than ever before, and parents are spending money on them. In a market glutted with kids' entertainment, Nickelodeon clearly positions its brand differently from its closest rivals. That Nickelodeon's products steer away from the violent action that characterizes Cartoon Network (*Dragonball Z, Samurai Jack*), Kids WB! (*Batman: The Animated Series, Jackie Chan Adventures*), or Fox Kids (*Medabots, Mon Colle Knights*) is a testament to the network's ability to combine the economies of commercial television with the components of a public service mandate. The network has created a brand sensibility centered on tolerance, diversity, and respect that is unique to children's cable programming and that resonates consistently through a viewer's entire childhood.

The cross-generational appeal and global popularity of the Nickelodeon brand begins with the network's series themselves, each segmented into various dayparts aimed at a specific kid demographic. Nick Jr. targets preschoolers (ages two to five) on Monday to Friday from 8 A.M. to 10 A.M. EST with educational, sing-along, puppet, and variety shows. The Nicktoons, Nickelodeon's signature animated programming aimed at its core demographic (ages six to eleven), airs every day primarily in the early morning, afternoon, and evening hours. Saturday night Nickelodeon or "Snick" consists of comedy and variety shows for tweens (ages nine to fourteen). Sunday night Nickelodeon or TEENick features live-action and animated programming, news, music videos, and on-line content for tweens as well. The late evening and overnight hours is the time for Nick at Nite, off-network sitcom reruns for the baby boomer generation. The ascendancy of Nickelodeon's brand worth or equity, despite the presence of these four distinct blocks, can be attributed to each daypart's ability to evoke the same brand sensibility while still retaining its own individual identity. In turn, the Nickelodeon experience, no matter the age demographic or time of day, still delivers nonviolent, multicultural, prosocial entertainment.

These respective values come together with the "empowering kids" agenda of Nickelodeon in unique ways for each daypart's programming. On the almost-commercial-free Nick Jr., *Blue's Clues* invites preschool viewers to help the host and his energetic female puppy Blue to solve the day's puzzles. Child actors offscreen respond to the host's questions, echoing the participation of kids at home. Todd Kessler, cocreator of *Blue's Clues*, describes the show's mission: "to challenge, empower and build the self-esteem of preschoolers, while making them laugh. Building self-esteem is linked to thinking skills and independent thinking."[20] Similar in nature is *Dora the Explorer,* a series featuring a seven-year-old Latina heroine living inside a computer who teaches viewers Spanish words or phrases to assist her in solving problems. Less interactive but equally innovative are the Nicktoons, whose stories dramatize the trials and tribulations of childhood from a kid's point of view.[21] *The Wild Thornberrys,* a series about a filmmaking family who travels the world making documentaries, features daughter Eliza who has the secret power of conversing with wild animals. Similar to *Rugrats* whose child characters can talk when their parents are not around, *The Wild Thornberrys* provides its fictional kids and nonfictional viewers an entryway into a world that their parents cannot access. This form of "kids only" experience was key to the 2002 Summer Pick Nick event, where kids could vote each morning on the Internet for the Nicktoons they wanted aired during the afternoon.

Later in the evening, Snick and TEENick often share programming aimed at the tween market. Snick and TEENick's animated and live-action series dramatize the experience of kids growing up in unique environments. The eponymous teenage hero in the animated *Pelswick* has an African American girlfriend and is confined to a wheelchair. *As Told by Ginger* centers on a sixth-grade girl living with a single mom. Live-action dramas include *Caitlin's Way,* a tale of a thirteen-year-old orphan living with a foster family on a Montana ranch, and *The Brothers Garcia,* which narrates the life of a Mexican American family in San Antonio, Texas, from the point of view of the youngest child. Exclusive to the Snick block of programming are variety shows hosted by teenagers. The sketch-comedy program *The Amanda Show* starring teenager Amanda Bynes contains parodies of popular culture like the court show Judge Judy ("Judge Trudy") and "Rock-a-Bye Ralph," a doll that will not stop telling you to go to sleep. *The Nick Cannon Show* is filmed in various locations nationwide and features Cannon in real-life situations, talking with real people as well as an assortment of celebrity guests such as Eddie Murphy and Joe Pantoliano. Cannon, once a member of the long-running, Nickelodeon sketch comedy *All That,* also hosts TEENick. Unlike Snick, TEENick contains interstitial segments of real tweens talking about their lives as well as *Nick News,* a newsmagazine show with Linda Ellerbee. In June 2002, Nickelodeon ran a controversial *Nick News: Special Edition* program called "My Family Is Different" which explored the issue of same-sex parenting with a group of kids and parents from straight and gay families. Prime time and late-night hours are reserved for Nick at Nite, a brand built separately from Nickelodeon.[22]

What is distinctive about all Nickelodeon fare, in particular the animation, is its aesthetic originality: each program or film has its own creator-driven look. *Bob the Builder* is stop-motion animation. *Jimmy Neutron: Boy Genius* is computer animation. *Hey Arnold!* is gritty realism.

The Fairly Odd Parents has a 1950s retro style to it. Yet each stays true to the integrity of its brand attitude: kid empowerment.

The challenge for Nickelodeon when extending its brand to new markets and new distribution channels—an expansion engineered in 1996 with its most popular show *Rugrats* and later, most notably, with *Blue's Clues* and *SpongeBob SquarePants*—is to complement the television experience in new and original ways while furthering an emotional connection with the consumer.[23] It is a matter of simple survival in today's highly competitive global media market, according to Nickelodeon executive vice president–general manager Cyma Zarghami. "Any major successful brand devotes resources to reinforcing its brand and positioning. If you don't do that, you allow [other brands] to creep up on you. And then you can't throw enough money at it to get that position back."[24] Viacom, like many other media conglomerates, has exploited its media properties for commercial gain. Yet Nickelodeon's commitment to learning, tolerance, and diversity—a brand attitude made possible by cable television expansion—makes globalization and superbranding a little less unscrupulous than Klein makes it out to be. The network neither resonates with nor specifically targets the eager-to-consume teens and twenty-somethings with disposable income that Starbucks, the Body Shop, and other multinationals covet.

Viacom builds brand recognition for Nickelodeon by taking advantage of the many channels of distribution and the array of consumer products managed by its subsidiary holdings. Coordinated synergies—cross-promoting and cross-selling the Nickelodeon name or Nickelodeon franchises among many of Viacom's media properties—heighten the awareness of a brand while transferring the editorial concept and personality of that brand to another venue. In every instance, the brand extension must always remain true to the integrity of what the original brand stands for with each child and adult consumer. Dan Sullivan, former magazine chief of one of Nickelodeon's first brand extensions, *Nickelodeon Magazine*, explains his formula for the publication:

> The content is for the most part original content that's inspired by the attributes of the Nickelodeon brand and what it means to kids. It's not just viewer support. We made a conscious effort, and succeeded I think, by choosing the right editorial mix. It's a humor and entertainment magazine. And the way in which it's presented graphically, in tone, and

choice of articles and [profiled entertainers] are all reflections of the brand quality itself.[25]

Nickelodeon Magazine, Nick Jr. Magazine, and *Rugrats Comic Adventures* all serve to reinforce the Nickelodeon brand to kids. The magazines are, in effect, pieces of Nickelodeon that kids can, in the words of Sullivan, "take wherever they want to go."[26]

The notion that Nickelodeon can be marketed and experienced anywhere, anytime, anyplace, lies at the core of synergy. As Norma Pecora explains in her essay in this volume, Viacom's empire includes CBS, Blockbuster Video, MTV Networks (MTV, Nickelodeon, VH1), Paramount Pictures, Paramount Parks, and Simon and Schuster. Simon and Schuster publishes the aforementioned magazines as well as *The Bestest Mom,* one of the many *Rugrats* paperback books. These publications provide behind-the-scenes coverage and support for Paramount Pictures films distributed under the Nickelodeon banner. Feature-length movies of television's *Hey Arnold! The Movie* or new live-action material like *Snow Day* will be available for rental or purchase six months later on Paramount Home Video. Kids and parents will be aware of their release date, as advertising spots for these films and other Nickelodeon properties appear on Blockbuster Video's in-store programming network and on sister cable networks MTV and VH1.[27] If a consumer does not have cable television, CBS airs Nick Jr. shows like *Bob the Builder* on Saturday mornings—a process known as "repurposing." One could also visit Kings Island (one of six Paramount Parks), which dedicates part of its amusement park to Nickelodeon Central, an area where kids can ride the Rugrats Runaway Reptar or play in the Green Slime Zone. Banner ads for the park can be viewed on Nickelodeon's websites, some of the most trafficked and interactive destinations on the Internet. The sites contain on-line entertainment like the *SpongeBob SquarePants* 3-D Game, as well as entertaining tools and services such as encyclopedia, weather, and calendar services. The on-line Nickelodeon Shop even contains exclusive Nickelodeon-branded merchandise and promotional offers only available to web visitors.[28]

However, Nickelodeon brand extensions are not only available through opportunities afforded by synergy. In many cases, Viacom grants permission to a company to manufacture products incorporating Nickelodeon's name, shows, or characters in return for royalties on each item. This process, known as merchandise licensing, occurs with many media

Extending the network brand: *Nickelodeon Magazine.*

products since a corporate parent does not own every avenue of production, distribution, and exhibition. Unlike AOL Time Warner, Viacom does not have a music division. So it licensed Warner Bros. to distribute the *Jimmy Neutron: Boy Genius* feature film soundtrack. Other licensed products have included: Farley's fruit snacks shaped to resemble characters from *Rugrats, CatDog,* and *The Angry Beavers*; Long Hall Technologies' *Rugrats* Talking Alarm Clock that awakens children to the theme song and a message from one of the five main characters; *Rugrats'* children's adhesive bandages from Band-Aid; Good Humor-Breyer's Green Slime ice pop; Reach's anticavity fluoride toothpaste with *Rugrats* packaging; and Mott's blue applesauce to celebrate the *Blue's Clues* birthday episode. Most licensed products share the same brand approach that toy companies use to develop products with the Nickelodeon attitude: toys that cross gender lines, that incorporate a kid's point of view, and that have no right or wrong way to play. Licensing pacts with Singing Machine's Nickelodeon Karaoke Cassette Recorder, Flying Colors' Nickelodeon Gooze Transporter Pack or Mattel's My First Uno Card Game featuring the Rugrats all embody the wacky, zany, fun attitude of Nickelodeon.

Most of the above products are manufactured by brandless entities. Critical to the success and growth of any brand is establishing strategic alliances with other brands sharing your brand attitude, a relationship for which Nickelodeon has many interested parties. For *The Rugrats Movie* in 1998, Nickelodeon struck a promotional partnership with Burger King and its Burger King Kids Club. According to Brian Gies, director of youth and family marketing at Burger King, "Both of the brand's business objectives are closely aligned when it comes to reaching kids and families in an entertaining manner. Nickelodeon has achieved remarkable success in its ability to talk with kids, not at them, which links up beautifully with our kids brand personality and what we've achieved with our kids club marketing efforts."[29] Later Burger King promotions included Splat calculators, a special apple-flavored "slime" dipping sauce for chicken tenders, and eight collectible toys from *Rugrats in Paris* that, when connected, simulate the experience of EuroReptarland from the movie.

Another frequent partner is Kraft Foods who, in conjunction with Nickelodeon in fall 1999, launched a promotional campaign called "Smell-O-Vision." Smell cards and 3-D glasses were placed in 100 million packages of Kraft and Blockbuster Video products with additional promotions on packaging of Kraft-owned Post cereals, Oscar Meyer

Nickelodeon undertakes promotional campaigns
in partnership with Kraft.

Lunchables, and Kool-Aid. Kraft provided in-store displays, on-package graphics, freestanding newspaper inserts, and media support. (More recently, Kraft produced SpongeBob SquarePants macaroni and cheese.) Nickelodeon then created specially produced Nicktoons that contained distinctive cues alerting kids to release different smells from their cards.[30] Recent cobranded ventures include a three-year promotional agreement with the family-targeted Embassy Suites Hotel chain, a public service announcement with Ford Motor Company and *Blue's Clues* on Internet safety, and a multiplatform alliance with The Islands of the Bahamas tourism agency.

Strategic brand management also includes staging special events for Nickelodeon viewers. Such events keep the brand fresh, as the creative ideas and themes associated with them resonate with a child's present world. Nickelodeon's TEENick Summer Music Festival is a concert festival for kids and families that tours the United States and Canada. The first two festivals (under the name All That Music and More) in 1999 and 2000 featured youth entertainers such as Monica, 98°, and B*Witched as well as advertising exhibitions that embodied the brand attitude of Nickelodeon. Perrier hosted "Drencher Adventure," a virtual whitewater rafting ride with a large-screen video monitor and sprinklers inside an air-conditioned tent. KB Gear promoted its new JamC@m digital cameras by taking digital photos of kids in a tent and sending them the pictures by e-mail after the event. In 2001, the 3rd Annual TEENick Tour, "Aaron's Party," starred teenage pop sensation Aaron Carter, his sister Leslie, and the Swedish girl-band, Play. Other off-air events have included floats at the Macy's Thanksgiving Parade and a live theatrical show featuring characters from *Rugrats* and *Blue's Clues*.

The most successful and longest-running brand extension is surely Nickelodeon's Kids' Choice Awards. Celebrating its seventeenth year in 2004, the show honors children's favorites in the realms of film, television, sports, books, and video games with kids themselves voting on-line or by phone. "It's one of the most important statements about kid empowerment," says Albie Hecht, president of film and television entertainment for Nickelodeon.[31] All the Nickelodeon brand attributes are there on display at the Kids' Choice Awards: interactivity with audience members, a laid-back, anything-goes attitude, and plenty of slime. In fact, the theme for the 2002 show was "bigger, louder, and messier." Stuntman Dave Mirra performed a backward somersault on a BMX bicycle into a four thousand gallon tank of green slime. Smashmouth and Pink performed their recent hit songs, presenters included kid favorites Frankie Muniz, Melissa Joan Hart, and Kirsten Dunst, and Janet Jackson received the second annual Wannabe Award, presented to a celebrity role model kids most "want to be." Special guest Adam Sandler got slimed on the show, an honor, states Cyma Zarghami, "for those who kids love the most," since the green goo is a Nickelodeon rite of passage for kids themselves.[32]

Celebrities as well as marketers are drawn to the event because they realize that an association with the Nickelodeon brand is the best vehicle to reach the youth demographic. "Nickelodeon has a very targeted, very devoted, very brand-conscious audience," explains Terry Press, head of marketing and promotion for DreamWorks, who used Matt Damon's appearance on the show to promote *Spirit: Stallion of the Cimarron*.[33] "The Kids' Choice Awards is designed as an awards show for kids, by kids. We think that even if we just get to stand next to them, we'll look good."[34] In addition to showcasing the hottest kid-friendly stars of the moment, Nickelodeon offers twenty different versions of the event in thirteen languages. Local hosts interview U.S. celebrities on the red carpet about their experience in those foreign countries. Spanish language versions of the event have a one-hour preshow special as well as award nominations tailored to Latino cultures. Brazil even has its own full version of the festivity entitled Premio Kid's Choice Awards.[35]

Fashioning the Kids' Choice Awards to serve the needs of international markets and consumers is just one component of Nickelodeon's larger globalization strategy. Available in 149 countries and territories via localized channels, branded blocks, and individual program sales, Nickelodeon serves over 300 million households worldwide with a combination of local productions, American originals, and regional acquisitions.[36] The company's strategy is to establish local partnerships and tailor programming country to country. "We're not pan-regional in concept," said Jeff Dunn, Nickelodeon's executive vice president for strategy and business operations. "Our mission is to create Nickelodeons around the world. It can't be Nickelodeon unless it really connects with kids and their own world."[37] For more recent international launches like China, Viacom struck a distribution deal with Beijing's Tanglong Culture Development Company to dub shows like *Kenan and Kel* and *Clarissa Explains It All*.[38] For more established areas, particularly those twenty-four-hour channels like Nickelodeon Australia, Nickelodeon in the CIS and Baltic Republics, Nickelodeon Latin America, Nickelodeon in the

Philippines, and Nickelodeon UK, indigenous programming promotions and events are organized to connect the Nickelodeon brand with regional and local audiences and cultures. Catering to different tastes, different backgrounds, and different cultures has made Nickelodeon not only a global network but an international children's lifestyle brand.

Nickelodeon: What's Next?

Nickelodeon's entire programming landscape in the United States—with the exception of the British *Bob the Builder*—is purely American in origin. The days of acquiring second-hand foreign fare like *Dangermouse* and *Adventures of the Little Koala* are long over for Nickelodeon U.S. as its American original series serve as the focal point for brand extensions and global expansion. To maintain Nickelodeon's level of brand awareness and ubiquity in the United States, Viacom created three new cable networks to fill any voids left undernourished by its flagship network. Less significant but still a vital force in promoting the Nickelodeon brand are Nick Too (a West Coast feed of Nickelodeon) and Nickelodeon GAS (Games and Sports), a plethora of reruns from Nickelodeon past bracketed with newly produced and hosted interstitials from Nickelodeon Studios at Universal Studios Florida.

More notable is Noggin/The N, a joint brand venture between Nickelodeon and Children's Television Workshop (now Sesame Workshop) launched in February 1999, which is a commercial-free educational television network and on-line service designed for kids aged two to fourteen. Similar to Nickelodeon and Nick at Nite, the broadcast day is broken down into two dayparts—a format instituted in April 2002:[39] Noggin for preschoolers from 3 A.M. to 6 P.M., and The N (an educational twin of Snick and TEENick) for tweens from 6 P.M. to 3 A.M. The network's mission, however, is more unified than Nickelodeon/Nick at Nite; it stresses fun, empowering, and educational programming for kids in both age-specific dayparts. Developing a cohesive brand attitude with two different but not altogether dissimilar brands is the challenge facing Noggin/The N, explains general manager Tom Ascheim. "Instead of trying to make education fun, we're going to try to make fun educational. We think that's going to give us license to create a brand that kids love and come to, not because they're supposed to, but because they want to."[40] Assisting this objective are the network's on-air slogans: The Noggin's "What Sparks You?" and The N's "Real. Life. Now."

It is too early to tell if this brand sensibility will emotionally connect with viewers as Nickelodeon has, but thus far, Noggin/The N is following the template laid down by its mother ship. As viewership and brand recognition grow, the network will branch out into more original programming. In 2002, Noggin/The N mainly drew from the libraries of Nickelodeon and Sesame Workshop. Noggin's preschool schedule includes Nick Jr.'s *Blue's Clues* and *Little Bear,* Sesame Workshop's *Sesame Street* and *Electric Company,* and the newly produced *Play with Me Sesame* and *Tiny Planets.* The N includes Snick's *The Adventures of Pete and Pete* and *Clarissa Explains It All,* MTV's *Daria,* Sesame Workshop's *Ghostwriter* and *Sponk!,* international productions *Degrassi: The Next Generation* (Canada) and *24Seven* (England), and the newly produced *A Walk in Your Shoes.*

A Walk in Your Shoes is most representative of the The N's attempt to eventually brand itself separately from Nickelodeon. Revolving around two real people from completely different backgrounds who swap their lives in front of the camera, the show examines social and educational issues such as race, deafness, and religion. After the 9-11 terrorist attacks, The N aired an episode where a Protestant teen from Boston spent two days with a New Jersey Muslim teen.[41] Diaries, photos, clips, and discussion boards of this and other shows were available on-line, serving Noggin's commitment to web and television convergence.[42] Such brand extensions as these follow Nickelodeon's brand-building formula. Noggin/The N's "fun but educational" attitude can be experienced through: special on-air events like the vintage R2-D2/C-3PO *Sesame Street* episodes to coincide with the release of *Star Wars: Episode II: Attack of the Clones*; cross-promotions like a kid being Aaron Carter for a day on *A Walk in Your Shoes*; and brand partnerships with entertainment and dining megaplexes like Jillian's.

As a global media conglomerate, Viacom risks very little in Nickelodeon's pursuit to expand its brand even further into the consciousness of kids and parents. The loser in all this, however, is PBS, who lost Sesame Workshop's *Play with Me Sesame* to Nickelodeon and continues to struggle financially as a network and a brand alongside cable expansion. "When PBS started in the '60s," stated Lee Hunt of Lee Hunt Associates, the marketing agency hired in 1999 to strengthen and expand PBS's branding efforts, "it had kids and science and other genres to itself, but these cable networks discovered they could make money doing what PBS had done."[43] Nickelodeon, in effect, became the branded network that PBS was striving to be. Despite PBS's entry into the digital cable universe with PBS Kids, the noncommercial, publicly funded network is not armed with an arsenal of cash or synergies (unlike its cable competitors) to produce new shows or build a variety of off-air brand extensions to heighten brand awareness among children of all ages. The dwindling significance of PBS to kids and its flagging Nielsen ratings are of deep concern to Carole Feld, PBS senior vice president of communications and brand management. "Kids watch Nick because it's a fun place to be. . . . That's their brand and kids respond. For us, it's the reverse. Kids love our shows, but there's little evidence we're on the radar screen. That's something we've got to change—not by compromising or abandoning our kids' mission.[44]

Exacerbating PBS's attempts to loosen Nickelodeon's as well as Cartoon Network's and Disney's stranglehold on the youth market are operational and staff cutbacks affected by the economic downturn, the fallout from September 11, and the pressure to meet Congress's digital conversion mandate for 2006.[45] Cuts in state funding have left PBS needing about $1 billion to meet the deadline for converting to a digital signal.

Without extra money from the government or pots of revenue from brand extensions, how can PBS compete with the commercial cable networks? Herein lies the downside of corporate branding. The ever-greater commercialization of the U.S. media invariably places too much economic, political, and cultural power in the hands of a corporate America whose current media policy is contingent on squeezing every available dollar from branded and synergistic properties. National networks like Nickelodeon have led to the decline and marginalization of nonmarket public service networks like PBS whose more than three hundred local broadcast stations cater to local and regional tastes. As a result, local programming and public participation in media culture have become virtually nonexistent as the commercial values of maximum profit have overwhelmed any remnants of public service broadcasting.[46] And despite Nickelodeon's success in embracing multiculturalism and diversity on an international scale, market-based globalization still primarily serves the needs and concerns of a handful of enormous and powerful profit-driven corporations. Those local or national firms incapable of synergy, unable to cross-promote and cross-sell their own media properties, find it impossible to compete in the global marketplace. Ultimately, then, the outcome of "superbranding," as Naomi Klein calls it, is the renunciation of "national habits, local brands, and distinctive regional tastes."[47] Not surprisingly, 75 percent of the programming on Nickelodeon's international channels is comprised of Nickelodeon U.S. originals. How ironic it is, then, that Nickelodeon's "A kid's gotta do what a kid's gotta do" attitude and empowerment agenda is so remarkably and singularly undemocratic.

NOTES

1. These prosocial descriptions are borrowed from Jennifer Kolter, "The Ingredients of Prosocial, 'FCC Friendly' Animation," *Animation World Magazine* (November 1998): 34–37. Available at www.awn.com.

2. Heather Hendershot, *Saturday Morning Censors: Television Regulation before the V-Chip* (Durham, N.C.: Duke University Press, 1998), 97–98.

3. Hendershot, *Saturday Morning Censors*, 105.

4. See the entry for *You Can't Do That on Television* at www.yesterdayland .com.

5. Quoted in N. F. Mendoza, "The Weird and Wacky World of Nick," *Animation Magazine* (September 1996): 29.

6. In actuality, the syrupy substance is a simple nontoxic prop comprised of applesauce and green food coloring (and sometimes oatmeal for good consistency).

7. The original logo was a man turning a crank on an nickelodeon, definitely not the brand image the network would soon be associated with.

8. Information gathered from www.yesterdayland.com and the Classic Nick website, www.johnsrealmonline.com/classicnick/.

9. Quoted in Ed Kirchdoerffer, "Kids in the U.S. Tune in to Animated TV with a Kid Feel," *Kidscreen*, 1 May 1998, 46.

10. Harry McCracken, "Just in the Nick of Time: A Review of the New Nick at Nite Toons," *Animato!* 22 (winter 1992): 49.

11. See Langer's essay in this volume.

12. Naomi Klein, *No Logo: Taking Aim at the Brand Bullies* (Toronto: Knopf Canada, 2000), 59.

13. Ibid., 5.

14. Ibid., 21.

15. Ibid., 68.

16. Nellie Andreeva, "'Ren' Resurrected at TNN," *Hollywood Reporter*, 22 July 2002.

17. Robert W. McChesney, *Rich Media, Poor Democracy: Communication Politics in Dubious Times* (New York: New Press, 2000), 22.

18. Gary Strauss, "Life's Good for SpongeBob," *USA Today,* 17 May 2002, 1B, 2B.

19. "Soaking Up Households," a chart in John Dempsey's "Nick's Toon Hits Its Target," *Variety,* 3–9 June 2002, 15.

20. Quoted in Lynne Heffley, "School for Thought," *Los Angeles Times,* 18 January 1998, 4. Surprisingly, Steve Burns, the host for the first four years of *Blue's Clues,* expressed disillusionment with the show's commercial aspects upon his exit in 2001. "I was surprised to see the degree to which children's television exists to sell toys to children. When you have the attention of that many kids, there's a lot of good you can do that doesn't involve the selling of products," he said. "But I always got upset when we got more press for the amount of toys that we have for sale as opposed to the educational value of the show." See "'Clue'-less Steve's Not Blue," *Newsday,* 2 January 2001, B27.

21. The Nicktoons, however, do not include *Animaniacs, Pinky and the Brain,* and *Tiny Toon Adventures.* They were first developed and syndicated through Kids WB! on broadcast television. Nickelodeon licensed these shows from Warner Bros. Television in spring 2001 to be aired through 2005. Cartoon Network, owned by AOL Time Warner, must have believed that these cartoons did not fit the network's brand attitude since it is the home of anime, super-heroes, Looney Tunes, and other theatrical shorts.

22. Nick at Nite may not empower kids the way the four other dayparts do, but it does frequently share the family-friendly nature of many of Nickelodeon's shows. *The Cosby Show, The Andy Griffith Show, Family Ties,* and *Leave It to Beaver* best represent this brand relationship. The more adult-oriented sitcoms *All in the Family* and *Cheers* may deviate somewhat from this mold.

23. Prior to 1996, *Rugrats* had been featured in promotions with Kraft Foods, General Mills, and Kellogg's. This year marked the first time that Nickelodeon made *Rugrats* a top priority in its licensing, offering the show in all major kids' products lines.

24. Quoted in Beth Snyder, "Rivals Attracted to Nickelodeon's Sweet Success," *Advertising Age,* 9 November 1998.

25. Quoted in Dale Buss, "Cross Pollinating," BrandMarketing Supplement to *Supermarket News,* August 1998, 22.

26. Quoted in Buss, "Cross Pollinating."

27. At one time, Viacom owned sixteen Nickelodeon theme stores as well as the Viacom Entertainment Store in Chicago, which carried branded products. The conglomerate closed the stores in 1999.

28. The media synergy for the release of the Nickelodeon series *CatDog* is described by Mariam Mesbah as follows:

Nickelodeon is promoting the series on its channel, as well as on its Web site (www.nickelodeon.com). The site has step-by-step instructions on how to draw CatDog, as well as an interview with Peter Hannan, the show's creator and artist. A *CatDog* short will be shown at Nickelodeon attractions in seven amusement parks across the U.S. this summer. It will also precede *The Rugrats Movie* in 2,000 U.S. theaters in November. Mattel will run a national television advertising campaign, and retailers will promote *CatDog* products in their catalogues and flyers. See "Property: *CatDog,*" *Kidscreen,* 1 June 1998, 55.

29. Quoted in Ed Kirchdoerffer, "A Whopper of a Deal for *Rugrats,*" *Kidscreen,* 1 November 1997, 11.

30. See Jim Cooper, "Beyond the Box," *Mediaweek,* 24 April 2000, and Virginia Robertson, "Nick Rockets into a New Season," *Kidscreen,* 1 September 1999, 66.

31. Quoted in Stuart Levine, "Kudocast Bring Out OshKosh B'Gosh," *Daily Variety,* 19 April 2002, A1+.

32. Quoted in David Ciminelli, "Slime Sticks in Fans' Consciousness," *Daily Variety,* 19 April 2002, A4. Other slime recipients include Tom Cruise, Will Smith, James Earl Jones, Carrot Top, the child cast of *Home Improvement,* and the current host of the show, Rosie O'Donnell.

33. Matt Damon narrated the feature-length animated film.

34. Quoted in Jon Burlingame, "Finding Their Inner Child," *Daily Variety,* 19 April 2002, A1+.

35. Ramin Zahed, "Global Auds Partake in Festivities," *Daily Variety,* 19 April 2002, A2.

36. Information gathered from the Nickelodeon section of www.viacom.com.

37. Quoted in Lawrie Mifflin, "Can the Flintstones Fly in Fiji?" *New York Times,* 27 November 1995, sec. D, 1+.

38. Elizabeth Cohn, "MTV and Nick Grow into Tricky Asian Regions," *Kidscreen,* 1 October 2001, 33.

39. Until then, the twenty-four-hour schedule was split into four blocks—preschool in the morning, all ages during the day, and six-to-twelve after school and in the evenings and late hours.

40. Quoted in Duncan Hood, "Noggin Brands Learning Fun," *Kidscreen,* 1 February 1999, 40. Tom Ascheim also says,

> What (tweens) tell us in their research is that their No. 1 challenge outside of class is who they are and where they're going. For them, life can be ridiculously embarrassing. What you wear is embarrassing. Your parents are embarrassing. You are embarrassing. You're not very comfortable asking questions. We like to be the destination that helps them. It's our educational mission.

See Jonathan Curiel, "Beam Set at Tweens," *San Francisco Chronicle,* 26 May 2002, 25.

41. The roles were not reversed, however, an exception for the series.

42. *Noggin* press release, "Muslim Teen Introduces Protestant Teen to Islamic

Faith to Dispel Misconceptions as *Noggin* & *Nickelodeon* Simulcast *Noggin*'s 'A Walk in Your Shoes' Sunday, February 10 at 8:30 P.M.," 6 February 2002.

43. Quoted in Richard Katz, "Hunt to Push PBS Brand Quality in New Campaign," *Daily Variety*, 25 February 1999, 26.

44. Quoted in Russell Shaw, "PBS Takes Off Kid Gloves: New Image Initiative Planned," *Electronic Media*, 14 June 1999, 8.

45. Andrew Grossman, "PBS Chief Bullish on Future of Net," *Hollywood Reporter*, 25 June 2002.

46. McChesney, *Rich Media, Poor Democracy*, 48, 64.

47. Klein, *No Logo*, 129.

3

"TV Satisfaction Guaranteed!"
Nick at Nite and
TV Land's "Adult" Attractions

Susan Murray

When logging onto TVLand.com, a viewer is confronted by what some might consider an archetypal postmodern vista.[1] While a vaguely sixties-inspired ditty plays in the background, aqua and orange cutout figures of Jackie Gleason, a go-go girl, a uniformed cop, a cowboy, and a *Mod Squad*–style detective donning an Afro sashay around the outline of a television and the TV Land logo. As these images fade, the site promptly reconfigures itself into an olive green screen containing a line of small television-shaped snapshots of Vivian Vance, Mary Tyler Moore, Susan Dey, and Martin Mull that are placed alongside a larger photo of television theme song writer and *Brady Bunch* creator Sherwood Schwartz at his piano. A few bars of the *Gilligan's Island* theme song ring out as a window hawking a "limited edition" *Get Smart* watch pops up in the upper-right-hand corner of the computer screen. Of course, this busy pastiche of pop culture styles, periods, and genres is not meant to be interpreted in isolation, but in the framework of TV Land's cable television identity. And from this we can catch a glimpse of the way in which the ideal viewer of this channel is addressed as a playful, childlike adult.

While the new cable channel, TV Land, and its predecessor the Nick at Nite programming block on Nickelodeon, haven't actually produced much that is new in terms of actual program content, TV Land and Nick at Nite have enacted quirky environments and unique spectator positioning for their distinctive collections of reruns. Promising "Better Living through Television" and "TV Satisfaction Guaranteed," TV Land/Nick at Nite's slogans disclose the homey, yet sardonically self-aware sensibility that the sister channels want their viewers to associate with their programming. Many of the slogans mimic the claims of comfort found in vintage ads for suburban communities ("Hello out there from TV Land— Your Home Away from Home!" and "After a long day, when you've been to heck and back, coming home to TV Land feels good!") while others offer diversion and a sense of timelessness ("Times Change, Great TV Doesn't"). Coupled with images of slippers, pipes, apple pie, and postwar living rooms, TV Land's interstitial programming[2] manages to convey a nostalgic or childlike vision of a bygone era of wholesomeness, while simultaneously allowing room for hip and ironic readings of the values, aesthetics, and narratives generated by representations of that period in American history.[3]

Scott Webb, a Nick at Nite creative director who oversees promotional campaigns, stated in 1990 that his channel serves "the TV generation— everyone who grew up on television and everyone who loves television." Webb likened Nickelodeon to "a curator of a television museum." This makes the channel's target audience and programming strategies sound terribly broad.[4] Yet it is apparent that the creators of both Nick at Nite and TV Land had quite specific viewers in mind. In fact, a 1996 in-house segmentation study found that Nick at Nite viewers could be broken up into three discrete groups: those "turned off" by the more adult-orientated prime-time content of *broadcast* networks (these viewers are "wholesome"); those looking for a less "intense" viewing experience than that provided by both cable and broadcast ("escapists"); and those who view the programs in a distanced manner ("ironic").[5]

Although TV Land is technically targeted to adults, much of its appeal lies in its playful and winsome call to the child within us all. But, as the Nick at Nite study implies, the inner child that responds to its siren song could be either one that is sincere, nostalgic, and seeking solace from the strains of the adult world, or, on the other end of the spectrum, one that is a troublemaking, playful imp. And the channels must provide for both possibilities. TV Land does so by presenting a pre-therapy, childlike vision of a black-and-white world of nuclear families and protected communities in which strict but well-intentioned social rules are joyfully adhered to. The meaning of this televisual world could be read in a number of ways, but the manner in which Nickelodeon's "adult" channel is packaged suggests that ironic and escapist viewing are the preferred reading strategies. This is achieved, in part, by the channel's stimulation and reconstitution of viewer memories through select programming, campy packaging, and retro commercials; the manner in which it encourages the purchase and collection of toys and faux-vintage keepsakes; and its construction of a nonlinear, nonhierarchal, irreverent, "pop-up" style history of the medium itself.[6]

Nick at Nite was a result of Nickelodeon's 1985 decision to extend its schedule into prime-time and late-night hours. After considering a variety of cheap alternatives—such as a family film channel, an "oldies" music video channel, a comedy channel, and a twenty-four-hour kid's channel— Nickelodeon execs eventually settled on a nightly lineup of select "classic" TV shows. Rich Cronin, general manager of Nick at Nite, stated that he and his staff felt this specific type of "repurposed" programming would help the channel draw an adult audience without alienating Nickelodeon's core demographic of children.[7] Sitcoms of the 1950s and 1960s seemed particularly appropriate because, as Cronin explains, "back when censors were so much tougher, shows were more wholesome so kids could watch, which also appealed to adults because they'd grown up with the shows and had strong emotional bonds to them."[8] Or, as another programming executive put it, the shows make both groups feel "safe and comfy."[9] It was also a smart move in terms of counterprogramming. Many cable stations and networks in the late 1980s and early 1990s were pumping out tabloid, melodramatic, or crime-based shows. With *Married . . . with Children,* the new network Fox had upped the ante on prime-time sexual innuendo, and the old networks were following suit. Even prestigious programs like *NYPD Blue*—apparently the opposite of Fox's trashy fare—were sprinkled with profanity and bare butts.

Nickelodeon was crafting a seemingly unadulterated haven from the "realities" of contemporary social concerns and issues. At the peak of the widely covered O. J. Simpson trial in 1995 Cronin boasted to the *Los Angeles Times* that Nick at Nite was "one of the only networks that's 100% O.J.-free. We never even mention O.J. There's something to that, a chance to get away from the world."[10] (TV Land was also explicit with such positioning in 2001 when it differentiated itself from reality-soaked network offerings with its "Unreality Summer" bumpers.) Prior to the advent of Nick at Nite other stations had broadcast episodes of *I Love Lucy* or *The Brady Bunch,* but they served as filler and were often sandwiched between contemporary and/or more recently syndicated programs. Nick at Nite, on the other hand, offered such fare exclusively, focusing primarily on sitcoms of the 1950s and 1960s (and, in time, the 1970s and

1980s) and ignoring other forms of "classic" television such as dramas, soap operas, or newsmagazine shows that might bring difficult issues to the fore. "We have a brand personality, a certain type of show as they channel surf," Cronin says. "They know what they're gonna get when they land on us: classic TV that's wholesome and quirky. It's a complicated, scary world, and we're a nice safe haven of classic wholesome TV shows that are light entertainment and an escape from scariness."[11]

The very embodiment of Nick at Nite's brand identity came out of one of its earliest program acquisitions, *The Donna Reed Show*. Originally aired on ABC from 1958 until 1966, the show is exemplary of the middle-class suburban sitcom that came to represent family life during the late postwar era. While many scholars have pointed out that this particular manifestation of the genre was out of sync with the larger cultural criticism of suburbia and middle-class values that was occurring at the time, recent generations have held up personas such as Donna Reed (who played Donna Stone, the perkily compliant wife and mother of two) as signifiers writ large of the quaintly misguided expectations for postwar femininity and the precepts of suburban life. Nick at Nite exploited that particular reading of Reed with such obsessive fervor that she became an unofficial mascot for the channel for almost a decade.

Nickelodeon packaged *The Donna Reed Show* in a way that poked fun at Reed's character's almost robotic dedication to domestic problem solving and child rearing. (One promo cheekily alleged, "You've gained ten pounds. There is a hole in the ozone. Your dog has worms. Donna Reed can help!") This strategy was taken to an extreme in 1991 when the channel hired thirty Donna look-alikes to run a marathon (holding dusters) through the Chicago loop in an effort to promote the weeklong programming marathon "The Donna-thon: Seven Days to Tidy the World."[12] Moreover, four years later, Nick at Nite Records released "Donna Reed's Dinner Party," a compilation of Donna-inspired songs (including Johnny Mathis' "Chances Are" and Bobby Vinton's "Blue Velvet"), which extended the Donna Reed "experience" even further from the initial viewing experience.[13]

The reading of postwar sitcoms fostered by Nick at Nite and exemplified by its use of the figure of Donna Reed ignores the contradictions embedded in such texts as well as the complexity of the historical moment. A number of media scholars have shown the ways in which supposedly "escapist" fare actually *did* address and mediate the social anxieties and concerns that were circulating at the time of their production.

Donna Reed, the Nick at Nite icon. Frame grab
from *How to Nickelodeon* video. © 1992 MTV
Networks.

George Lipsitz, for example, has shown that early ethnic working-class
sitcoms "arbitrated complex tensions caused by economic and social
change in postwar America."[14] Lynn Spigel reveals similar intricacies in
the customarily disparaged form of the 1960s "fantastic family sitcom"
(such as *Bewitched, The Addams Family,* and *I Dream of Jeannie*), not-
ing that these texts were filled with "contradictory ideas, values, and
meanings concerning the organization of social space and everyday life in
suburbia."[15] This research speaks to just how much meaning hinges on
extratextual and intertextual context, since discourses constructed by and
through publicity material, press reports, public events and debates, and
the reception of other media texts inform a program's reception. Furthermore, as Jonathan Thornton Caldwell reminds us, aesthetics and style—
not simply overt content—also need to be considered in relationship to
their own contemporary discursive and economic contexts.[16]

For a television historian, the content, flow, and packaging of TV
Land/Nick at Nite present an epistemological and pedagogical conun-
drum. While the channels have helped familiarize a new generation of
viewers with "classic" programs that they might not otherwise have had
the opportunity to see, they also recontextualize them in a manner that
strips them of their original historical and cultural meanings. (One TV
Land executive producer went so far as to liken his product to putting
"40 years in a blender.")[17] Spigel has discussed the problems that this has

caused in her television history course, which covers the changing representations of women.[18] Although she warns students to avoid such teleological arguments, she finds that, without fail, students hand in essays that compare female characters from 1950s programming with current female characters, ultimately asserting the supremacy of the latter. Spigel contends that Nick at Nite's ironic and potentially derisive take on classic programs encourages students (and viewers in general) to "remember the past in order to believe in the progress of the future."[19] Derek Kompare, who makes a similar argument, also finds that TV Land/Nick at Nite supplies us with "a sense of heritage, which simultaneously honor[s] the television past while mocking our interest in it," thereby promoting "the interpretation of the cultural past as both crucial and outmoded."[20]

I would add that TV Land/Nick at Nite contributes to the reification of particular images of the past and allows those images to stand in for historical exploration and knowledge.[21] The result is that popular memory is often reduced to a vague sense of decades, style, and nostalgia while historical reflection is reduced to condescension for the naïve simpletons of yesteryear. (This might be particularly true for those viewers whom Nick at Nite has labeled "the ironics.")[22] Nick at Nite can even take a culturally relevant show like *All in the Family*, which in the words of John Thornton Caldwell is exemplary of "zero-degree" televisual style, and reverse its stylistic and social intentions.[23] Instead of being the politically engaged, culturally challenging, and highly literate text that it was understood to be in the 1970s,[24] the show is positioned as a wacky look back to a fashionably problematic and endearingly earnest period in television history. Archie's ratty chair and linguistic faux pas, Edith's high-pitched hysterics, Mike's sideburns and lefty proclamations, and Gloria's short skirts and ditzy demeanor all stand in as the dislocated signs of a program stripped of its original context.

The heads of Nick at Nite balk at the term "nostalgia" whenever it is applied to their channel. Since the word carries with it a feeling of regret, longing, or desire for what one has lost, it is fairly apparent why it is so strenuously resisted in this context. There is an indirect call for the audience to withhold affect while viewing Nick's classic television: rather than be moved in a dramatic way, they are to distance themselves from the experience before them. There is certainly room for play and involvement, but not for serious contemplation or investment. The ironic, detached viewer enjoys revisiting his or her childhood in theory, by watching vintage television, but does not enjoy the shows *too* much. To truly enjoy such programs would be "childish."

This move away from emotional engagement, coupled with the reification of fictional historical images, also lends itself to the practices of collecting and consuming products, artifacts, and trivia which are understood to denote (perhaps sardonically) the sensibilities of the past, and which are conveniently available for sale at TVLand.com. The acquisition of objects such as spy-watches and lunch boxes is not about play, a youthful activity, but rather about "collecting," a legitimate adult activity. "Collected" toys are displayed, and perhaps even increase in value. What could be more grown-up? This odd coalescence of childish and adult modes of viewing (you watch to be childlike, perhaps, but not childish) and purchasing (you buy toys to access your past, but not to be immature) comes out of Nickelodeon's desire to maintain continuity throughout its adult and children's programming marketing strategies; its investment in its three different types of viewers; and its wish to stimulate consumer-based fan practices.

The packaging and marketing of Nick at Nite and TV Land position viewers as playfully youthful and yet distanced television connoisseurs and experts. However, the promotions and marketing staff also work to get the audience to engage personally and sometimes even physically with textual and historical signifiers in order to create an accessible and all-encompassing material manifestation of Nick's brand identity. One of Nick at Nite's most notable promotional techniques was its 1989 national "TV Land Mall Tour," which enabled regular and potential viewers to explore the Nick at Nite sensibility in a tactile and interactive manner. Part museum exhibit and part old-fashioned road show, the tour was designed to publicize the addition of *Green Acres* to the nightly lineup. Visitors to the shopping mall-based exhibitions were invited to ask questions of a (live!) Mr. Ed look-alike horse; get an autograph from and speak to a *Green Acres* cast member; compete for a chance to (digitally) appear in a *Green Acres* episode; participate in TV trivia contests; record themselves singing TV theme songs in a 1950s-style recording booth; and wander through displays of vintage TV memorabilia and life-sized reproductions of American living rooms from the 1950s, 1960s, and 1970s.[25]

Although such elaborate and expensive publicity stunts are extremely rare these days, they were quite common in the early years of television.[26] In 1950, for instance, Desoto and NBC hired Groucho Marx impersonators to drive convertibles through one hundred and seventy towns nationwide to promote both the car and the premiere of *You Bet Your Life*.[27] Events such as the Donna-thon and the TV Land Mall Tour harken back to these types of postwar publicity tactics. While the broadcast networks used local promotion for the express purpose of solidifying their relationships with affiliates, Nick at Nite, as a basic cable station, is not driven by that particular economic imperative. Instead, Nick at Nite is ingratiating itself into the everyday environment and material world of the local cable customer in order to attract local advertisers and to further familiarize audience members with its "fun and kitschy" worldview. It is also working to develop a particular relationship with current and future classic television fans.

These kinds of promotional techniques were escalated and extended with the advent of Nickelodeon's second classic television channel, TV Land. In 1996, almost a decade after Nick at Nite had proved itself to be an abiding and profitable venture, Cronin launched TV Land for Viacom as a round-the-clock "retro-contemporary" channel. He told reporters that "TV Land will do for pop television culture what MTV did for the record industry."[28] This time, however, the company branched out from its vintage sitcom template and added variety shows such as *Sonny and Cher,* Westerns like *Gunsmoke,* dramas such as *St. Elsewhere* and *Hill Street Blues,* and the newsmagazine show *60 Minutes Classics* to its lineup. "Retro-commercials" were placed alongside contemporary spots, a few original programs were produced, and Cronin's staff worked with the curators of the Museum of Television & Radio to unearth obscure shows that would form the basis of monthly specials. The new venture and its generic reach afforded Viacom additional and more extensive opportunities for synergistic merchandising and cross-promotions. For example, the media conglomerate also exploited the TV Land/Nick at Nite concept through its Paramount Pictures division with theatrical releases such as *The Brady Bunch Movie* and *Austin Powers,* which were in turn heavily promoted on TV Land.[29] The creation of TV Land also helped Nickelodeon to fine-tune its classic TV brand identity and to further hone its construction of and attraction to its ideal viewer.

Both TV Land and Nick at Nite have aggressively courted audience interaction and input with what they call their "guerrilla marketing" techniques. One explicit and early instance of this was Nick at Nite's "I Wanna Be Manager of Acquisitions" contest, which urged viewers to send in their resumés to the channel and addressed them as fans and couch potatoes: "Imagine having to watch TV all day for a living!" cried the contest's promotion.[30] Diane Robina, an employee of Group W Cable in Manhattan, won the job and by the mid-1990s had risen from acquisitions manager to senior vice president for programming at TV Land/Nick at Nite. Robina was already in the TV business and was no doubt qualified to win the 1987 contest. But the hype and advertising around the contest sent a clear message, that all Nick at Nite viewers become television experts and historians through their engagement with its programming and that, as a result, there is little separation between those who watch the channel and those who run it. As Scott Webb declared, "We give our fans access, we're not executives on high."[31] The contest also held the promise that a viewer could enter into not only the visual world of TV Land/Nick at Nite, but could actually access and gain control within the inner workings of the channel's production process. Just as Nickelodeon encourages kids and parents to envision any type of audience interactivity as "empowerment," TV Land/Nick at Nite's purported leveling of hierarchical institutional power relations seems to insinuate viewer agency.

Producers and publicity managers work to construct viewers who see themselves (and the channel's staff) as trivia buffs, fans, collectors, and catalogers. Geraldine Laybourne described her target audience as "people who make TV-referential jokes. They know the theme songs. TV is part of their vocabulary."[32] Yet if a viewer doesn't already have those proclivities before coming to the channel, TV Land/Nick at Nite offers to train him or her extensively in such practices and sensibilities. Through multiple merchandising channels, TV Land/Nick at Nite provides an array of extratextual materials that weave the audience's classic TV experience into its everyday life. Indeed, the TV Land website is essentially a guide on how to be a good consumer and fan of classic TV. The site not only offers products, but also games, trivia, and archives of programs, promos, and retro-commercials. Certainly, basic program and scheduling information is posted as well, but unlike other network websites, TV Land/Nick at Nite also provides detailed plot summaries and episode guides, which can be used to catalog and collect program material (particularly when used in conjunction with marathon block programming formats). Since TV Land/Nick at Nite envisions itself as both a television resource and a museum, it also uses the site to "teach" its viewers about little-known producers and directors, the origins of theme songs and show ideas, the biographies of and interviews with "classic" sitcom actors, and small behind-the-scenes details of programs.

This focus on a history based in trivia, factoids, lists, and gossip is reiterated in much of the merchandising offered on TVLand.com's on-line store. The *TV Land to Go* book is described as "the BIG book of TV Lists, TV Lore and TV Bests. . . . [It] delivers opinionated, informed and, most of all, humorous takes on everything television!" The *Blast from the Past* CD-Rom promises that a buyer will "feel like an actual contestant on a TV game show," as "past TV celebrities appear live on video and ask challenging questions about their TV shows in a very entertaining and comical way." And the *I Love Lucy Trivia* board game affords viewers the opportunity to "challenge your knowledge of the show while enjoying hours of nostalgic laughter as you recall the hundreds of outrageous scenes." Most of TV Land's products are arranged on the site according to program (only ten programs are associated with complete merchandising lines) and are not exclusively game-based. For example, the "*Bewitched* Shop" contains *Bewitched*-inspired, 1960s-style mugs, cookie jars, "TV tins," salt and pepper shakers, address books, and wall clocks. Some of the less explicitly trivia-based products, such as the *I Love Lucy* "Grape-Stomping Pajamas," fetishize certain textual moments, contributing to the process of cataloging and textual distillation. Fans are encouraged not only to be collectors of mass-produced memorabilia (which brings TV Land and its mission into the realm of lived experience), but also to be collectors of facts, figures, and other historical minutiae. Textual and extratextual information, in other words, are not seen as contributing to a larger social historical narrative or as a connector for a more organic network of fans, but rather as a grouping of isolated bites to be processed, rehearsed, and then regurgitated.

Susan Stewart describes the ways in which an object must be divorced from its origins in order to stimulate a collector's desire. She writes:

> The collection does not displace attention to the past; rather, the past is at the service of the collection, for whereas the souvenir lends authenticity to the past, the past lends authenticity to the collection. The collection seeks a form of self-enclosure which is possible because of its ahistoricism. The collection replaces history with classification, with order beyond the realm of temporality. In the collection, time is not something to be restored to an origin; rather, all time is made simultaneous or synchronous within the collection's world.[33]

A promotional poster for TV Land illustrates the
ways in which the cable station combines iconic
television images from various decades and
places them in a singular ahistorical landscape.

Stewart here addresses material objects rather than the more ephemeral
mechanism of trivia, but her observations do astutely characterize how
TV Land collectibles function, replacing history with classification. Those
who collect and catalog classic television-related items are not doing so
to better understand or form new connections with television history. Instead, television history lends a very basic organizing structure to their
collection.

However, for TV Land fans the collection of facts and objects does not
end at accumulation. The channel promises to reward them for their effort in a number of ways—all of them based on interactivity. An overt
example is TV Land's 1999 "Ultimate Fan Search," a five-month-long

nationwide television trivia competition. The winner received not only a new car and a television set for every room in his home, but also the opportunity to program and host his own weekly block of shows for an entire year.[34] Fans are rewarded for their accrual of knowledge in more subtle ways as well. The focus on trivia and behind-the-scenes tales in the channel's promotions and merchandising obliquely implies a direct relationship between the amount of information accrued and the amount of pleasure a fan can take in a text. Intertextual and extratextual references enable the viewer to find additional layers of meaning in both the programs themselves and the promotional spots that surround them and help them take on a knowing or ironic stance. Some promos contain call-in games, and contests raise the stakes even further as they claim to test viewers on the extent of their knowledge and investment as viewers and fans.

Despite the fact that many of TV Land/Nick at Nite's ploys for audience engagement can appear rather superficial or silly, many adult viewers have responded enthusiastically to them. Nick at Nite's series of audience polls is a striking example. A poll asking viewers to call to vote via a 1-800 number on "Who has the greatest powers, Jeannie of *I Dream of Jeannie* or Samantha of *Bewitched*?" received 1.4 million responses in a week.[35] While it's possible that kids and teenagers made up a percentage of those who answered this weighty question, since the Nick at Nite target audience is the coveted eighteen- to forty-nine-year-old demographic we have to assume that a large number of the respondents were grownups; or rather, adults playing at being children. It would seem that the ultimate reward for a fan's trivia and material collections is the promise of interactive play and institutional recognition of his or her skill and textual investment.

In its promotional and marketing campaigns TV Land/Nick at Nite tinkers with the boundaries between what is traditionally considered to be adult behavior and what is thought of as childish. Certainly, the packaging and content of programming invite the viewer to return to a more innocent and playful state of mind, but they also require him or her to retain a mature distance from both the fantastical and the realist claims of the text and its surrounding promotions. This straddling of viewing positions is essential to the meaning-making functions of TV Land/Nick at Nite; the playful yet mature viewer is the foundation of the very type of "nostalgia" that TV Land/Nick at Nite is attempting to inspire. While Nickelodeon executives may eschew the term nostalgia in relation to their programs, it seems that they encourage a feeling of nostalgia for a *notion* of childhood itself in their adult viewers. In engaging in this particular form of classic television programming, viewers are given the chance to retreat to an unadulterated, naively uncomplicated, and exultant vision of childhood, family, and home, without having to encounter the mercurial and often confusing emotions that an actual child would experience. The coupling of detachment and play in TV Land/Nick at Nite's sensibility enables it to attract and retain the three types of viewers it has targeted (wholesome, escapist, and ironic) and to take a portion of that audience into a world of tie-ins, merchandising, collections, and consumer-driven fan interactivity.

The coupling of detachment and play in TV Land/Nick at Nite's spectator positioning also resonates with what some scholars have identified as a cultural shift toward a postmodern childhood. Partially a result of the collapse of mythic narratives about the historical and social role of the nuclear family and partly a result of the intergenerational address of the current media landscape, the current construct of childhood is said to exist in a liminal state. As Joe L. Kincheloe has argued, "Children have become 'adultified' and adults 'childified.' Boundaries between adulthood and childhood blur to the point that a clearly defined, 'traditional,' innocent childhood becomes an object of nostalgia—a sign that it no longer exists in an unproblematic form."[36] In other words, in a postmodern space such as the world created by TV Land/Nick at Nite, *playing* with the conventions of "childhood" and its various idealistic connotations becomes more important than actually *being* a child. And the longing to return to an idyllic past is tempered by an awareness of its ultimate inaccessibility. Moreover, an adult viewer's even temporary existence in this "childified" state fosters ahistoricism and the depoliticization of cultural and personal memory. This is only possible because, as Henry Jenkins points out, as a culture we believe that "children exist in a space beyond, above, outside the political."[37]

TV Land/Nick at Nite's aesthetic and narrative sensibility is certainly an enchanting and tempting one. It asks us to see our personal and social histories as a curious and misguided (yet ultimately innocuous) series of dislocated styles, feelings, and flashpoints that can be mobilized to validate our current sociopolitical actions, values, and aesthetic choices. More specifically, it also works to comfort parents longing to idealize the experiences of their children and to connect with and understand them via their own memories of childhood. But if we as viewers, consumers, parents, and "childified" adults allow ourselves to slip into such a historical and political fugue, we run the risk of alienating ourselves from the complexities, contradictions, and imperatives of our past, and ultimately from our own sense of agency.

NOTES

1. TVLand.com, July 2002.

2. Interstitial programming refers to short spot segments produced by a channel or network to promote its regularly scheduled programs and specials, or used for overall channel identification.

3. Cronin claims that those responsible for creating the look of TV Land studied old programs and commercials at the Museum of Television and Radio. Betsy Sharkey, "Pure Pop for Now People," *Mediaweek,* May 27, 1996: 17.

4. Edward Guthmann, "Corner on the Comedy Classics: Nick at Nite Provides Wacky Setting for '50s, '60s Nostalgia," *San Francisco Chronicle,* July 8, 1990: 45.

5. Guthmann, "Corner," 17.

6. "Pop-up style" refers to a narrative concept that originated with VH1's program *Pop-Up Video,* in which animation and text bubbles were used to provide tidbits of behind-the-scenes and other tangentially related information on the music video at hand.

7. Repurposed is a recent industry euphemism for recycled programming.

8. N. F. Mendoza, "Nick's Nites to Remember," *Los Angeles Times,* June 25, 1995: TV Times, 4.

9. Seth Margolis, "Comfy Old Shows Charm a New Audience," *New York Times,* July 12, 1998: section 13:4.

10. Mendoza, "Nick's Nites," 4.

11. Ibid.

12. Lauren Lipton, "Out There in TV Land . . . Still Crazy and Campy after Six Years, Nick at Nite Airs Promotions Matching Its Philosophy," *Los Angeles Times,* June 30, 1991: 81.

13. Robert Hilburn, "Donna Reed's Dinner Party," *Los Angeles Times,* July 15, 1995: F22.

14. George Lipsitz, "The Meaning of Memory: Family, Class, and Ethnicity in Early Network Television Programs," in *Private Screenings: Television and the Female Consumer,* ed. Lynn Spigel and Denise Mann (Durham, N.C.: Duke University Press, 1992), 71–110.

15. Lynn Spigel, "Domestic Space to Outer Space: 1960s Fantastic Family Sitcom," in *Close Encounters: Film, Feminism, and Science Fiction,* ed. Constance Penley et al. (Minneapolis: University of Minnesota Press, 1991), 205–35.

16. John Thornton Caldwell, *Televisuality: Style, Crisis and Authority in American Television* (New Brunswick, N.J.: Rutgers University Press, 1995).

17. Frederic M. Biddle, "TV Land Turns Back the Clock," *Boston Globe*, April 29, 1996: 29.

18. See Lynn Spigel, *Welcome to the Dreamhouse: Popular Media and Post-war Suburbs* (Durham, N.C.: Duke University Press, 2001), 357–80.

19. Ibid., 362.

20. Derek Kompare, "I've Seen This One Before: The Construction of 'Classic TV' on Cable Television," in *Small Screens, Big Ideas: Television in the 1950s*, ed. Janet Thumim (London: I. B. Tauris, 2002), 27.

21. The term "reification" refers to a process whereby social objects, images, and ideas come to seem natural, fixed, or unquestionable in their role and/or definition.

22. For more on popular memory and television, see George Lipsitz, *Time Passages: Collective Memory and American Popular Culture* (Minneapolis: University of Minnesota Press, 1990).

23. Caldwell, *Televisuality*, 55–59. Caldwell defines "zero-degree" television as a style of production that eschews flashy or artistic aesthetics in order to highlight its literary connections and social relevance.

24. See Janet Staiger, *Blockbuster TV: Must-See Sitcoms in the Network Era* (New York: NYU Press, 2000).

25. Other such publicity events include Nick's 1963 Suburbafest party in New York and its eighty-city "The Partridge Family: Back on the Bus Tour."

26. Wild stunts were also common in the early days of film. See, for example, Richard Koszarski, *An Evening's Entertainment: The Age of the Silent Feature Picture 1915–1928* (New York: Charles Scribners and Sons, 1990), 36–41.

27. Jack Benny Papers, UCLA Film and Television Archives, Jack Benny collection, Box 91, folder 1, "Promotion," 1950.

28. Biddle, "TV Land Turns Back the Clock," 29.

29. The 1999 release of *Austin Powers* was cross-promoted with a "Retro Spy Marathon" of *It Takes a Thief, The Prisoner, The Man from U.N.C.L.E.,* and *The Avengers*.

30. Kim McAvoy, "I Love Television: Robina Won a Fan's Dream Job in a Nickelodeon Contest," *Broadcasting and Cable*, April 30, 2001: 76.

31. Behnoosh Khalili, "New Media: Nick at Nite Brings TV's Past to the Web: Re-Launch Offers More Content," *Electronic Media*, July 28, 1997: 16.

32. Andrew J. Edelstein. "Nick at Nite Offers up a Real Nostalgic Feast," *St. Petersburg Times*, July 5, 1987: 15.

33. Susan Stewart, *On Longing: Narratives of the Miniature, the Gigantic, the Souvenir, the Collection* (Durham, N.C.: Duke University Press, 1993), 151.

34. Chris Kaltenbach, "Tune up the Tube Trivia," *Baltimore Sun*, May 31, 2000: 4E.

35. Samantha was ultimately deemed the more powerful. Brian Lowry, "It's Amazing What New Wrappings Can Do," *Los Angeles Times*, December 10, 1996: F1.

36. Joe L. Kincheloe, "The New Childhood: Home Alone as a Way of Life," in *The Children's Culture Reader*, ed. Henry Jenkins (New York: NYU Press, 1998), 170–171. See also Stanley Aronowitz and Henry Giroux, *Post-Modern Education: Politics, Culture, and Social Criticism* (Minneapolis: University of Minnesota Press, 1991), and Steven Best and Douglas Kellner, *Postmodern Theory: Critical Interrogations* (New York: Guilford Press), 1991.

37. Henry Jenkins, "Introduction," in *The Children's Culture Reader*, 2.

PART II

The Production Process

4

The Early Days of Nicktoons

Linda Simensky

On Sunday morning, August 11, 1991, three animated series premiered on Nickelodeon. This "Nicktoons" block, consisting of *Doug, Rugrats,* and *The Ren & Stimpy Show,* would become the first of many Nicktoons series that would help make Nickelodeon one of the premiere forces in animation, particularly in the 1990s. Many animation fans and historians are familiar with the impact of Nicktoons since 1991. Few, however, know the planning and analysis that went into the decisions that were made during the franchise's formative period, 1988 through 1991.

I worked at Nickelodeon from 1986 through 1995. I started as a summer intern for a producer in 1984, and I returned to Nickelodeon in 1986 as a scheduler in the programming department, where I was charged with the task of putting together the daily program schedule. I was known around the network as an animation fan, and as the network pondered a move into animation, I mentioned that I was very interested in working in that area. In 1989, I started helping out the animation producer, Vanessa Coffey, and by the end of the year I had become the second member of the new animation department. This put me in the unique position of being able to witness the decisions that were made, while also influencing the end product.

In 1989, Nickelodeon, under president Gerry Laybourne, made the decision to develop and produce four animated series to form a block on Sunday mornings. Enormous resources were made available, and the network decided that the animated shows would be creator-driven, which was quite different from what was being produced for the rest of children's television at the time. Crucially, we would also start out by developing and producing short pilots to test, rather than simply jumping into expensive show production. While the pilot system was standard for most television shows, it was very unusual for television animators to take this approach.

Consider the landscape of children's television at the time. The broadcast networks—ABC, CBS, and NBC—ran their animation on Saturday mornings. Popular shows of the era included *Teenage Mutant Ninja Turtles, The Smurfs, Garfield, Disney's Adventures of the Gummi Bears,* and *Beetlejuice.* The majority of the popular shows of the time were based on presold properties, such as toys, books, or movies, or featured celebrities or bands; these properties did not always translate well into the medium of cartoons. In some cases, the shows were merely half-hour "commercials" for the properties they featured. The independent channels ran syndicated fare in the early mornings and after school, usually toy-based programs such as *G.I. Joe,* older shows in reruns, or programming imported from Japan. At this time, the relatively new Fox Network was starting to develop animated shows for Saturday morning as well as after school. In the late 1980s, the networks had a few bright spots, for example CBS's *Pee Wee's Playhouse* and Fox's *Bobby's World,* but for the most part the networks did not program particularly exciting or groundbreaking animation.

At the same time, there were two cable channels for children: Nickelodeon, which was a basic cable channel, and the Disney Channel, which was a premium channel. The Disney Channel mainly ran reruns of shows it owned, various packages of its animated shorts, live action programming, and preschool programming. There was no emphasis on developing new animated programming for the Disney Channel at that time.

By the late 1980s, Nickelodeon was quite successful as a channel. Some of its success came from its lack of competition and enviable position as the only basic cable channel narrowcasting to the two to eleven age group. But the network also succeeded because it had put a great deal of emphasis on development and production, and on understanding its audience and what it wanted to see. In the earlier years, Nickelodeon had found success with coproduced programs such as *You Can't Do That on Television,* which was a live action skit show from Canada, and with acquired animation such as *Dangermouse* and *Count Duckula,* both from U.K. producer Cosgrove Hall.

But the biggest success in the 1980s came from *Double Dare,* a game show that was created, developed, and produced in-house by staff members at Nickelodeon. This was followed by more success with other in-house innovations, such as talk show *Don't Just Sit There,* sitcom *Hey Dude, Kid's Court,* and several more game shows. By 1990, in live action, Nickelodeon was developing even more unusual, innovative programming, including *Clarissa Explains It All* and *The Adventures of Pete and Pete.*

By the late 1980s, Nickelodeon had clearly honed its "big idea," a philosophy which could be summed up as "Us versus Them." The basic idea was that kids lived in a grown-up world, and that it was tough to be a kid when you had to follow all the grown-up rules. Either you were part of "them," the authority, and expected kids to be quiet, behave, and follow the rules, or you could be part of "us," referring to kids, or in this case, Nickelodeon. The "us" believed kids should be free to play around, have fun, and stand up for themselves.[1] Nickelodeon positioned itself as understanding kids, being for kids, giving them what they wanted to see, and giving them a place where they could be kids.

The executives at Nickelodeon used a fair amount of focus group research to determine this philosophy. A great deal of time was spent listening to kids talk about everything from shows they liked to how they felt about the world. Nickelodeon discovered that, contrary to popular belief, kids did not want to grow up quickly, but instead they wanted to enjoy being kids. This research would inform every aspect of Nickelodeon's approach to programming and production. The network even applied the philosophy to its own place in the media universe. Positioned against stodgier and more established networks with well-entrenched procedures, Nickelodeon seemed to have its greatest successes flying in the face of conventional network wisdom, doing the opposite of what everyone else was doing.

Meanwhile, another important development in the late 1980s was the rising popularity of animation among adults. The Disney studio's 1988 release of *Who Framed Roger Rabbit?* featuring guest appearances by almost every well-known animated character ever, reminded adults of how much they had loved these characters and renewed adult interest in animation. In addition, the Fox Network had been running *The Tracey Ullman Show,* which featured animated shorts of Matt Groening's Simpsons family. By 1989, Fox had gone into production on the series *The Simpsons,* and the show would become the first adult animated series to succeed in prime time since *The Flintstones* and *The Jetsons* in the early 1960s.[2] At the same time, Disney had released *The Little Mermaid* to much fanfare, and it suddenly seemed that animation was "hot" again.

It made sense that Nickelodeon would find its way into producing original animated shows. After all, kids loved animation, and it seemed natural that animation could be a mainstay of a network devoted to the two to eleven age group. However, Nickelodeon did not jump into animation immediately. Rather, it dipped its collective toe into the pool for a couple of years before taking the plunge. After some success with acquired animated programming, it seemed that Nickelodeon should premiere animated shows made by and for the network. The reason often given at the time was that there was no original programming being produced elsewhere that seemed right for Nickelodeon. So the network was waiting until there was enough funding to afford to produce its own shows.

Meanwhile, Nickelodeon dabbled in animation, somewhat cautiously. The first original animation came with a Christmas special from Ralph Bakshi Productions, called *Christmas in Tattertown,* which premiered in December 1988. Debby Beece, the senior vice president of programming at Nickelodeon, was the executive who oversaw this project. *Christmas in Tattertown* featured a girl named Debbie, her dog, and her doll, Muffett. While reading, the three of them are sucked into the book, and emerge in Tattertown, a place "where everything you've ever lost winds up," explains the narrator, a saxophone. Everything that lands in Tattertown becomes real, so the town is packed with anthropomorphic toys and items running through scenes. Muffett, now alive and angry, decides she does not want to be Debbie's doll anymore and takes off. Debbie, meanwhile, sad that she is missing Christmas, sets out to explain Christmas to the residents of Tattertown.

Perhaps the most notable aspect of this special was the look, which was decidedly 1920s Fleischer-influenced rubber-hose animation. The full animation and design are enhanced by moments of surreal animation that are unfortunately counterbalanced by a slight story, a lack of humor, and the doll's somewhat unmotivated mean-spiritedness. The special does have a happy ending, with Debbie playing a Victrola recording of "White Christmas," while Muffett ends up in jail for trying to ruin Christmas. It did not feel like a particularly good fit for Nickelodeon, as it seemed more appropriate for adults than children in some ways. Perhaps this should not be surprising since Bakshi, the show's producer, was best known for animating *Fritz the Cat,* the first X-rated cartoon.

The next undertaking would test if Nickelodeon could successfully produce animation while overseeing the creative process. In 1989,

Vanessa Coffey was hired to produce a special called *Nick's Thanksgiving Fest*. Coffey had come from Los Angeles, where she had worked for the art directors at Marvel on shows such as *Muppet Babies*. She had also worked on the first five episodes of *Teenage Mutant Ninja Turtles* before moving to New York.

Nick's Thanksgiving Fest was comprised of two shorts about Thanksgiving, surrounded by interstitial Thanksgiving-themed gags. The first short was "Thanksgiving Nightmare," which opens with a family finishing a Thanksgiving meal and going out for a walk.[3] The mice and roaches in the house then comically fight over the leftovers, while the cat tries to keep them from the food, knowing that he will be blamed for any missing food. The family is depicted in the generic television animation style of the late 1980s, while the rodents look not unlike Mickey Mouse.

"Thanksgiving Dreams," the second short, featured a Depression-era family depicted in a saccharine 1940s style of overly cute animation.[4] After going to bed on Thanksgiving eve, the two children, Sam and Emily, have a Busby Berkeley-influenced dream about a fabulous Thanksgiving meal. In the dream, the kitchen becomes alive, food becomes anthropomorphic, and the vegetables dance to 1940s-style jazz. After accidentally knocking extra yeast into the bread dough, Sam and Emily fight a huge dough monster, eventually vanquishing him with pepper. Of course, the children wake to a full Thanksgiving meal, and their mother is completely baffled as to where the food came from.

The two shorts were held together by Joey Ahlbum's interstitial Thanksgiving gags, which were probably the most successful part of the special. They were brightly colored, silly, designed in a style similar to what Nickelodeon viewers were used to, and probably gave the best sense of what animation on Nickelodeon could look like. Despite a lack of humor for the most part, and only average ratings, *Nick's Thanksgiving Fest* still gave Nickelodeon executives the confidence they needed to get the animation department started.

While the Thanksgiving special's production had been going on, executives at the network were developing a philosophy that would lead to the creation of the Nicktoons. Sometime in 1989, a meeting took place at Gerry Laybourne's house in Montclair, New Jersey, where Nick's animation development philosophy was articulated; the results of this meeting would be referenced constantly during the early years of Nicktoons. The meeting included several key individuals who had thus far shaped the network's success: Gerry Laybourne; Geoffrey Darby, senior vice president of production for the network; Debby Beece, senior vice president of programming; Herb Scannell, vice president of programming, who oversaw development; Fred Seibert of Fred/Alan, a consultant for the network; and Kit Laybourne, Gerry's husband, an animator himself.[5] According to Scannell, at this meeting they watched tapes of other animated shows that were running at the time and made observations about what was right or wrong with each show. They also discussed what they loved about the Looney Tunes.

The problem with contemporary animated children's shows, the group determined, was that they all looked alike; the shows appeared to have been made by a "cookie cutter process." Mostly created by such companies as DIC, Marvel, and Hanna-Barbera, all the programs seemed to be cut from the same cloth. The efficient production process was valued over creativity, and making animation had become an assembly line process.[6] Unlike the cartoons of the 1930s and 1940s, which were made by teams of animators who could write, draw, do gags in storyboard form, and bounce ideas off each other, the newer cartoons were produced impersonally, the writers, storyboard artists, and animators rarely interacting with one another. In some cases, the storyboard artists and writers felt pitted against each other, because the writers felt the board artists did not follow their scripts and changed the stories. Similarly, the artists often felt the writers overwrote the dialogue and that dialogue needed to be edited or shortened to make room for more gags and physical comedy.

Gerry Laybourne believed that the best characters lived inside the hearts of their creators, referencing Jim Henson's Kermit the Frog, Walt Disney's Mickey Mouse, and Warner Bros.'s Bugs Bunny. The group was faced with a number of challenging questions: How do you put the creator back front and center? How do you put the fantastic back in cartoons? How do you put emphasis back on music and score? How do you have diversity of design? The answer, they decided, was to have creator-driven shows with completely new and original characters.[7] In typical Nickelodeon fashion, the answer would entail the same kind of "Us versus Them" philosophy that had fueled so many other decisions that Nick had made. Nickelodeon would do the opposite of what conventional wisdom dictated.

Creator-driven shows keep the creator of the show in a key creative role throughout the entire production process. Ideally, the creator of an animated show would have a background in animation and would be able to oversee every aspect of the show from writing and design through production. At the time, network shows rarely kept the show creators attached to their series, because the presence of a creator with a very specific vision tended to make the production process less efficient and harder to manage. The decision to have original characters made perfect sense in that it would allow Nickelodeon to differentiate itself from the broadcast networks. For the most part, the broadcast establishment had little interest in original characters, instead opting to play it safe with easily recognizable marquee characters, such as M. C. Hammer, the New Kids on the Block, and Macaulay Culkin. Nickelodeon's original characters would be funny, and the cartoons would be eleven-minute stories instead of the standard twenty-two-minute stories. These shorter cartoons would allow for more character comedy[8] and would avoid the violence and staid formulas that were typical of network cartoons at the time. The shows would not be gender specific and would stay away from the typical good guy versus bad guy stories. Also, the shows would be targeted to children eight to twelve years of age, which was slightly older than the typical network skew toward the five- to eight-year-old age group. The designs would need to be different from what was out there, different from each other, and more sophisticated than what was usually produced for the target audience.

As the network's vision of original animation came together, what probably helped the most was that Gerry Laybourne believed in animation. And it was no small matter that her husband, as an animator, was equally passionate about animation. No doubt his influence and animation expertise greatly benefited the network's animation and philosophy. Thus an animation department was born. Herb Scannell was put in charge of the department, which fit in with his duties handling development for the network. Scannell saw himself not necessarily as an animation fanatic, but as a champion of the vision the network had for animation.[9]

The broadcast networks generally paid production studios license fees for Saturday morning shows. The networks did not own the shows, and that tended to keep them from feeling invested in the shows. For financial reasons, according to Scannell, Nickelodeon made the decision to create a library for the network by fully funding and owning all the shows. This would allow the network to amortize the high costs of the shows over many years. They also decided that the network would have an in-house team that would oversee the development and production of each show, just as Geoffrey Darby's production department oversaw the game show and sitcom production. Animation production, of course, is expensive, so the next step was to figure out how to rationalize such an ambitious plan to the company, MTV Networks (and parent company Viacom). Tom Ascheim from the business development department was given the task of figuring out the financial scheme to allow the company to see that the investment would eventually provide returns.[10]

How could Nickelodeon get the funding it needed to pursue its vision? MTV Networks had succeeded as a company by running music videos, which were free, and by figuring out branding ideas, which mainly involved creating images from promos and running over-the-top promotions and contests. "The idea of spending big money was anathema to MTV Networks," observes Scannell. "Why make shows when you could buy them?"[11] Spending between $1 million and $2 million on pilots alone was a big bet. Laybourne would eventually have to convince the company that Nickelodeon would be successful at this endeavor because Nick would do it differently, the new shows would fit with the Nickelodeon environment where the existing shows out there did not, and the Nick shows would be better. Ultimately, she would be correct, and the success of the shows would fuel Nickelodeon's success and growth internationally. Of course, no one knew that at the time, and Laybourne skillfully managed expectations within the network, as one must with any start-up endeavor.

Once the network got the go-ahead to move into animation, a department got started and a mission, based on the meeting in Montclair, was articulated. The department would be comprised of just two of us, Vanessa Coffey, the producer, and myself. I moved over from programming and became the coordinator of animation development, a relatively low-level job. However, because there were only two of us, I handled the majority of the pitches and much of the paperwork. Coffey, who had worked on most of the initial development, would oversee creative direction and pilot production.

The assignment we had back in late 1989 and early 1990 was to find talent. The goal was to find creators with concepts for shows—either animators hidden in the studio system who had ideas deep in their brains, boutique studio animators, or independent animators who felt there was no place for them in the television animation industry. By the end of the year, we needed to produce eight five-minute creator-driven pilots, which would lead to four animated series. The pilots would be carefully tested in focus groups of kids, and partially from those results, series would be chosen. The series would premiere in a block on Sunday mornings, and the goal was to start them in August 1991.

In the early 1990s, Joey Ahlbum's singing dinosaurs, along with George evelyn's Big Beast Quintet, defined the look and feel of Nickelodeon as a network. © 1988 MTV Networks.

The first step was to take advantage of Nickelodeon's existing animation connections. Up to this point, Nickelodeon had only produced the aforementioned *Christmas in Tattertown* and *Nick's Thanksgiving Fest.* Yet through its on-air promotions and station identifications, the network had a rich tradition in animation. Independent animators and quirky animation studios had been producing station IDs for Nickelodeon, as well as MTV, for years. In many cases, Nickelodeon's image was more clearly articulated by the animated IDs than by the shows themselves. Probably the best known of those IDs were the Doo-Wop-A-Saurs, the singing dinosaurs designed by Joey Ahlbum, and the Big Beast Quintet designed by George Evelyn of animation studio Colossal Pictures. Since these two sets of characters were so closely identified with the network, it made sense to develop both into pilots for the network.

Joey Ahlbum was a New York–based animator who had worked on *Eureeka's Castle* for Nickelodeon and *Sesame Street* for Children's Television Workshop. The singing dinosaurs he designed for Nickelodeon helped define the look and feel of Nickelodeon as a network, and his designs seemed to be tailor-made for the network. His look involved simple drawings, wide-eyed smiling characters, dinosaurs wearing sneakers and sunglasses, and bold, bright colors. The pilot he developed and wrote with Mark Catapano was based on these very designs and was called "The Thunder Lizards." The Thunder Lizards were a pop band comprised of three dinosaurs named Dina, Desi, and Billy, who walked upright, played instruments, and dealt with a lazy, winged-beatnik roadie named Pter. In the pilot, the band is set to play a huge concert called "Dino Fest," at Crater Stadium, a concert venue packed with cheering dinosaurs of all sizes, munching on "red-hot tree snacks." (Yes, trees.) Their agent, Sammy, reminds them that they had better not be late, so naturally the youngest member of the band, the rebellious Billy, runs off to skateboard around Mt. Fire, an active volcano. The volcano starts erupting just as Billy gets near the top. As a rock comes rolling after him, Billy is rescued by Pter who flies up, saves him, and gets him back just in time for the concert. The band performs a pop song called "Thunder Lizards," and the crowd cheers. Focus group members told us that while the style, feel, and color of the pilot were very Nickelodeon, they did not find the pilot particularly funny or relevant to their lives. Some of the children didn't like the music that much and others thought it looked like it was for younger audiences. We realized the things we found the most amusing, such as Pter reading "Howl," were more amusing to adults than they were to our intended audience. After the first round of testing, Ahlbum and Catapano took a crack at redeveloping the idea as a series and putting more kid-oriented humor in it, but they never quite got it to the right place.

In the meantime, Colossal Pictures began work on their "Big Beast Quintet" pilot. Colossal had produced a number of IDs—as well as other projects—for the network. Colossal, a San Francisco–based studio, had started in 1976 and ultimately would become best known for two shows they would go on to produce for MTV, *Liquid Television* and *Aeon Flux*. George Evelyn, a director and designer at the studio, had created the Big Beast Quintet for a Nickelodeon ID that featured five brightly colored, simply designed animals walking down the street in orange shirts. Each shirt had some seemingly random letters on it. As they walked, they changed places, dashed into an open-backed yellow television set in the middle of the road, and by the time they had finished changing places, their shirts spelled out "Nickelodeon."

For the pilot, the Big Beast Quintet now worked as a team of roving reporters for a news show on Channel Zero in the town of Animatropolis.[12] The five reported to the one-eyed Nero Zero, a mercurial boss who literally had a "nice-mean" switch on his head. His assistant, Bombat, would change the switch at whim, leading to mood mayhem that the Big Beast Quintet had to deal with. In the pilot, the five reporters were sent off to Ice Cube Island to find the "Abominably Animated Man," a sasquatch-type character. The Quintet can't find him and end up faking their news reports from a stage set at the Wiki Tiki Lounge. They fake being lost, but Big Beast himself, feeling guilty, goes off to find the Abominably Animated Man alone. When Nero Zero comes to save them, he finds four of them on the set. He calms down considerably when Big Beast walks in with the Abominably Animated Man, who turns out to be quite friendly.

The look of the pilot was busy, colorful, and silly, but the story was perhaps a bit confusing and over the heads of the intended audience. The aesthetic was pure Nickelodeon, but the story, which boiled down to faking a news story and having a mean boss, was not compelling for the eight- to twelve-year-olds who saw the pilot. The network worked with Colossal to tweak the idea, but the revised series pitch, now called "Channel Zero," never quite seemed funny enough, and we realized how important—and how difficult—it would be to create original shows that would click with our young viewers.

At the same time, two pilots in LA started up. The first pilot, "Ren Hoek & Stimpy in Big House Blues," was the brainchild of Los Angeles–based Canadian animator John Kricfalusi.[13] When Kricfalusi pitched the series to the network, those in the room knew without a doubt that it fit the "creator-driven" philosophy perfectly. The original idea had been tailored to the broadcast networks and was a typical "kids in the neighborhood" show called *Your Gang*. In that version, Ren Hoek, a high-strung asthmatic chihuahua, and Stimpy, a naïve and not-too-bright red cat, were merely two of the characters in the show. In the initial pitch, Coffey felt Ren Hoek and Stimpy alone would work better as a show. The pilot showed Ren and Stimpy getting picked up by the dogcatcher. After seeing one dog, Phil, being taken away, Ren finds out that Phil is going to "the big sleep," and flips out. Later, while sleeping in their dog pound–style jail cell, Stimpy has a hairball that covers Ren. Ren is angry until a girl sees them and asks for the "poodle." Ren realizes he is free, but then looks back to see Stimpy waving sadly. "You can't have me unless you take Stimpy too!" he yells, and the two end up in a suburban house. Ren is given a sweater, and Stimpy is given cat litter. "My first material possession," Stimpy gasps.[14]

This pilot tested moderately well, but Coffey and others at the network were so supportive of it that it was destined to go to series, no matter how it tested. In retrospect, the show contained many patently adult elements, but at the time the show was described as "kid-friendly" because the characters had "a life-long friendship and a knack for getting into trouble." As network promotional materials would note, "Come to (Ren and Stimpy's) cartoon party and experience classic animation madness—taken to the cutting edge."[15] Within the network, the pilot received mixed reactions, but when the show aired and was extremely successful, even the biggest detractors remembered being "huge supporters" right from the very beginning.

Not far from Kricfalusi's Spumco studio in Los Angeles, the Klasky Csupo animation studio was hard at work on the five-minute "Rugrats" pilot. Klasky Csupo started out in 1982 doing graphics, commercials, and title sequences, getting its biggest breaks with Fox, for the *In Living Color* title sequence and the Simpsons segments on *The Tracey Ullman Show*. The company also produced the first few seasons of *The Simpsons*.

This is the one pilot of the eight that I can claim any real involvement in finding. In early 1988, when I was still working in the programming department, I had seen a small ad in *Millimeter* magazine for Klasky Csupo Animation, and I saw that it was the studio which had produced the *Simpsons* shorts. The ad said, "call for our reel," so I did. I got a call back from the head of sales, Larry LeFrancis, who sent me the reel and kept in touch. Shortly after that, when LeFrancis was in New York with Gabor Csupo, they came by to visit me at Nickelodeon. I felt a little guilty that I was merely a scheduler and was not going to be hiring them for animation anytime soon. But we kept in touch, and a year later I was calling them to tell them that I had moved into the new animation department, and suggesting they pitch ideas to Nickelodeon. I introduced them to Vanessa Coffey on their next visit to New York, and on her next trip to Los Angeles, she sat down with them. That was the meeting where they presented twelve pitches, the last of which was an idea for a show about the world from a baby's perspective.

The idea behind the show was, "What do babies do when the adults leave the room? What if they can talk to each other?"[16] The idea was a very personal one for Arlene Klasky and Gabor Csupo, as they had two children, and at the time one was a baby and the other son was slightly older. Clearly, this was a topic that was on their minds, and they included a fair amount of teasing about new parents' nervousness and dependence on baby experts. The idea became *Rugrats,* Nickelodeon's megahit show. In the pilot, "Tommy Pickles and the Great White Thing," Tommy witnesses the toilet for the first time and thinks it is alive. None of the babies are quite sure exactly what it is, so Tommy decides that he will go back that night to find out. In a slapstick scene, he ends up climbing up a plunger, pulling on a bathroom curtain and dropping it in the toilet, causing an overflow and generally creating mayhem. When the mess is discovered, Tommy is long gone, having hopped on the dog Spike's back to ride into the den to watch television.[17]

The pilot captured the world from a baby's perspective, but also seemed to have an "Us versus Them" feel, which made the babies' predicaments relevant to older viewers and appropriate for Nickelodeon. Additionally, the pilot presented a look surprisingly different from other animated shows on the air at the time. The original pilot had an unusual purple-pink-orange color palate, and an Eastern European–influenced animation style. The character outlines in the pilot were rough and hand drawn–looking, with shadow lines and even more extreme angles and exaggerations. One scene in the pilot showed Phil talking to Lil, but the perspective is from the back of Phil's mouth, and shows his teeth and his tongue moving. The short tested well in focus groups, and along with "Ren & Stimpy," was chosen to go into series production. The look of the Rugrats world changed slightly as it moved into series production, with the character designs looking more polished and the extremes not quite as extreme as those in the pilot.

Two more pilots started up in New York. The first one was "The Weasel Patrol," based on a humorous comic book. The characters, created by Ken Macklin and Lela Dowling, were a team of seven technology and prop-wielding weasels whose motto was "Protect, Serve, Run Away." Although they positioned themselves as the world's greatest crime-fighting force, they were quite inept. In their comic books, the Weasel Patrol generally won out through a series of random events that would inevitably work to their advantage. Finding a pilot story from the comics proved difficult, as each story had an adult element that rendered the story inappropriate for the Nickelodeon audience and needed to be removed. Ultimately, the pilot story was cobbled together with elements from different comic book stories. The completed story involved an attempt to keep top secret hot chili peppers, which were to be used as rocket fuel, from a smuggler. Both sides were incompetent, but good accidentally won out over evil, in the most confusing way possible. The idea ultimately seemed to be the most commercial and generic and perhaps the most "Saturday morning" of the pilots.[18]

The reaction of the focus groups was quite negative. In fact, I remember one nine-year-old boy commenting that he'd rather stare at a blank screen than watch this show. The comic books were quite funny, so the negative reaction had less to do with the charm of the characters and more to do with what the pilot lacked. The story was convoluted and unclear and should have been written from scratch as a pilot, rather than being pulled together from existing stories. Also, the pilot had seven weasels, two bad guys, and an alien creature—too many characters to absorb in five minutes. In addition, the weasels did not have developed personalities. A few had names, but it was hard to connect with them beyond that. After testing so badly, the pilot turned out to be a learning experience for all involved.

The next pilot produced in New York had a very different outcome. The idea was created by Jim Jinkins, a writer, actor, and illustrator who had been connected to Nickelodeon through the show *Pinwheel* in the early 1980s and who, more recently, had worked on Children's Television Workshop productions. He had written and illustrated an unpublished children's book about a boy named Doug. The design had the feel of an Ink Tank ad, with simple shapes, wavy lines, and water-colored backgrounds. The character was an eleven-and-a-half-year-old boy named Doug Funnie, who felt painfully average and unsure of himself. The comedic stories were told from Doug's perspective and showed how he, along with his overactive imagination, got through confusing or awkward situations.

In the pilot, Doug is about to attend his first dance, a costume party.[19] His dance partner is Patti Mayonnaise, a girl he has a crush on. Doug's nemesis, Roger Klotz, attempts to convince Doug that he can't dance and shouldn't even bother showing up at the dance. Roger volunteers to take Patti instead. Nevertheless, Doug attends, dressed as a slug, and while Patti teaches him to dance, Roger, dressed as a hammer, hassles Doug. When tripped, Roger's hammer head lands on Doug's foot, causing Doug to jump up and down in pain. The empathetic Patti begins to dance like Doug, calling it the slug hop, and soon everyone at the dance is doing the slug hop.

It was a somewhat old-fashioned story, but it was simple, character-driven, and easy to follow and relate to. That helped the pilot score the highest of the eight pilots with focus group members. The show was the most comfortable for the audience, and the easiest to understand, but it was the least risk taking and the most similar to stories viewers most likely had already seen. What helped make "Doug" work was that the creator, Jim Jinkins, and Doug were in many ways the same person, and the cartoon was the creator's story. We found that the creator's connection to the character was crucial to making the show a success.

The final two pilots were made with Cosgrove Hall Productions, an animation studio founded in 1976 by Mark Hall and Brian Cosgrove in Manchester, England. The studio was known for both its 3D model and 2D cel animation. They had created and produced *Dangermouse* and *Count Duckula* for Thames Television, and both shows had been acquired by Nickelodeon in the 1980s. Gerry Laybourne had maintained a good relationship with Cosgrove Hall, and so the decision was made to have them create two of the pilots. Their first one was called "The Crowville Chronicles." It featured a crow named Clarence T. Crow, and his photographer, Ozzie, a koala. The newspaper editor was a curmudgeonly rabbit. At the start of the pilot, the editor complains that there is no story for the front page and says that Crow has ten minutes to find one. After some slapstick frenetic action in which Crow runs around the office, he finds a large photo of a rhinoceros. He asks Ozzie to snap a picture of him in front of the rhino photo so he can write a story about carrying out a rescue in the jungle. As he stands there, the photo becomes real, and suddenly he is being chased by the rhino. They eventually jump out of the photo, but the editor doesn't believe the jungle rescue is a real story, and he storms off. Then the rhino runs through the room. In testing, kids didn't like the show much, finding it to be generic and uninteresting.

The slightly more promising of the two pilots was "Trash," a 3D stop-motion ("model") animation piece that took place on an all-trash planet. The main character was a little green man named Crash Morgan, who looked a bit like Marvin Martian. He was a superhero whose job it was to frequently save the world. He resided in Trashtown, where the local big guy was a tyrant named Boaster T. Strut. In the pilot two aliens in search of a vacation on the planet Bermudox accidentally land in a garbage dump in Trashtown. An intruder alert sends a group of tiny soldiers called "nutters" after the aliens. It's never quite clear why the aliens don't leave the planet as easily as they ended up there, but they don't, and they end up in jail. A "To Be Continued—If They're Lucky" sign flashes, and the pilot ends, unresolved. We had expected viewers to

respond negatively to the model animation, as historically this kind of animation has appealed mostly to younger viewers. However, the audiences
responded merely with indifference. Ultimately, the critique of the two
Cosgrove Hall pilots showed that the characters were a bit too formulaic,
and the creators, who had already been successful selling shows for years
in the United Kingdom, perhaps lacked the necessary passion to create interesting and believable characters that the audience would care about.[20]

In the course of developing these initial eight pilots, and in the next few
years, it remained difficult to find the right projects for the network. The
idea of creator-driven shows was foreign to the majority of people pitching properties. Most had trouble believing we were doing shows any differently from the rest of the networks. When we first went out looking for
ideas, we made the point that we were looking for projects that were unusual and different from what was already on, and it turned out that
many people did not believe us! It was only after the shows had premiered
that people seemed to understand our objectives.

On the other hand, after seeing *The Ren & Stimpy Show,* some people
thought that we would accept any ideas that seemed odd and offbeat.
Others felt that because they were animators or creators, and had strange
ideas, their shows would automatically work within the creator-driven
show philosophy. They never kept in mind that their idea would have to
resonate with the viewing public as well.

The next step for Nickelodeon Animation was selecting three shows
from the pilots to produce as series. "Rugrats," "Doug," and "Ren &
Stimpy" were chosen, and we found that we were one short for the two-
hour block that we had set out to develop. We had attempted to move
"Thunder Lizards" and "Channel Zero" to the next stage of series development, but neither ever seemed funny enough for the Sunday morning block. The network went ahead and premiered with an hour-and-a-
half block that got high ratings and generally positive press. The block
also had, for the most part, a positive reaction within the animation community. As an added bonus, the shows even attracted adult viewers. The
network had put approximately $11 to 12 million into the first round of
series production, and by the end of 1991, it announced an additional
$40 million investment for additional episodes of all three series. The
press release announcing the investment quoted Gerry Laybourne as saying, "Nicktoons has already paid off in terms of ratings and reviews. We
were confident that animation that was entertaining without being violent, and economically worthwhile without being purely commercial,

would be attractive to viewers and critics alike."[21] Herb Scannell today comments that, in retrospect, the success of the three properties validated the choices that had been made about going with creator-driven properties rather than presold and well-known ones.[22]

By coming out of the gate with three successful properties, Nickelodeon had made animation development and production look easy, at least to outsiders unaware of the behind-the-scenes process. Perhaps some of my motivation for writing this essay was to point out that while a "three out of eight" success rate is great, there were still five projects that, for various reasons, never moved ahead. In 1993, I attended a panel discussion about contemporary animated television series and one of the panelists, a knowledgeable animation historian, commented that clearly Nickelodeon had known exactly what they were doing when they developed the three pilots. He noted that they were particularly smart going for three completely different alternative animation looks: the animated ad look (*Doug*), the Eastern European animation look (*Rugrats*), and the Hanna-Barbera meets Tex Avery on drugs look (*The Ren & Stimpy Show*). At that point, I raised my hand, revealed that I had worked on all eight pilots, and said we had no such plan. I explained that we did eight pilots, of all different styles, and these were the three that had tested well. The audience seemed surprised that we had made eight and only ended up with three series.

Two years later, I was invited to give a presentation at the Society for Animation Studies conference in Greensboro, North Carolina. Michael Frierson, who was running the conference, had requested a presentation on "the Nick pilots that never made it." Having just left my development job at Nick, it seemed fitting for me to take the chance to sum up what I had worked on at Nickelodeon. I showed the five nonseries pilots mentioned here, as well as four others. I recall that the audience, mostly animation professors and historians, also seemed shocked that there were so many pilots that had never made it past the initial pilot stage. They also seemed particularly amazed that some of them were even made. I kept explaining, as I had at the panel two years earlier, that we had not always gotten it right in development. I made the same point again, that animation development is difficult.

And yet, ultimately, our lack of experience in some ways may have helped. We were happy that viewers liked any of the shows, and that creator-driven shows did indeed work. We were lucky to have had the chance to make pilots, rather than going straight to production. The animation piloting process is, after all, a luxury in an industry where a season of show production takes at least a year. Doing pilots requires great planning and forethought, putting at least two years aside for development and pilot production before there is any chance that a show can become a series. But the piloting process clearly was crucial for allowing Nickelodeon to come out of the gate with three hits.

The process allowed us not only to test characters, but in essence to test the entire creator-driven process. It allowed us to see which creators had the passion to make characters that connected with the audience, as well as to see if creator-driven ideas would work as series ideas. The piloting process also allowed us to see if the audience would accept shows which looked different from what was on television at the time. It may be hard to believe now, but the styles that Nickelodeon came out with in 1991 were considered risky.

Risk taking, scary as it is, is crucial to the advancement of the animated medium on television. The more risks you take, the more often you will end up with unusable material. But there is also a greater chance for success. I certainly benefited from the network's attitude at the time, as they were willing to take risks on both employees and show ideas. I was merely an animation fan from the scheduling department, and I was guided more by my love of animation than by any particular experience in developing shows. But that sort of risk taking was commonplace in the early years of Nickelodeon, and it paid off for many of us who worked there at the time.

The Nicktoons have been successful, and in the early 1990s were extremely influential as well. Creatively, the early Nicktoons had a great deal of stylistic influence on the animation of the early 1990s. *Ren & Stimpy* copycat programs, such as Disney's *Schnookums and Meat* proliferated in the early 1990s. Even more "crazy mismatched duos" were pitched but never made it to pilot. These were followed by shows more influenced by *Doug* and *Hey Arnold*, such as Disney's *Recess* and *Pepper Ann*.

Nickelodeon benefited from its early success in animation, and has continued producing one to two new animated series a year. There were eventually enough original cartoons for the network to create a digital channel called Nicktoons TV. The channel, which was launched on May 1, 2002, has a library of more than twenty-two hundred hours of animated programming, which, of course, was the goal promised by Gerry Laybourne early on. The Nickelodeon channel itself seems to run mostly

Nicktoons as well, as the animated series seem to generate the highest ratings and most attention for the network.

Most importantly, Nickelodeon has proved that creator-driven shows can work in the long term. Rather than being driven by toy companies and marketing concerns and finding (at best) short-term success, animated shows for kid audiences can succeed in a much greater way when driven by creative forces. Not surprisingly, then, in the mid-1990s every network attempted to produce creator-driven shows. At that time, even Hanna-Barbera, derided by many as one of the most formulaic of the television animation producers, began a creator-driven shorts program to develop pilots under the leadership of Fred Seibert.

Soon, however, the realization set in for many networks that creator-driven shows were extremely difficult. The degree of trust necessary sometimes requires years of commitment to a particular artist before finally creating a series, and networks rarely have that kind of time. By 1992, even Nickelodeon struggled with the creator-driven philosophy. In a well-publicized drama, John Kricfalusi was fired from *The Ren & Stimpy Show,* which begged the question of how to call it a creator-driven show without a creator. Several creators ultimately found the creator-driven process confusing, wondering why, if they were really the creative minds behind their shows, they had to take notes from network executives. The struggle has continued, with some creators naturally assuming positive leadership roles within their teams, and others becoming demanding dictators. The network itself seemed to stumble a few times, with shows such as *CatDog* which had little impact on its audience. The network has found, though, that *Spongebob Squarepants,* which in many ways has the energy and creativity of the early Nicktoons, is its biggest success since *Rugrats* and *Hey Arnold!*

The success of the Nicktoons, and of Nickelodeon in general, most likely influenced Turner's decision to start up his Cartoon Network. And of course, Cartoon Network's development process, considered by many (including my biased self) to be one of the most artist- and creator-friendly in the industry, was greatly influenced by Nickelodeon's process. Animation historians would point out here that I myself am a link, given that I learned how to develop shows at Nickelodeon, then moved on to Cartoon Network in 1995. I was so impressed by Cartoon Network's original programming that I moved over to the network and, along with head of programming and production Mike Lazzo, have structured the Original Animation department with most of the original philosophies that we had at Nickelodeon back in 1989 and 1990. Clearly, I was greatly influenced by Gerry Laybourne's big vision back in 1989. My own goal has remained the same as the one I was charged with back then. Find the best creators to make smart and funny cartoons, create enduring characters, and get people to laugh.

NOTES

I thank Herb Scannell for his excellent memory, and Khaki Jones for her invaluable assistance in preparing this essay.

1. Scott Webb and Donna Friedman (producers), *How to Nickelodeon* (New York: MTV Networks, 1992), 5.

2. See Jason Mittell, "The Great Saturday Morning Exile: Scheduling Cartoons on Television's Periphery in the 1960s," and Wendy Hilton-Morrow and David T. McMahon, "*The Flintstones* to *Futurama*: Networks and Prime Time Animation," in Carole A. Stabile and Mark Harrison, eds., *Prime Time Animation: Television Animation and American Culture* (New York: Routledge, 2003), 33–54 and 74–88.

3. "Thanksgiving Nightmare" was written and directed by Kevin Altieri.

4. "Thanksgiving Dreams" was written by Terrence McDonnell and Jim Carlson, and directed by Joe Pearson.

5. Kit Laybourne is probably best known for writing the animation classic, *The Animation Book* (New York: Three Rivers Press, 1998).

6. Herb Scannell, telephone interview with author, July 3, 2002.

7. Ibid.

8. Ibid.

9. Ibid.

10. Ibid.

11. Ibid.

12. The "Big Best Quintet" pilot was created by Japhet Asher and George Evelyn, written by Asher, and directed by Evelyn.

13. Up to that point, John Kricfalusi had been best known for his work on *The New Adventures of Mighty Mouse* with Ralph Bakshi, the *Harlem Shuffle* video for the Rolling Stones, and the *Beany and Cecil* remake in the late 1980s.

14. The Ren Hoek and Stimpy pilot was written by John Kricfalusi, Bob Camp, and Jim Smith, and was directed by Kricfalusi at Spumco, their Los Angeles–based animation studio. Stories of Kricfalusi's frenzied pitching style of acting out gags set off a trend of frenzied pitching at the time.

15. "Nickelodeon the #1 Network for Kids Explodes into a World of Animation" (New York: Nickelodeon Public Relations pop-up brochure for Nickelodeon's original animation, 1991), 2.

16. The idea was not much different from the National Periodical Publications/DC comic book *Sugar and Spike*, which had been produced from 1956 to 1971.

17. The pilot was written by Ben Herndon and Paul Germain, and directed by Peter Chung, who would go on to create *Aeon Flux* for MTV shortly thereafter.

18. The "Weasel Patrol" pilot was produced through Mark Zander Productions and was directed by Norton Virgien, who afterwards became a *Rugrats* director.

19. The "Doug Can't Dance" pilot was written by Jim Jinkins and Joe Aaron, and directed by Tony Eastman.

20. Scannell, interview.

21. "Nickelodeon Reorders All Three of Its Original Animated Series" (New York: Nickelodeon Public Relations press release, November 19, 1991), 1.

22. Scannell, interview.

5

"You Dumb Babies!"

How Raising the Rugrats *Children Became as Difficult as the Real Thing*

Mimi Swartz

Over the past decade, Arlene Klasky and her former husband, Gabor Csupo, have become two of the most highly regarded animators in Hollywood. In the late eighties, they helped create *The Simpsons,* a prime-time cartoon show based on Matt Groening's dark, deadpan comics about a modern family, and they went on to originate several successful cartoon series. In 1989, with the producer Paul Germain, they developed *Rugrats,* which was—until *SpongeBob SquarePants* came along ten years later—the most popular children's television cartoon show in the country. It has won three Daytime Emmy Awards, and *The Rugrats Movie,* a feature film based on the show, was a blockbuster in 1998. *Rugrats* stars a group of preternaturally adventurous toddlers: Tommy Pickles, a sweet-natured one-year-old; Chuckie, his two-year-old neurotic friend; and the year-old twins from next door, Phil and Lil. The children are far more precocious than their parents could ever imagine (they talk and conspire as soon as the grown-ups leave the room) but nevertheless often find themselves at the mercy of Tommy's malevolent three-year-old cousin Angelica, the unreliable emissary between the world of the children and that of adults.

Klasky, however, did not seem completely sanguine about *Rugrats* when I visited her in her austere office at Klasky Csupo, Inc., the animation studio she runs with Csupo. Her wide eyes, generous mouth, and abundant curly hair give her the pleasant, reassuring look of an earth mother, but her manner was guarded and anxious as we spoke. When I asked her about Angelica, she shrank back in her swivel chair. "I think she's a bully," she said. "I never liked Angelica."

This confession is somewhat surprising, since Angelica is one of children's favorite *Rugrats* characters. It is also largely through her that Klasky Csupo established the edgier, more sophisticated children's-cartoon style that is the studio's trademark. For millions of kids, Angelica is their icon of mischief—a direct descendant of Spanky McFarland, Dennis the Menace, and Eloise. Angelica was invited to promote the movie on *The Rosie O'Donnell Show,* and she was given a speaking role in a Ford Motor Company commercial. She has been honored by Girls, Inc., a nonprofit educational group formed to inspire young women to be "strong, smart, and bold," and her spin-off videos, *Angelica the Divine* and *Angelica Knows Best,* are strong sellers. Producers of children's programming regard her as completely bankable—the cartoon equivalent of Julia Roberts. They've been known to exhort writers and animators, "Get me more characters like Angelica!"

But Angelica was a source of dissension at Klasky Csupo. Although the idea of a baby show originated with Klasky, Angelica was not her invention, and Klasky never fully approved of the way Germain and the show's first team of writers developed her character. In the early years of the series, Angelica sued her parents, ran away from home in her baby convertible, framed her friends for crimes that she had committed, and terrorized innocents. (In one episode, she convinced Chuckie that his stomach was going to explode because he had eaten a watermelon seed.) Her trademark line became "You dumb babies!" and her only real friend was a ratty doll named Cynthia. "She's really nasty to Tommy, Chuckie, and the twins," notes U. C. Knoepflmacher, an authority on children's literature who teaches at Princeton University. "But, on the other hand, her manipulation of her businesswoman mother and her resourcefulness are tremendously attractive."

In a sense, Angelica embodied the approach to children's television pioneered in the late eighties by Geraldine Laybourne, then the president of Nickelodeon (she is now chairman and CEO of Oxygen Media). Laybourne wanted shows that were smarter and funnier than the standard children's programs, without being offensive or inappropriate for grade schoolers. So the network recruited writers and animators with a sharper sensibility, and then struggled to contain their darker impulses. It was a risky strategy, and it produced some anxious moments—notably, in *The Ren & Stimpy Show,* a manic cartoon series in the Ralph Steadman style about a cat and a chihuahua. Its creator, John Kricfalusi, was an irascible eccentric who was eventually removed from the series because his material was deemed too violent and scatological. With *Rugrats,* discord among the staff arose from the show's effort to be both cutting-edge and age-appropriate, and the angriest battles were fought over Angelica. In fact, the conflict over Angelica was in many ways responsible for the breakup of the original *Rugrats* creative team.

I first became aware of Angelica the way most parents do—when I was wandering in and out of the room while my son, then five years old, was watching television. *Rugrats* wasn't like the shows I had watched as a kid. In the world inhabited by the Pickles family and their friends, the children were precocious, and the dialogue was knowing, with sly references to everything from *Our Gang* to Sigmund Freud and sci-fi movies like *Fantastic Voyage.* The parents were ambitious, self-absorbed, and addicted to experts and gadgets. The babies had an addled, homely look that made them hipper than their smooth, glossy counterparts on other kids' shows. Tommy was good-hearted and brave, but he looked as though he'd been hit over the head with a blunt instrument. Angelica had tight yellow pigtails, saucer eyes, and a pointy little nose, and she spoke out of one side of her face, in a high, wrenching whine that evoked angry kittens. Chuckie, with his Swifty Lazar glasses and convulsed red hair, was a walking nervous breakdown.

The show projected a jaded view of family life and consumer culture. Aside from a somewhat dyspeptic Grandpa Lou, there was no wise Robert Young figure to offer protection and guidance. In one episode, Tommy's father, the scruffy, hapless inventor Stu Pickles, and his dithering but well-intentioned wife, Didi, took Tommy to a child psychologist. Stu had vehemently resisted seeking help, but once they arrived he talked compulsively to the doctor about his own psychologically deprived childhood, unaware that Tommy had crawled away to make trouble elsewhere in the high-rise office building. Another show introduced Angelica's parents—Drew, an investment banker, and Charlotte, an executive with Mergecorp who was always pictured in a suit and screaming into the cell phone at her assistant, Jonathan. "Charlotte, something's wrong with the fax machine!" Drew yelled in one scene. "Use the one in the bedroom!" she called from another part of the house. The show, in sum, is clearly designed with an intergenerational audience in mind.

Particularly in the show's first season, Angelica was mischief unchained, a child as shrewd as she was narcissistic. She was prone to

Rugrats appeals to both kids and adults. In this promotional campaign
Nickelodeon courts the adult audience with a pro-reading message.

malapropisms and liked to pontificate about the wider world. ("When you're rich, you can pay someone else to be scared for you.") At the end of each episode, Angelica received her obligatory comeuppance, yet she remained unrepentant from show to show. Her nastiness was funny, and, for Klasky at least, that was often a problem.

"Arlene didn't like Angelica," Germain told me. "She never did." When I visited him in his office, at Disney's studios, and asked about the show, he sounded like a man who had lost his kids in a custody battle, and in Hollywood terms he had. Germain is tall, pale, and rather intense, and has a passion for precision. In 1992, when the executives at Nickelodeon suggested a *Rugrats* Hanukkah special, Germain felt compelled to argue that a Passover special was a funny idea, but that a Hanukkah special was not. ("They wanted the Jewish version of a Christmas episode. I told them, 'You know, that's not an interesting story.'")

Germain is a native of Southern California, and studied economics at Berkeley in the late seventies. Before he was thirty, he was in charge of development for James L. Brooks, who created *The Mary Tyler Moore Show.* In the late eighties, Brooks produced the *Tracey Ullman Show,* and he hit on the idea of interspersing Ullman's skits with cartoons. Brooks admired the work of the Portland cartoonist Matt Groening, whose strip "Life in Hell" was just taking off with the grunge set, and he asked Germain to find a way to animate it. Germain turned to Klasky and Csupo, who were then still relatively unknown. Klasky had been trained as a graphic designer, and Csupo was a Hungarian émigré whose sensibility had been shaped by everything from Disney's fairy-tale classics to Ingmar Bergman's films and Frank Zappa's music. Germain took a chance on them: *The Simpsons* became an instant hit. Soon afterward, in 1989, Germain left Brooks to work as a development executive for Klasky Csupo. "We wanted to do intelligent stories for intelligent children," he told me. "I had worked with Jim Brooks, who wasn't gonna do crap, and I wasn't gonna do crap."

Later that year, Nickelodeon asked Klasky Csupo to pitch some ideas for shows. The night before the scheduled meeting with Nickelodeon, Klasky, who was on maternity leave, called Germain with one last suggestion. "What about a show about babies?" she asked. Germain was dubious, but then, he says, he went to bed thinking of a way to make it work. "Finally, it came to me," he recalls. "My pitch would be a show about little babies, but the minute adults leave the room the babies cognate and can talk." The next day, Germain and Csupo met with Vanessa

Coffey, who was then creating an animation department for Nick-elodeon. They proposed a show about a boy trying to escape his barren life at a gas station on another planet. Then they suggested one (prescient in retrospect) about life inside a bug city. Coffey wasn't buying. Finally, Germain pitched the idea for a series about babies' lives from the baby's point of view. "Great," Coffey said. "Let's do that one."

Germain, Klasky, and Csupo set out to create the squiggly and near-dissipated characters of Tommy Pickles; his dog, Spike; his parents, Stu and Didi; his Grandpa Lou; and the twins Phil and Lil. Their pilot, "Tommy Pickles and the Great White Thing," played to the insatiable ap-petite of children for toilet humor and touched on themes that would be-come *Rugrats* trademarks: exceptionally savvy kids (after his parents tuck him in for the night, Tommy grabs a hidden screwdriver to escape from his crib); oblivious parents (Stu is too busy with a high-powered din-ner party to notice that Tommy is on the loose); and knowing references to popular culture (after laying waste the bathroom, Charlie Chaplin–style, Tommy plops down in front of the television and changes the channel from a mindless commercial to a head-banger music video). Nickelodeon loved the pilot, and so did a majority of the kids in the test audience. The network ordered thirteen episodes.

To sustain the series, however, the creators needed more characters. Chuckie was added, as Tommy's cautious sidekick, but, according to Ger-main, "we decided we needed a bully, because to me childhood is about dealing with bullies." As a kid, Germain had been ruthlessly tormented by a girl. It was decided that the bully should be a spoiled little girl with self-absorbed parents. Her name would be Angelica.

The special appeal of animation is that there is no limit on mischief. If you can imagine it, you can do it—drop someone off a cliff, mash him into a pancake, twist his arm like a corkscrew. Legendary animators, such as Chuck Jones at Warner Bros., were masters of such mayhem and were scrupulous in their attention to aesthetic details. The fast action was ex-pensive, but that was of little concern during the Depression, when labor was cheap. There were some guidelines regarding "good taste," which ruled out toilet humor, but there was no concern about showing violence. Cartoon characters like Bugs Bunny, Daffy Duck, and Sylvester and Tweety were not regarded solely as children's fare. Cartoons ran as pre-views to movies, and were made to work on several levels.

It wasn't until the institutionalization of Saturday morning children's television in the 1960s that studios came under pressure to tone down gratuitous violence and "imitable" behavior in cartoons. At the height of Vietnam, and in the wake of the assassination of Robert Kennedy, concerns about representations of violence on television increased, and the networks increased the power of their Standards and Practices departments. Children's shows were now closely scrutinized. Kevin S. Sandler, the editor of the lively book *Reading the Rabbit: Explorations in Warner Bros. Animation*, explains how, in the 1970s, television censors persuaded Warner Bros. to cut cartoon scenes in which characters shot guns, drank gasoline or alcohol, made cowboy-and-Indian or other racial jokes, or received electric shocks. The number of times a character could be pounded into the ground had to be reduced from, say, six to two.

In the early days of television, most of the cartoons shown were drawn from the studios' enormous collections of thirties and forties classics. As original production increased, however, animation became more costly for the networks. Eventually, much of the production would be sent overseas. Still, cartoons were so expensive by the 1980s that animators often had to make a deal with a toymaker before they could create a show. As a result, Saturday morning became a wasteland of gender-segregated tie-in programs, like the refurbished *G.I. Joe* for boys and *My Little Pony and Friends* for girls. There was no incentive to make any changes until 1990, when the Children's Television Act required that networks be held accountable for the quality of children's programming or risk losing their licenses.

Meanwhile, animation for adults had become racier. Ralph Bakshi came up with a surprise hit in *Fritz the Cat*, in 1972, and sixteen years later Roger Zemeckis directed the sexy, successful *Who Framed Roger Rabbit?* In late 1989, *The Simpsons* combined animation and adult humor during prime time, and was followed by the far more cynical *Beavis and Butthead*, in 1993. These shows proved that grown-ups were perfectly willing to watch cartoons as long as the scripts were clever. They also demonstrated that children would watch far more complex material than they had been getting on Saturday mornings.

Nickelodeon's goal, in the late eighties, was to find a fresh way of entertaining six- to eleven-year-olds without patronizing or corrupting them. "We wanted to change the face of animation," Vanessa Coffey, who now develops children's programming for King World Productions, says. The company's buzzword was "sophisticated." "When I was growing up, *Bugs Bunny* was for kids and *Donna Reed* was for adults,"

Mitchell Kriegman, a former *Rugrats* story editor for Nickelodeon, says. "Which one was the more sophisticated? *Bugs Bunny* had classical references; *Donna Reed* was for morons."

But Nickelodeon knew it had to police content. The network took pains to avoid scenes that could be construed as dangerous to children. "Could we have the babies going down the staircase on a vacuum cleaner? No," Coffey says. "Could we have babies going out the window? No." Nickelodeon also addressed the issue of children's self-esteem—it didn't like characters calling each other "dumb" or "stupid"—and, appropriately for a company run predominantly by women, the issue of gender roles. Some *Rugrats* writers felt they were spending so much time creating confident and employed female characters that the men, devoid of advocates, began to look wimpy and ineffectual.

The aim, explains Craig Bartlett, who was a story editor on *Rugrats* and went on to create Nickelodeon's *Hey Arnold!*, was to be surprising and risky enough to get children's attention but safe enough so that "parents could leave it on all day"—unlike, say, "Fox, where kids would see a promo for a murder." In 1991, Nickelodeon launched "Nicktoons," which consisted of three new animated shows: *Doug*, a sweet, almost melancholy series about a suburban middle-school student; *The Ren & Stimpy Show*; and *Rugrats*.

"We set out to be *The Simpsons* of kids' shows," Paul Germain says. Germain wanted plot-driven shows with well-developed characters. But, almost immediately, Angelica's incorrigibility became a problem. Cheryl Chase, the voice of Angelica, had trouble being mean enough in line readings. One of the writers, Steve Viksten, who subsequently codeveloped *Hey Arnold!* with Craig Bartlett, would try to put her in the right frame of mind, saying, "Look. You're the J. R. Ewing of the show."

During the first season of *Rugrats*, in 1991, Klasky responded to Angelica's antics more as an overanxious parent than as a working animator. "With everything that came out, I'd ask, 'How would I feel if my kids were watching that?'" she told me. Many of the show's writers, some of whom also had children of their own, found her caution constricting. "*Rugrats* didn't take this view of childhood as innocent," one of them told me. In the second episode, the script called for Angelica to throw the babies' ball over a fence, precipitating an expedition to the neighbor's yard. Why, Klasky reportedly asked, did Angelica have to be so mean? In another episode, Viksten thought it would be funny if Angelica lost her temper and screamed, "You dumb babies!" Klasky didn't want the characters gratuitously insulting each other, but the line would eventually make it into a script and become a *Rugrats* signature.

Tensions escalated in a subsequent episode called "The Trial," which satirized recovered memory. Angelica urged Chuckie to confess that he had broken Tommy's favorite clown lamp, even though he didn't remember having done so. "That's where we established her," Germain says of Angelica. Klasky later told me, "I felt strongly that we needed a bully, but that we needed to counter how mean-spirited she was." The writers ended the episode with a Perry Mason moment in which the other *Rugrats* drew a confession out of Angelica. "I did it and . . . there's nothing you babies can do about it 'cause you can't talk," she taunts. Unfortunately, Didi overhears, and Angelica gets "the chair," a.k.a. a time-out. From that point on, Klasky frequently complained that the babies were too grown-up. Many of the writers mimicked the *Rugrats* characters, and Klasky sometimes lapsed into baby talk in voicing what she wanted. "By the end of the first season," one former staff member says, "she was driving some of us crazy."

After its first year, *Rugrats* won a Daytime Emmy Award for Outstanding Animated Program. Yet by its second season, in 1992, the show was being run by warring generals. What's more, Csupo and Klasky's marriage was collapsing. Both of them, however, continued to work on *Rugrats*, and Csupo often tried to mediate between his wife and the writing staff. Csupo, writers remember, tended to agree with them. "I was always pushing as far as good taste allowed," he told me.

By then, the show's growing popularity was inspiring comparisons to *Our Gang*, even though one of the show's former story editors, Joe Ansolabehere, recalls, "Paul always hated *Our Gang*. To him, the point of *Our Gang* was to give kids lines they would never say, watch them screw it up, and that's the joke." The *Rugrats* writers were actually more closely in tune with *Peanuts*. Craig Bartlett explains, "That was a major breakthrough in giving characters a psychology. Up till then it was anvils falling and shit." He goes on to say, "Charlie Brown was dealing with his depression, Linus was obsessed with his blanket—these were post–Dr. Spock ideas. . . . I thought, Holy cow, there's a cartoon character that's bummed out. Bugs Bunny was never bummed out."

"You know what I'm tired of doing?" Germain asked at the beginning of the *Rugrats*' second season. "These 'wreak havoc' episodes. They're never any good." (The episodes were described to me as "The Rugrats go to an office building and wreak havoc, the Rugrats go to a toy store and wreak havoc, the Rugrats go into a grocery store and wreak havoc.") Germain wanted to explore emotions: Why was Chuckie so afraid? Why was Angelica such a rotten kid? The writers look back on this as "the Golden Age of *Rugrats*," though a Nickelodeon story editor at the time sometimes criticized the adult-oriented *Rugrats* scripts as being "too *Thirtysomething.*" In later shows, the source of Angelica's brattiness was revealed: viewers met her parents, who were too busy with their careers to raise her properly. In "Runaway Angelica," she floods her father's home office with paper from the fax and copy machines, and when she is sent to her room she plots to run away. Hiding out in Tommy's yard, she shakes down the other Rugrats for cookies, and then spies her father inside next door. She overhears him musing that it is nice to occasionally escape the responsibilities of parenthood. Angelica bursts into the house, sobbing, and apologizes for all her past transgressions. "Take you back?" her father asks. "Honey, I didn't even know you were gone!"

When her meanness was exposed as neediness, Angelica became, if not nicer, then more complex. "She's an extremely vulnerable girl," Coffey assured me. "She's just hostile and angry." But her essential unpleasantness remained unchanged. In "Pickles vs. Pickles," Angelica sued Charlotte and Drew for making her eat broccoli. ("I think I can get your parents kicked out of the house," her lawyer assured her.) By now, some of the tensions on the show were finding their way into the scripts. For example, the writers parodied Klasky's passion for child-care experts by making Didi Pickles ever more slavishly dependent on a pompous child psychologist named Dr. Lipschitz.

By 1993, as *Rugrats* neared the première of its third season, the situation reached its predictable Hollywood conclusion: Germain was out (he eventually went to work for Disney, where he developed the highly rated Saturday morning cartoon series *Recess* for ABC), and the members of his writing team who hadn't already left the show did so in his wake. (The *Rugrats* creators are now prohibited by a legal settlement from discussing their split.) Despite winning a second Emmy, *Rugrats* appeared to have run its course, and in 1994, Nickelodeon ordered no new episodes. Still, Germain had left one extremely valuable asset behind: there were sixty-five episodes, the number required to send a show into syndication at Nickelodeon.

The year that *Rugrats* ceased production was also the year that it became a hit. Nickelodeon's president, Herb Scannell, who is a programming wizard, decided to broadcast the show every evening around dinnertime, and, as any parent can tell you, small children delight in repetition. Almost overnight, *Rugrats* became one of the most popular programs on cable, with 23 million viewers a week. Advertising and licensing deals took off, and in 1996, after two years of steady reruns, the show went back into production. Klasky and Csupo were repeatedly described in the press as creative geniuses, and their consistent failure to fully credit Germain compelled eight former *Rugrats* writers to sign a letter of protest to the *Los Angeles Times*.

Today, Klasky Csupo's animation studio takes up almost half a city block. Two battleship-gray buildings are decorated with cartoon characters from their shows, including their latest Nickelodeon hit, *The Wild Thornberrys*. Csupo's office displays *Rugrats'* three Daytime Emmy Awards, and a foot-high stack of issues of *Variety* with Klasky and Csupo on the cover; Burger King Kids Club Meal *Rugrats* toys share a shelf with boxes of Kraft's *Rugrats* macaroni and cheese. Csupo, a smallish, laconic man with a Mephistophelian beard, is more philosophical than his ex-wife is about the break with Germain. "It happens in every single production," he says, of the personality conflicts.

When *Rugrats* resumed, Klasky Csupo hired the writing partners J. David Stem and David N. Weiss, whose previous experience included CBS's *Cybill* and Nickelodeon's *Roundhouse*, as well as a final polish on *Anastasia*. They then hired the husband-and-wife team of Jon Cooksey and Ali Marie Matheson, whose "strong suit," according to a Klasky Csupo book about the making of *The Rugrats Movie*, is "heartfelt moments." The new episodes of *Rugrats*, which began airing in 1997, have some daring turns, but the edge has been softened with sentimentality.

The new team claims to love Angelica just as much as Germain did, but it seems to be a tough love. "She's actually my favorite," the story editor Kate Boutilier says. "I try to monitor how many times she says 'You dumb babies!' because it makes her look cruel, and she isn't cruel." (Boutilier also watches Angelica's weight. "I always count how many times she's motivated by food," she says.) "Some people around here felt you can't soften Angelica, but I just think it lends a whole new element," Boutilier explains.

In 1996, when Klasky Csupo got approval from Sherry Lansing, at Paramount, to develop a *Rugrats* feature film, the new team worked up a standard adventure tale that owes a great debt to Disney. The color is lush, there are dramatic, cliff-hanging moments, and it has a hip sound-track, featuring artists like Jakob Dylan, of the Wallflowers. The sly jabs at yuppie values have mostly been replaced by pee and circumcision jokes, one of which struck my son as so funny that he almost had to be resuscitated. Angelica is, once again, the catalyst. Fed up with the babies' squalling and fighting over Tommy's new baby brother, Dil, she sends them careering out of the house in the Reptar Wagon, one of Stu Pickles's strange inventions. But then, while the other Rugrats are having adven-tures in the woods, Angelica simply brings up the rear, tracking the ba-bies because she believes that they've kidnapped Cynthia, her beloved doll. Her only big scenes would have been considered out of character a few years ago: she now bravely steps between the babies and a hungry wolf, and then weeps when she believes that the wolf has mortally injured Tommy's dog, Spike. In the second *Rugrats* feature film, Angelica reverts to type, conspiring to get Chuckie's dad to marry a nasty amusement park executive. (To win his affection, the nefarious Parisian pretends to be lac-tose-intolerant, and even woos her would-be husband with a gold-plated asthma inhaler.) Even so, by the end Angelica is repentant. Children who once thrilled to Angelica's nasty schemes may be disappointed by her soft-ened personality. But Klasky is delighted. "I think she's great for the show," she told me. "I love Angelica."

NOTE

An earlier version of this chapter originally appeared in *The New Yorker.* © No-vember 30, 1998, by Mimi Swartz. Reprinted by permission of the author.

6

Diversifying Representation in Children's TV
Nickelodeon's Model

Ellen Seiter and Vicki Mayer

How do the producers of children's entertainment envision children as an audience? We interviewed children's producers, writers, agents, and other executives to analyze degrees of self-consciousness about gender and ethnic representation in children's programming, and how such awareness—or lack thereof—affects the development of new programs. Nickelodeon's programming in the 1990s challenged the accepted wisdom on marketing to girls and to boys. Nickelodeon's programs also expanded the representation of Latino, Asian American, and African American children on television. Our primary research, carried out in the summer of 1997, involved more than twenty in-depth interviews with producers, agents, writers, software developers, and other executives in cable and network television.[1] We wanted to test an informal hypothesis that more girls were being seen on television because more women, and mothers, were in decision-making positions in the industry. Seiter had formulated this hypothesis in the process of consulting for children's television and software developers, and attending events where industry professionals and academics are brought together to worry publicly—and with much publicity—about the impact of the media on children. Often these events are intended to sanitize and uplift the image of some of the major participants in the children's television industry. This chapter investigates the increasing attention and sophistication brought to bear on questions of stereotyping in the current marketplace for children's television programs.

As argued in the book *Sold Separately*, many aspects of children's toy and media worlds have remained unchanged since the 1950s; white, affluent children are the most desirable demographic group, and children's culture is largely dominated by male characters and action figures.[2] Gender stereotyping, and the symbolic annihilation of girl characters, has proven to be one of the most durable features of children's media. A fairly radical breakthrough took place in the 1990s, however, when Nickelodeon cast girls as leads, without losing the audience of boys—as industry wisdom predicted would happen. Onscreen, Shelby Woo, Alex Mack, Clarissa, and Angelica were intelligent, adventurous, and physically daring. Offscreen, Nickelodeon's ranks were full of smart women, who had a high degree of feminist consciousness—and happened to be mothers, much like Gerry Laybourne herself. Could the presence of these women at Nickelodeon be the simple explanation for the change in children's programming to include more female characters? Does increased representation of girls follow simply from the increased employment of women?

There are more women in senior level positions in kids' programming today than in all other types of programming. However, there are more men in animation and in writing and production—positions that arguably have the strongest influence on the final product. Within the television industry, kids' programming is considered less prestigious than other types of programming no matter what the salary, and for this reason, it has historically been more open to women. None of the women we interviewed complained of discrimination against them in other segments of the television industry. Yet they attributed the stronger presence of women in children's television to networking among women, women hiring women, and women's interest in kids' programming. Typical of the perception of women's leadership in the industry were the remarks of consultant David Kleeman:

Question: There seem to be a lot of women in charge of kids programming. Was it always like that?

Years ago that would have been unusual. Gerry Laybourne was the president of Nickelodeon and now is president of the Disney Cable Network. She used to be the only one. Now most are women. Margaret Loesch at Fox. Lucy at CBS. . . . There's only one guy I can think of.[3]

Laverne McKinnon, director of Children's Programming at CBS, gave this account of her own career and the advantages of working in kids' programming:

> In senior level management, there are more women than men to be sure in children's programming than any other prime-time section. In part, I think women are here because they're networking more. In another way, children's programming is seen as the stepchild of the programming groups. It's all about revenue. Even Fox Kids, which brought in huge amounts of money under Margaret Loesch, didn't get the respect they deserved from the rest of Fox. We're always the underdog. I got into children's programming because I saw some fantastic opportunities that were not being exploited. You can be more entrepreneurial in children's programming. Be a pioneer. It's so much more difficult in prime-time sitcoms where everything is so formulaic.

On a similar note, Halle Stanford, executive developer for Jim Henson Productions, Creative Affairs Division, viewed the large number of women in the business as related to opportunities for greater creativity:

> There are a lot more women now in the development business than men. In fact, the women are in charge. That proves there are some really strong women attracted to this field even down to the agents. [pause] At my level, everyone is a woman. There are lots of moms.

Nickelodeon is universally recognized as the pioneer in programming with girl leads, and some executives attributed this explicitly to the "agendas" of women working in the industry. Most people we talked to were either more cautious or more pessimistic about the increased representation of girls on children's programs—others were blatantly resentful of Nickelodeon's success. For example, when asked about the presence of girls, Roland Poindexter, director of Programming and Development for Fox Kids Network, answered:

> We all have our own agendas. But if you talk to most women in Saturday morning programming, they are not looking for just strong girl characters. You have to understand TV first. They know that traditionally, boys will watch boy programs but they won't watch girl programs. So you have to create a show that addresses both sides of the audience.[4]

Poindexter also gave a practical, business explanation for Nickelodeon's legendary success, linking it to the network's freedom from advertisers seeking a majority of boys (ages six to eleven) in the audience. The message was that it worked for cable, and for an all-kids' network, but was unrealistic as a business strategy for network kids' shows:

> Nickelodeon had such a success with girl-centered programs only because everyone else was so disproportionately focused on boys. Also, when Nickelodeon started, they just needed a number. They took shows that would never have made it at most of the networks because [they] wouldn't get the numbers we're used to. *Clarissa* would never have survived on Fox Kids because it wouldn't get a boy audience over the age of five. The younger boys would watch the program, but you still need a majority boy audience. [pause] The average program has 60 percent boys and 40 percent girls. A show like *Animaniacs* is more balanced, but still it gets something like 55 percent boys and 45 percent girls. If you can get that ratio in the audience, that's great. But at this point, girls are not drawn to the television the same way boys are. They start reading earlier, and talking to their friends. Boys can watch television until they're much older, and they go buy the stuff too. Girls don't typically buy the toys after a certain age. We don't want to alienate the girl audience, but we can't sacrifice the boy audience either.

The theme of girls' lesser interest in children's television was echoed by Nancy Steingard, executive vice president of Universal Cartoon Studios: "The networks tell us that boys won't watch girls' programs, but girls will watch boys' programs. I've also heard networks say that boys will stay with animation longer. Girls mature faster so they watch cartoons less after a certain age." The logic of the market, often reinforced in the trade press,[5] is readily available as a rationale when producers are challenged about the politics of representation.

Other executives were openly hostile to the pressures on gender representation they felt in the wake of Nickelodeon's success. One executive producer for an independent supplier of cartoons, for example, took off on a rant about political correctness:

> The problem is now you're getting into the politically correct arena. It's very ephemeral. It's popular now to have strong female characters. But you have to go to the other side too and ask are we emasculating our

male characters? You've got to have all kinds of characters. Who's going to create a wimpy girl character now? The real challenge is to have all sort of characters, male and female. On one of our shows, we have a strong female protagonist, but we also have a female who's totally unsure of herself. There are going to be girls watching who identify with the less confident girl, and in a way we're telling girls, it's ok to feel confused. Not everyone is born to be a leader. You have to be aware of the p.c. police now.

Some women in program development were openly cynical about the extent of any changes in gender stereotyping. According to Halle Stanford:

They all say they are [interested in girls' shows] but they're not. . . . The networks are starting to be more concerned about girl shows. But they all say they want them and then don't broadcast them. We've been taking them stuff—really quality stuff—and they don't pick it up. I guess you could say there's more of a commitment but everyone's still scared.[6]

Unexpectedly, Corey Stern, of Saban Entertainment—famous for action-superhero series—was especially frank about the limitations of Nickelodeon's first successful female leads:

There are some girl leads that appeal to both boys and girls. *Clarissa*'s and *Alex Mack*'s success means there are more girl leads, thank God. Still, no one's willing to say they're putting on a show for girls. Of course, there's a lot of shows that are aimed just at boys, but no one would say it that way. As soon as someone takes a chance on it, there will be shows for girls. The networks, but even more so the advertisers, are worried if you market a program for girls, you're instantly going to lose half the audience—that is, the boys. They're also worried that the girl show might break up the programming pattern in the block of programs. The majority of toys are bought by boys. Girls are pickier with their products. The perception out there is that boys will buy the action figures and so they're worth more money. Girls buy more books and advertisers don't sell books on television.

Nickelodeon executives were not eager to take credit, however, for their own success with innovations in the arena of girl characters. Rather, they seemed to follow a party line aimed at widening their potential advertisers and marketers, reiterating in all interviews that their shows were really about character and interesting story lines. The following is from an interview with Cyma Zarghami, senior vice president of Programming and general manager of Nickelodeon:

Question: Why are there so many girl protagonists?

There aren't any more girl protagonists than boy protagonists. It just feels like a lot because we have some. We care less about gender in our programs and more about kids. Our demographic research shows that boys will watch programs with girl protagonists, so we've shattered that myth. *Clarissa* was our first big success with girl protagonists. She ran from 1989 to about 1991. She was so successful, though, because her issues were not specific to girls but to all kids: school, friends, and homework. Her best friend was a boy too.

Question: When you create a girl character though, what are you looking for in terms of how she looks or acts?

We pay more attention to her attitude than the physical aspects. We want someone who could be a kid's friend, not someone more pretty or popular. We also don't want a character to be overly feminine because those are not typical girl characteristics. Those factors influence the way we cast.

This same Nickelodeon "party line" extends to the ethnic and racial representation on the shows. Here again, Nickelodeon is proud to take the lead over other producers, but carefully avoids sounding like its goal is political correctness or "green vegetable shows"—television that is good for you.[7]

Nickelodeon's record on racial and ethnic diversity is noteworthy. From its preschool morning block, Nick Jr., to its prime-time live-action shows, its characters are strikingly diverse. Nickelodeon developed the live-action sitcom *The Brothers Garcia,* with Latino producer Jeff Valdez and Latino director Mike Cevallos. Now entering its fifth year, it is at the top of Nickelodeon's ratings for live-action shows. Nick followed that success with *Taina* (which premiered in 2001, and doubled its ratings in 2002). The producer of *Taina,* Maria Perez-Brown, is a former attorney (and producer of *Gullah Gullah Island* for Nick Jr.) who has publicly argued for the importance of affirmative action for the project of diversifying representation on television. Both Perez-Brown and Valdez believe that one reason Nickelodeon has invested in two shows with Latino characters when other networks shy away from offering any, is that the executive in charge of programming happens to have a Puerto Rican mother.[8] In addition to these two prime-time shows, Nick Jr. offers *Gullah Gullah Island, Little Bill, Kids Say the Darndest Things,* and *Dora the Explorer.* Nickelodeon reports a concomitant steady increase in Latino and African American audience share.

Similar to the Nickelodeon line on gender representation, however, is an express disavowal of the politics of representation. As Patti Miller of Children Now says, echoing the Nickelodeon line, "The interesting thing about these shows is that race isn't the major issue. They're about kids of different backgrounds learning from, and interacting with, one another."[9] Race, in this rhetoric, is a "difference" on par with having a single mother, or living in an apartment, or being gifted with a special talent. Circumstantial and personality traits are equated with racial and ethnic differences as factors that might cause a child to have a "different background."

Nickelodeon's more inclusive representational practices followed from its audience research techniques, which emphasized a diverse pool of children. According to Bruce Friend, vice president of Worldwide Research and Planning, minority kids were deliberately sought out for focus group testing—always a core element in Nickelodeon's strategy to keep the network in tune with children's everyday realities:

> We oversample a bit with minorities. We've had some distinct groups of minorities as test groups. We skew the norms in terms of their representation in the population. But the multicultural focus groups give us different kinds of information. We ask them how Nickelodeon fits into their lives. We don't have a problem with representation and thus need the focus groups. It's the opposite. We're very strong in this area. We want to further our understanding of our appeal. We recognize our audience is not homogeneous.

At the time of our interviews in 1997, Nickelodeon's multiethnic character list included Shelby Woo, African American and Asian American characters on *Rugrats,* and Kenan and Kel on *All That.* We asked John Hardman, executive developer of Klasky and Csupo Productions (the creators of *Rugrats*), whether Nickelodeon planned any shows specifically for Latino, African American, or Hispanic kids.

We're trying to develop some shows which are ethnically diverse. One of them is specific for African Americans. *Rocket Power* is very ethnically diverse. The show has Hispanic, Asian and African American characters. We made a conscious effort to reflect the diversity of the people who do extreme sports in Southern California. So Klasky and Csupo decided to do research there and looked around at the people. We feel some sort of responsibility to be accurate.

Question: Did Nickelodeon ask for more ethnically diverse shows?

There are some African American characters on *Rugrats*. The response Nickelodeon has gotten to those characters on the program has been phenomenal. Nick wanted us to put those characters in their own series. But we're not going to do that. They were created for *Rugrats,* and if we put them in their own series, they couldn't hold it on their own. Their flaws would show too much. That's why we're doing our own program now.

By comparison, producers from other networks exhibited a defensiveness about racial and ethnic stereotyping. Typically, there was an emphasis on race having to fit into the "program's world," which seemed to translate into African American characters (often cast as "clowns") belonging only in urban, hip hop settings, loosely based on the 1970s Bill Cosby production *Fat Albert.* Everyone acknowledged the paucity of Latino and Asian American characters. Some answers were cagey; others offered stereotypical or dismissive views of children of color in their audience.

When the ABC network was premiering *Doug* and *Pepper Ann,* we asked Jonathan Barzilay, vice president and general manager of Children's Programming, if ABC was aiming for racial diversity in its shows.

That's something we look at in every episode of every program. We have a broadcast standards department that looks at each episode. This issue is more applicable to some programs than others. *Doug* has dealt with the issue by making all the characters different colors: blue, yellow, and green. But in shows about animals, it's not an issue. I mean on *Winnie the Pooh,* is "Tigger" a minority? I don't know how to answer that.

In fact, Disney has populated its cartoons with more racial caricatures based on animal types than any other media producer—but animals and fancifully colored characters is one of the primary ways that the politics of representation are avoided (or at least masked) in children's media.

In an attempt to represent African American children, Warner Bros. was experimenting with *Waynehead* at the time of our interview with Christopher Keenan, director of Children's Programming for Kids WB!:

> We have *Waynehead*. It's produced by Damon Wayans. It's about a ten-year-old urban black youth, named Damie Wayne, growing up on the Upper East Side. He's supposed to be modeled on Damon Wayans as a child. There's also an African American cast on that show. [pause] Aside from that, *Batman* and *Superman* both have a multiracial cast. Renee Montoya on *Batman* is Hispanic. We make a conscious effort to have human characters on our dramatic programs that are multiracial. Even on *Sylvester and Tweety,* they travel often to nonwhite countries in Asia and Africa. In those cases, most often the voices are by nonwhite actors.
>
> *Question: So has WB thought at all about Spanish-language programs?*
>
> It's funny. Until recently, we had the Warner Channel in Latin America. They were supposed to work with us to create bilingual products, but the project never went anywhere. The money got invested into translating the library and not developing original programming. So it's been talked about but nothing's been done. And our audience is really not Spanish speaking.

Avery Cobern of the Standards and Practices department at Fox gave similar answers to these questions. That year Fox also planned one show with an inner-city setting:

> Right now we have a program *C. Bear and Jamal* on Saturdays that takes place in the inner city — actually it's supposed to be South Central LA. It's full of African American characters with some white kids thrown in for good measure. *Spiderman* has an African American story editor. *Goosebumps* has lots of kids of different races. I think it's just most important to show everyone.
>
> *Question: Any chance for any Spanish programs?*
>
> Well we caption everything, but I don't think there will be anything specific. *Power Rangers* will have a Latino character. He is really hot! I've seen the actor, who plays soccer, and he'll be on in the fall. In Los

Angeles, I don't know how it is in the rest of the country, but here it's really important to represent the population.

Both *Waynehead* and *C. Bear and Jamal* lasted only one season. One non-network producer predicted at the time: "What we're seeing more of is city kids' shows which have a mix of ethnicities, African American kids, Hispanic kids. . . . But those shows don't generally succeed. The ratings are too low. It's hard to preach to kids. Comedy is more successful."

A supplier of programming for PBS gave one of the most off-handed—and therefore revealing—comments on whether there were any thoughts of making Spanish-language programs for Latino audiences:

> If you're talking about a program in Spanish, that depends on the financial logistics. There are a certain number of producers who make programs for the Spanish-speaking population in the United States and abroad, but I'm not planning on it. We do have these two Latino characters [on one of our shows] which reflects the growing Spanish-speaking population in the United States.
> *Question: And do they speak Spanish?*
> It's more of a seasoning than anything else. There's some Spanish language and they have fiestas and holidays. PBS asked for the Latino characters. So they're interested in recognizing that part of the U.S. population, which I'm not sure is a good idea. But we did it.
> *Question: Why wouldn't it be a good idea?*
> Because we should leave their culture alone. You know what I mean? Actually, I retract that. We are the great American melting pot, so it's okay.

A more critical perspective on the topic of Latinos on television came from Roland Poindexter at Fox Kids:

> *Question: Do you think Latinos are less represented than African Americans?*
> Without a doubt. In the last ten years, you can point to at least five or six programs that prominently feature African Americans. Latinos are totally more unrepresented. If I could speculate, it's a matter of arrogance and ignorance. A significant portion of the Latino audience speaks Spanish predominantly and watches Spanish-language television. So

they have been ignored. The industry, though, also ignores that many Latino communities have been here forever, as long as the United States. These communities want good programs. They contribute to the marketplace and deserve to be represented. The challenge in my job is not to get more minorities to watch television programs, but to get the mainstream to watch more multiethnic programs. I want to develop programs that cross racial and class boundaries.

Question: Has there been any talk of more bilingual programs?
  We've talked about it. On *C. Bear,* we've talked about throwing in more Spanish words. . . . But I don't think bilingualism is an agenda. To be quite frank, the common language of our audience is English. Other communities need to learn English. It's the "language of commerce," as they say. If we use bilingualism, it can't be condescending. We put it in if it fits with the themes of the show. We won't make it specifically a focus.

While distinctive changes in gender representation seem to be widely recognized by those working in children's television, the interpretation of these changes and their significance are widely contested. A handful of executives attribute the increase in girl characters to the feminist agendas of women working in the industry. But Nickelodeon's example has produced resentment over the perceived pressure to change business as usual, and a defensive rationalization of the status quo based on business imperatives. The subtext running through our interviews is the level of tension between network (and traditional Saturday morning programmers) and cable, and between the mass market versus the higher end of "quality" children's programming.
  Curiously, professionals used the "worldwide" marketing of cartoons to explain the limited ethnic representations in children's programs. Steingard at Universal Cartoon Studios said, "One issue that I've heard some people say is that the minority programs won't win over a foreign audience. It's harder to sell a program for American minorities overseas." Here, global distribution of children's TV production justified keeping the programs as "white" as possible to represent American children abroad. The timidity around increased representation stems from the hugely increased pressure all these executives feel in the economic climate of today's television industries. Industry changes are killing some of these executives, whose jobs are more competitive and cutthroat than ever.

Some, like CBS, sound like their network might cut them altogether. NBC shies away from kids' programs now, concentrating on dominating the preteen market instead.

Furthermore, vertical integration has had a huge impact on the children's television market. Each network only buys from its own studios or demands part of the rights to syndication from the few independents still operating in the market. One result is that major studios can only go with highly familiar, oversaturated cartoon characters because of pressure to provide the network with a reliable cash flow. An already recognized cartoon character is less risky and promises more reliable licensing opportunities than the more creative work of an independent producer introducing a new character. Another result is that all the major studios shoot for simultaneous release overseas. Satellite distribution agreements throughout Europe, Latin America, and Asia ensure that new releases have to promise global appeal—since the footprint is so wide, the cartoons must appeal across nations and cultures. Cable is a huge force but really has turned out to be another venue for large corporations with network stations. Fox is moving to cable and WB has Cartoon Network, now a competitor for Nickelodeon's audience.

A number of possible explanations for Nickelodeon's more diverse characterizations emerge from this study. One key factor is the network's lack of emphasis on Saturday morning as a time slot; Nickelodeon conceived of itself from the beginning as a continuous channel, a home base that would extend throughout the week. This eliminated the imperative of direct competition with the networks. By declining to compete on Saturday morning, it also freed itself from the domineering interests of toy advertisers. Nickelodeon ruled out violent action in its programs from its inception, and thus opened itself up to a larger pool of creative talent who provided more diverse representations, while currying favor with parents, critics, and educators. By turning down commercials based on weapons and action figures early on, it saved itself from the kind of enslavement to the ratings for boys six to eleven that dominates other programmers. Nickelodeon's policy of presenting characters who were normal, flawed, and unspectacular worked well with the agenda of "broader-casting": girls were never too good to be true, African Americans and Latinos avoided being model minorities, implausible tokens. Nick's rejection of superhero material also meant that the dark-skinned villains and Aryan protagonists—types that plague *Batman, Superman, X-Men,* and *Spider-man*—were excluded. Its emphasis on creating a space for "kids only" made Nickelodeon steer clear of sexual references as well as sexualized racial stereotypes. Further, Nick's comic approach helped save shows from the charge of political correctness.

At the start of the 2002 fall season, Nickelodeon had the highest percentage of up-front advertising sales in the children's market. Having eschewed the narrow interests of toy advertisers from the beginning, Nickelodeon now bargains with over one hundred parent companies, rather than individual brands. Nickelodeon's programming is far more diverse and more child-friendly than Cartoon Network—its closest competitor, who actively courts adolescent and young adult males as its core viewership.[10] One contradictory result is that many producers so fear any further erosion of their market share that they are wary of any innovation. Maintaining position in the ratings is the top priority for children's television executives, more important than anything else. Meanwhile Fox and NBC have so despaired of making money on children's ad sales that they have leased off their Saturday morning blocks to second parties—4 Kids Entertainment and Discovery Communications, respectively.[11]

Nickelodeon's success must be appreciated in light of the fact that children's TV is one of the most competitive and fickle of all types of programming. In short, Nickelodeon has far outpaced other children's television producers—and most prime-time producers as well—with its record of creative programming that reflects some facets of diversity in the children's television audience. The largest gains have been made in increasing the representation and variety of female characters: here the ideological commitments of individuals working at Nickelodeon have dovetailed nicely with market trends toward taking girls more seriously as a media and advertising market. With the representation of Latinos, Nickelodeon has deliberately sought qualified producers and conscientiously pursued Latino families as a potentially lucrative market: here Nickelodeon has positioned itself favorably and is well ahead of the networks, most other cable channels, and most advertisers. The returns on this investment in terms of brand recognition and consumer-viewer goodwill are likely to determine whether other children's producers follow suit in developing live and animated programs that feature child characters of color, as they did in the area of developing new cartoon properties featuring girl characters (even as boys continued to hold most of the starring roles).

Surveys of television prime-time content over the last few years have noted increasing numbers of Anglo main characters, even on situation comedies.[12] This undoubtedly predisposes children to favor those few genres of television programming where diversity is commonplace but content is often inappropriate for children, namely, wrestling, reality programs, and news programming, which tends toward especially threatening images of children of color and girls as victims of crime. Nickelodeon's model of diverse representation, sensitivity to age-appropriateness, and avoidance of violence and explicit sexuality becomes even more significant when viewed in this context of the deteriorating options for the child audience on the prime-time network schedule. We can only hope that more television producers—in children's and mainstream programming—will follow Nickelodeon's lead.

NOTES

1. The interviews included personnel from CBS, ABC, Nickelodeon, Fox Network, Columbia Tri-Star, Jim Henson Productions, Universal Studios, and Mattel. Vicki Mayer also made a site visit to Nickelodeon studios in New York.

2. Ellen Seiter, *Sold Separately: Children and Parents in Consumer Culture* (New Brunswick, N.J.: Rutgers University Press, 1993).

3. Telephone interview with David Kleeman, exec. director, American Center for Children's Television, 6 July 1997.

4. Interview on 29 July 1997. At this time Poindexter had been director of Programming Development at Fox Kids for nearly five years.

5. David Tobenkin, "Syndicators Programming to Girls: At Least Four New Kids' Shows Feature Female Leads," *Broadcasting & Cable*, 28 November 1994, 25–26.

6. Telephone interview with Halle Stanford, executive developer for Jim Henson Productions, Creative Affairs Division, 16 July 1997.

7. The term is Geraldine Laybourne's. See Jenkins's interview in this volume.

8. Comments made at the professional panel, "Everything You Ever Wanted to Know about Hispanics but Were Afraid to Ask," Latino Laff Festival, San Antonio, Texas, 30 June 2001.

9. Chuck Barney, "Kids' Channels Beat Networks to Diversity," *San Diego Union Tribune*, 3 August 2002, D1.

10. *Electronic Media*, 7 August 2002, 8.

11. *Electronic Media*, 18 March 2002, 11–12.

12. *Fall Colors: Prime Time Diversity Report 2001–2002*, Research Report Children Now, 2002. www.childrennow.org.

7

Interview with
Geraldine Laybourne

Henry Jenkins

Geraldine Laybourne has been a leading figure in American cable television since 1980, when she was first hired as program manager for Nickelodeon. She worked her way up through the ranks at that network, becoming its executive vice president and general manager in 1984 and the network president in 1989. She was named vice chairman of MTV Networks in 1992 and left the company to become president at Disney/ABC Cable Networks in 1996. She is now the chairman and chief executive officer of Oxygen Media, which she founded in 1998. Prior to entering television, she was a teacher at the Concord Academy in Concord, Massachusetts, the cofounder of the Media Center for Children in New York City, and a partner at Early Bird Specials, an independent TV production company. Henry Jenkins conducted this interview with Laybourne at her offices at Oxygen Media on July 22, 2002.

Geraldine Laybourne: Let me tell you a secret about Nickelodeon. We had a mission!

Henry Jenkins: Tell me about it.

GL: I had been a teacher of media education and was fascinated with the way kids saw the world. I had two kids of my own, and in watching television with them I was very disappointed in the range of TV available. It felt to me like there was this conspiracy, and I say that with a big smile on my face. But it felt to me like there were four animation studios in Los Angeles who were churning out very formulaic, look-alike stuff for kids and that there was no chance for an independent filmmaker to come in with a fresh idea. So how was the young Jim Henson ever to find his way into TV? And I had come from a background of testing stuff with kids and having my own production company. My own production company's goal was to market the work of independent filmmakers to television.

I had a lot of theories. One was to involve kids in the process. And another was to introduce new creative voices, since Hollywood does not have a lock on kids' programming. Being a total outsider, it appeared to me that people in Hollywood were going into the kids' arena because that was a way into television—they weren't really in love with kids or with kids' programming but it was a way to pad their resumé. We had these crazy theories that if you wanted to work at Nickelodeon, you had to love kids and want to do the best for them. But we had a rough start.

HJ: How did you first get involved with the network?

GL: When I joined Nickelodeon, I was an independent producer. They had hired me to do two pilots for them on a show called *Video Dream Theatre*, which was taking kids and animating them into their own dreams using various production techniques like color photocopying. Pretty interesting for a parent or a filmmaker, but it was excruciatingly bad television. But they hired me in the first year of its existence—1980. Nickelodeon was just a venue at that time. They had five shows on the air that ran in a loop—*Video Comics, Pinwheel, Front Row Features, America Goes Bananas* and *Hocus Focus*. There were no commercials and a mime filled in time between programs no matter how long the gap! It was really like "put on a show" time—it was very primitive.

Warner Amex—Nickelodeon's parent company—hired Cy Schneider and me on the same day. He was the new boss and I was two rungs down the ladder. I had been a teacher. He had been an advertiser who had put Barbie and Hot Wheels commercials on television, and he had a lot of desire to do something good for kids in a kind of "green vegetable" way. He did a lot to professionalize Nickelodeon, but he brought conventional thinking with him, hired Hollywood producers, and told kids what to do. His slate of shows consisted of *Reggie Jackson's World of Sports*, Leonard Nimoy's *Standby: Lights, Camera, Action*, and *Against the Odds*. He believed in an advertising approach that said to kids in a booming voice, "This is fun! Come watch us!" The kids heard a male voice saying, "Come watch us," and tuned it in, but it wasn't fun and it was "good-for-you-green-vegetables" so they felt betrayed by the "This is fun!" Yes, we got off to a rocky start.

Simultaneously, Bob Pittman was figuring out what MTV was going to do and I was fascinated because this was the first time I saw a landscape approach to television. He was creating a home base for teenagers. It was very hot, very sexy while Nickelodeon was "Woe is me." I think we had invested only $20 million in its development by the end of 1983, and we remained a last choice for kids. If there were nothing else on, kids would tune to Nickelodeon. My own son hid his Nickelodeon hat in the closet and lied to his classmates, telling them I was a housewife because he was mortified that I worked for this goody two-shoes, baby network!

HJ: Explain how you came to take over the network.

GL: At the end of 1983, Bob Pittman was made the head of the company, and it was clear that Cy, who was at least twenty years his senior, was uncomfortable with this crazy, "idiotic," approach to "home-based" television. Cy left in early 1984 and Bob looked at me and said, "We don't know what to do with you, we know not to fire you but we're gonna look, so just do your thing." I took that as a clear mandate for us to make this a successful business (smile) and I gathered a great team—Debby Beece, Geoffrey Darby, Scott Webb, Anne Sweeney, and Linda Kahn. We took everybody from the network on a retreat—it was only about twenty people—and we said, "What are our problems? What are we going to do about it? How are we going to approach this? And do you want to be on this team?" Most of the people wanted to be on the team, but about five people clearly didn't and were divisive and problematic. Eventually those five left. They were counseled out.

We started working with Fred Seibert and Alan Goodman—both very instrumental in creating MTV—who were wonderfully talented, brash, arrogant, fantastic people who would not allow us to get away with fuzzy thinking! We started with the assumption that we were going to create a home base for kids. We did focus groups where we showed kids ads from other people's products and listened to them, and that's when they validated our new approach. We were crazy about kids, and we thought they deserved the best. We clearly had to be on their side, and they told us very clearly that they didn't want to be told what was fun or funny. "Don't tell us what this is; let us discover it." "You have to BE it; you can't just say it." "Whatever you say about yourself, please be that and don't try to fool us." And that's the other side of this. . . . A lot of television has a low view of its audience, but we didn't think we could get anything by with kids. Maintaining our integrity meant we couldn't sell kids out. We needed to stay true to them.

HJ: Those orange logos were absolutely central to the branding of the new Nickelodeon. How did they come about?

GL: Scott Webb was the first new person that we hired in the on-air group. He brought to Nick a different way of seeing things—Scott literally had a degenerative sight problem—and the large, clear graphics have everything to do with the fact that he could see them! There was nothing frou-frou about this—his vision was bold and strong.

This was a big departure from where we were. Cy commissioned a silver ball logo with big, fat logotype in rainbow colors, and if there is anything condescending to a kid it's this notion that you do rainbow colors in lettering! Cy managed things very close to the vest, and he did not include any of us in the process of coming up with this new look. Granted, it was a big improvement over the mime that was hardly professional, but it went from this very crazy loosey-goosey artsy thing to this very slick silver ball. The logos offered a very stereotypical view of kids with pinball machines and arcades and an old-fashioned idea of what kids thought was fun. There was nothing cool about it, and there was nothing that a kid could attach to himself or herself. Then the takeover happened, and the inmates got to run the asylum! We wanted to get rid of that silver ball as fast as possible. Fred and Alan brought in a terrific guy named Tom Corey who went on to design a lot of logos. He created many show logos and was a force behind many cable networks—he worked with us to develop Nick at Nite and he worked with me at ABC, too. Tom was a very gifted guy who began each project with a holistic approach asking, "Who is the audience? How do we somehow take the audience into consideration as we develop? How do we represent the graphics at Nickelodeon?" Tom, who focused on the graphic side, often worked with a terrific guy on the music side named Tom Pomposello. They wanted to come up with something that morphed the way a kid's brain morphs, something that is just as free as the way a kid's brain associates. Tom Pomposello brought the "doo wop" sound to Nickelodeon.

So the notion was born that the logo needed to be orange and use a particular letter type, but could take on any shape as long as it was animated, could move and morph and have a sense of humor with it. We thought the constant changing shapes would be extra punctuation for humor. According to every graphic designer we dealt with in the first three years, we picked what was probably the ugliest color in the Pantone Matching Systems catalog—I think it was PMS 21. It ended up being a great choice because Nickelodeon now "owns" orange. You see orange, and you think it's a trademark violation if it doesn't have Nickelodeon on it! So we picked orange and against every good graphic designer's advice to change it, we didn't. But we had strict enforcement of our loose guidelines. Our goal was to get any creative person who worked on Nickelodeon ideas to put their work for us at the front of their "reel." We wanted them to be proud of what they did for us. We weren't trying to manhandle them. MTV had pioneered the way with the early MTV graphics. They used a group of suppliers, people like Drew Takahashi of Colossal Pictures, Eli Noyes, and Kit Laybourne, and wonderful, crazy, wacky Charlex. Fred and Alan managed the process and gave the animators free range. They said, "Here's the box you have to work with, but have a nice day, show us what you have and we'll say yes or no." We did more or less the same thing, and in a period of three months we received some of the best creative work I've ever seen in terms of ideas because there was freedom within the environment and it wasn't micromanaged. It was a very important premise of Nickelodeon—if we let you do your best creative work, we think it will be better for kids.

HJ: What are some other ways the network started to change?

GL: We changed the schedule. We got rid of our checkerboard schedule of *Against the Odds, The Third Eye,* and *Standby: Lights, Camera, Action*—all those kinds of things—we bought some animation from Europe, *Belle and Sebastian,* and we bought *Lassie,* which was a classic. Part of the reason kids weren't watching us (we had a .5 rating) was they never knew what was on. They couldn't count on us. So we went for a more series-based approach. We still had a mission, and we never put anything on that was violent or harmful to kids in any way, but the stuff we put on was more entertaining. It wasn't a lot of new stuff—it was mostly this new environment that was more playful. When we did an ad for *Lassie* it was a funny ad, even though *Lassie* wasn't a funny show. At least we got humor into our interstitial pieces, and by January we had doubled our rating to 1.

We moved from having *You Can't Do That on Television* as our one good show to developing *Turkey TV*. That was (I call it) the greatest "head fake" in the history of television because we put all our hopes on *Turkey TV*—we thought this was going to transform television. But you probably haven't heard too much of it since. *Turkey TV* was a pretty great example of trying something, having an early failure, and saving the company a lot of money. The idea was we were going to do comedy clips for kids the same way MTV had done music clips. And later on, HBO tried to launch a whole network based on comedy clips, but we learned on $1.5 million what they learned on close to $100 million—that mix doesn't work on television. The thing that's great about comedy is that it pays off, it builds, it pays off, it builds, it pays off, and when you're only getting the payoffs, it's obnoxious and jarring. There isn't as much funny material as you'd expect. The notion of *Turkey TV* was to take excerpts from all over the world—Norwegian commercials, Italian game shows, and classic footage—black and white stuff—and put it together with VJs in a transforming way. It would always be fresh due to running it in new combinations.

As Geoffrey Darby and I focused on programming and Debby Beece and her group worked on building a home base, the company heard that the Arts Network was no longer going to lease the end of Nickelodeon's day. My bosses, Domenic Fioravante and Bob Pittman, had to figure out what was going to be the back end of Nickelodeon and spent almost seven months looking for a program director from a local television station to come in and run nighttime programming. That person never materialized. We were busy trying to fix Nickelodeon, and they were constantly trying to fix the Nick at Nite problem, but they ultimately didn't have a plan, and we had to take it over.

Then Debby and I went and worked on Nick at Nite and *Turkey TV* coasted home. By Memorial Day, we got the cassettes of *Turkey TV* delivered to our house. My son thought it was awful. "Mother you will never work in television again." And it was horrible. So we spent two weeks reediting everything, making it passable so that at least it got a .8 rating, but there was no great solution. Everybody's focus was on *Turkey TV*. Meanwhile, Debby's group got a chance to figure out what Nickelodeon was gonna be all about. *Turkey TV* was a bomb in my mind; everyone else thought it was an "okay nothing." So we went from there to "Well, let's figure out how we're going to do production. Let's bring the good challenges in-house for a while, because clearly we don't know how to supervise outside production companies very well." That was the result of *Turkey TV*.

HJ: Double Dare was an important part of the rebranding of the network. Tell us some of the thinking behind it.

GL: Geoffrey worked with Dee LaDuke—a very, very smart creative person who happened to be our receptionist—and two on-air promotions producers, Bob Mittenthal and Michael Klinghoffer, and they spent that summer making us play this game they invented, *Double Dare,* in our offices. They came up with this truth or dare game and we all became involved. The whole company got behind it. This wasn't just a side project—this was how we came up with a definitive, completely delicious kind of show. We went through seven different phases of pilots and interviewed a large number of possible hosts until we found Marc Summers a week before we shot the pilot. We went to Philadelphia to produce it at WHYY, and it was a disaster the first day. It did not look like there was any way this show could be produced, but by the next Monday it was smooth sailing. We went on the air with *Double Dare* on a Monday, and with no promotion we got a .6. It went to a 1.8 by Thursday and eventually went to 5.6. It was "lightning in a bottle!"

HJ: Let's go back to the beginning. You mentioned that some years ago, you and your husband did some work getting kids involved in producing their own media. I was curious to learn a little more about what kind of work you were doing, what kind of media you had kids produce, and in what contexts?

GL: We used these great big video portapacks and had the kids doing little news programs, animation, storyboarding, learning how to tell stories, doing flipbooks . . . sometimes very primitive stuff!

HJ: And this was done through the schools while you were a teacher?

GL: My husband was a leader in this. First, he worked out of the American Film Institute and started their secondary school program. Then he went to

Double Dare was an important part of Nickelodeon's rebranding under Laybourne's direction.
Frame grab from *How to Nickelodeon* video. © 1992 MTV Networks.

a Title One program in inner-city schools in Philadelphia. I went to graduate school in Philadelphia and followed what he did. We moved to Concord, Massachusetts, where I taught high school students how to teach younger kids how to make movies. That was great because my students were bringing a new skill into the classrooms for teachers who were overburdened. It was high interest material for kids, and every age group likes to make media. In urban areas where Kit taught high school, kids who couldn't communicate through writing or speaking could make brilliant movies.

HJ: How did that work impact your thinking at Nickelodeon? It sounds like from what you're saying a lot of your faith in kids and their critical capacities comes out with that period of your career.

GL: If you talk to third graders about making a news show, they know exactly what to do. They know what the segments are. They're savvy little media consumers. Part of the process was getting to know what they know. They know what a story is. They know what a beginning, middle, and an end is, so what we tried to do was give them a voice—give kids a chance to help shape the kind of media they consumed.

HJ: And a lot of the early Nick successes were shows where kids were active in one way or another. From *Kid's Court* to *Double Dare*, they're on camera and often exercising some control over what's taking place.

GL: In *Double Dare*, for instance, every stunt we did was preapproved by kids and pretested. With *You Can't Do That on Television*, kids had the veto power, so if they didn't think something was funny, if they thought it was corny, they would refuse to approve it, which was good—it was humbling to the writers. Geoffrey was the creator of *You Can't Do That on Television*. But it was an interesting process to give kids power.

HJ: So how did that work? Walk us through an episode.

GL: First of all, Geoffrey and his writing partner, Roger Price, weren't necessarily casting for specific roles. They cast for kids who had personalities that they thought were quirky. And they put them into acting school. They weren't your standard Hollywood or Broadway acting kids who had decided early on that they wanted a career and they were going to go out there and do this great dramatic presentation. We were looking for everyday kids, and we wrote the episodes around these kids. Moose was Moose. That was her real personality. She wasn't forced to play Moose on TV. It was the essence of her real personality you saw. Writers based their scripts on what they knew about these kids, and then they would go into a table reading, and if the kids thought it was corny they would say, "No" and these guys would have to go and rewrite it. Then they would rehearse it, perform it, and tape it. Geoffrey and others tell a story about slime, which I'm not sure is true . . . but it's a good story. After a while, the kids began to act uppity, and to give them their comeuppance the producers decided to slime them because that seemed like a funny punishment for being an uppity kid. But I later learned the kids were paid $50 extra to be slimed!

As for *Kid's Court*, we tried three different versions of it, and it was very difficult for us to throw anything away. As a kid, my favorite shows were *Divorce Court* and *Queen for a Day*, so I mentioned this once and people thought it was hilarious and asked why don't we do a "kid's court"? We never developed a successful *Kid's Court* because it was an idea that couldn't work. If kids took trivial issues to *Kid's Court*, the audience thought they were trivial issues which they could have solved outside of the courtroom. And we couldn't take serious issues to *Kid's Court* because it was *"Kid's Court."* We just couldn't figure a way around it, so it didn't last very long.

HJ: Some of the shows that I remember admiring the most in those days featured Linda Ellerbee explaining news to kids or representing things real kids were doing out in the world. Those shows fostered a conception of children as citizens.

GL: We wanted to do a news program, and we wanted to actually have a news department. We brought Linda in to be the mother of *Nick News.* We had no idea how hard it was to do news. Linda was originally going to do it for two years, but after the first year we said, "You know what? This is your baby." The goal was to raise better citizens—it was that simple. Actually, it was to raise better candidates. It was a seditious plot on Linda's and my part to try to get kids thinking about important global issues, but in relevant terms. When you talk about Northern Ireland you do it from the standpoint of Protestant and Catholic kids who want to be friends, and how do you go about it? How do you approach it from the standpoint of a kid? Linda is one of the most gifted, most humane journalists I have ever seen, and she was able to put herself in the head of the kid and ask herself, "What are the issues here? What do I need to know about?" And the show must now be approaching the twelve-year mark, but, yes, we tackled some really great things.

When Magic Johnson came out as HIV positive, I called David Stern, Commissioner of the NBA, and said, "If you want to talk to kids about this, you know we are here." Several months later he said, "You know what? Magic does want to talk to kids." Linda was going through breast cancer at the time and had a double mastectomy. Ten days later, she was on the set with Magic. She needed to do it. I was fully prepared to cancel it, but that was a good example of her bravery.

The most contentious moment that Linda and I had on the show regarded a sign on the set that said, "Question authority." I came on the set and I said, "You know I really don't like that sign." And she was sure she had a bad network executive on her hands and I said, "I think it should say, 'Question everything.'" And that was when she understood that I was on her side.

HJ: I still sometimes teach the L.A. Riots program that Linda did, which was one of the best discussions of how the Rodney King tape became manipulated during the trial and about the impact of racism on American culture.

GL: I think plenty of adults found her show to be incredibly important for its ability to talk to their kids and to understand issues.

HJ: Did you get any fallout from airing some of those more risky shows?

GL: We were careful about doing this AIDS special with Magic Johnson. I hired a woman to come in and train twenty Nickelodeon employees on how to answer hostile questions because we had never done anything this controversial. So we had a daylong training session on taking calls and how we could talk about it. We gave an 800 number on the set, "If you have any concerns about this, please call us," and gave it to cable operators. We had a hundred calls, and only two were negative.

HJ: It raises a larger question about the way in which children's television constantly has to negotiate between adult expectations and kid expectations.

GL: We never did. We believed our duty was to kids, and we didn't compromise that very much. We did in news, but that was because they were going to be watching with their parents. We were a network for kids; we were on their side. My basic belief was that parents would like us if their kids were in better shape after they watched us. I think parents loved us because their kids were happy and funny, and maybe a little sassy; but they weren't doing sword fights and saber rattling after watching Nickelodeon.

HJ: So a lot of what you were calling "green vegetables" in earlier Nickelodeon programming was an attempt to appeal to parents almost exclusively at the expense of what kids wanted.

GL: In fairness to the previous administration, the first job of Nickelodeon was to get cable carriage for those networks which were started by the cable division at Warner Cable. The local cable operators needed to be able to promote what they were doing for children when they were negotiating local contracts. In the previous administration's mind, Nickelodeon's first job was to be "good" programming for kids for the cable operator. The cable operators were almost our only audience and our only source of revenue. We didn't take advertising until we took sponsorship in 1983, and then, in 1984 we started taking [regular] advertising.[1] I will be very frank. . . . In those early years, the ad sales people would have been very happy if we had acquired a violent cartoon library. But we always had more revenue on the affiliate side than the advertising side and so we could always say to the advertising side of our business, "We can't do that because of our commitments to our affiliates." It helped us stay on the side of nonviolence. In our first year of taking advertising there was an advertiser who wanted to buy $1 million worth of advertising on Nickelodeon. You have to understand that our entire budget was $3 million. So, $1 million worth of advertising time would have meant wall-to-wall ads for a product called Laser Tag, a game where kids put a shield on their head or heart to register hits. The advertising was incredibly violent. Boy, I didn't want to do that—I didn't want to go in that direction. We were trying to keep the trust of parents, the Peggy Charrens of the world, and the cable affiliates. Imagine their response if we started taking advertising with guns. This very violent ad was going to be everywhere, and we would have been "owned" by Laser Tag, so I objected to running it . . . which was not popular with the ad salesmen due to it being one third of their budget! In the end, Laser Tag went bankrupt after a kid was killed in a fluke accident . . . and I don't think anyone received payment for advertising. But that decision was very useful in the early days for setting the standards about what kind of advertising we were going to accept and where we drew the line.

HJ: You mentioned Peggy Charren just now.[2] What can you tell me about the relationship Nickelodeon had with Action for Children's Television and similar reform groups?

GL: Peggy was nervous when we started taking advertising. She always liked the people at Nickelodeon and grew to like the network because we did things like *Nick News* as well as doing good things for kids in general. But she was leery about Nickelodeon for a lot of reasons, and rightfully so. When we first started, we had 1.5 million subscribers, and she didn't want broadcasters to be let off the hook. They had been given this valuable license, and she didn't think they did much programming that had a higher purpose for kids—except for the occasional history minute. She was afraid of Nickelodeon in the early days because the broadcasters would say, "Well we don't need to do that because Nickelodeon does that." Since she knew the poorest kids were not going to get cable television for a long time, she became an effective watchdog.

She brought the issue of toy-based programming to the American people. This was an egregious way to make programming, and it resulted in nothing good. It started with *He-Man*.[3] *He-Man* was a gigantic success out of the box. So everybody, of course, acted like lemmings; everybody ran toward doing toy-related programming in the mid-1980s. At one point, there were close to sixty-five toy-related programs available in syndication. The creative problem was impossible to solve because you had to get your sixty-five episodes of the series done and produced in time for the toy launch, so you never had enough time to develop anything good. You had to write the story around the toy, which didn't have the deepest history in the world. Eventually, kids turned their backs on it, but in the meantime, Peggy Charren did a good job of getting everybody riled up.

HJ: Those arguments have resurfaced more recently. Some Republicans in Congress argue against funding public television on the grounds that there is ample programming for kids on cable.

GL: I don't think that public television has suffered any worse in the kids' arena than it has in any other. Cable TV networks like Arts & Entertainment, Discovery, and BBC America have eroded all of PBS's franchises. I'd say public television has a hard job of figuring out what it's going to be for the American people, and it's having an even tougher time getting the support it needs. They had brilliant early years with kids' programming, but Children's Television Workshop (now called Sesame Workshop) really hit a homerun with *Sesame Street* and then a bunch of singles. PBS's station program cooperative is a difficult system for getting a show on the air; and there are some insidious problems for all public television, not just kids' programming. I'm a strong believer in public TV and what it can be for independent voices.

HJ: We've talked a little bit about the green vegetable period; let's talk a little bit about the green slime period. A lot of the programming you're describing, like *You Can't Do That on Television*, could have been read as disrespectful to adults and as engaging in scatological humor, and that's very different from the images of childhood that tend to crop up in the green vegetable period.

GL: For me there's probably no more important show psychologically for kids than *You Can't Do That on Television*. It was a real lightbulb over my head. We put it on the schedule simultaneously with *Spread Your Wings* and *Going Great*—two Canadian coproductions that we were doing. *Going Great* was about five different stellar kids in each episode who did fabulous things. They could draw naturalistic owls in charcoal, build things with clay, sail a boat, etc. They were extraordinary kids—prodigies. But when we took the show to focus groups, it made kids depressed. Their common response was, "Well, I'll never be that good so I won't try that." Simultaneously, we were going to focus groups watching *You Can't Do That on Television,* and there was a sigh of relief. We were never making fun of adults—we were making fun of adults who find fun unbearably loathsome. We were making fun of authority figures, such as a father who was completely unfair or a principal who took the kid down into the dungeon and put him into manacles. Watching this, the kids at home were saying, "Wow, my life's not so bad. So my dad's a little stiff, at least he doesn't act as bad as the Dad on *You Can't Do That on Television*." And there was this recognition that we were there to build confidence. We were there to say to kids, "You know what? There are a lot of funny things that happen in your life and there are a lot of hard things. And adults will approach these things, and they'll be unfair, and that's gonna happen, but you are not in bad shape because look at the kids on this show!" And it worked. We also used reverse psychology—there is no better way to teach a kid than through reverse psychology. Parents on *You Can't Do That on Television* screamed, "You can't have that orange juice till you've had three sodas!" That made clear the point that orange juice was better nutrition than soda!

HJ: On the Nick shows, kids have bodies and they often didn't have any bodies, any appetites, any desires in some of the shows that came before. The kids on the *Ding Dong School* didn't have appetites.[4]

GL: Our goal was to be slightly naughty but not to go over that line. We had some shows like *Ren & Stimpy* where finding the appropriate line was agony. Here we had a brilliant creator, John Kricfalusi, who just did not understand our stance on kids, so we had to fire him. This was after the whole movement into creator-driven animation—which was a dream come true for me. That's why I started in the business, but it took us twelve years to get there. We went across the country with the theory that there were really good creators out there. We imagined they had ideas they had tried to sell in their bottom drawers. Because if it wasn't *Care Bears* or something else that was based on a toy, it wasn't going to get sold. Vanessa Coffey, a very talented young woman, went on a hunt, and she found eight properties from which we chose three to take to series— *Rugrats, Ren & Stimpy,* and *Doug.* All three were fabulous successes. I mean, no one has that kind of batting average. But we probably should have given *Ren & Stimpy* to MTV, and John could have done with *Ren & Stimpy* exactly what he wanted to do. But we were too new and we didn't have enough success under our belt to be generous. It was a battle with him. He would have had a million fart jokes per second. To me, a lot of it was gut, what's going too far and what's not, what's funny and what's overkill.

HJ: You've mentioned a connection with MTV a number of times, and I'm wondering whether Viacom put any pressure on you to prepare the Nick viewers to become MTV viewers?

GL: No, we had this wonderful free reign. Viacom, Frank Biondi, and Sumner Redstone were very interested in the bottom line and performance; but as long as we performed, there was no interference. In fact, MTV was very nervous about how we could attract older kids and how close we could get to their target age group. There was more nervousness than strategy. I don't know how Nickelodeon is doing with its older programming now. I was of the school that we should be a kids' network and never violate that. Once a kid starts thinking about driving and sex, Nick shouldn't be there and shouldn't be doing that programming. Nickelodeon should stick with what it knows about kids; it should be a safe place for kids.

I didn't tell you the story about Hartford, Connecticut, in 1984. We went there to figure out what kind of language to use on air to talk to kids. In Hartford we did four focus groups, and we asked kids the simple question, "What do you like about being a kid?" And holy Moses, did we get an earful. I mean these kids were feeling so pressured. They'd heard about drunk driving, teenage suicide, etc. They thought that when you turned into a teenager, your brain shrunk! They possessed all these myths. These kids were the first generation growing up in households where their moms were working and caretakers were raising them.

So we asked, "What could Nickelodeon be to you?" And they answered, "Well, you could be a place where we could have a childhood," which became the resounding thought of the day. And that's when we came up with "us versus them." We were going to be a safe harbor where kids could be silly, where they could have a sense of humor, and where there were no double entendre jokes. Nickelodeon has had to do that with their feature movies, though, like *Rugrats in Paris,* because they need to get adults into the theaters too.

HJ: I was going to ask you about movies, the franchises that have gone on in recent years. You were talking about the debate around television programs that were half-hour commercials for toys. Nickelodeon now seems to be part of a much larger transmedia phenomenon—the shows become movies, become Happy Meals, and become toys. Is that consistent with the spirit of the network's earlier years, or do you cringe at the direction things are going?

GL: I think Herb Scannell has done a great job in staying true to what we dreamed Nickelodeon would become. You know, God, *Sesame Street* is the master licensing vehicle, but the *Sesame Street* product is consistently great. You always feel good about having Elmo in your home. To me, it was first things first—create the character in its fullness so that you have something that's worth having. I remember making a speech at a Viacom retreat in 1987, a time when Nickelodeon was an annuity that had not yet begun to pay off for Sumner Redstone, and I spoke about wanting to be the Disney of the 1990s, which is exactly what happened. So it was always logical. You create great characters that kids want to sleep with or take to school or color in coloring books. You will have a franchise, but you'd better get the product right first and not design the product for the toy world. I think they've been really true to that. I think *SpongeBob SquarePants* is very charming, and I didn't have anything to do with it.

There were so many things we haven't covered and I'm afraid our time is running out. *Blue's Clues* and Nick Jr.—you know, we made some really good decisions about Nick Jr. early on. Because of the experience with my son thinking that Nickelodeon was a baby channel—he was all of six years old—and wanting to make sure that older kids knew that Nickelodeon was for them, we created that boundary with Nick Jr. The older kids would be safe from the little kids. And first we did *Eureeka's*

Castle, which was a really sweet, very multilayered puppet show that was technically ambitious and complicated, but we learned a lot. We saw what happened with *Barney*; those very simple love messages, irritating as they were to adults, did something right, which was speak directly to kids. We found a crazy Englishman who had invented the Borg-Warner educational system and invented an interactive television "wand." He was convinced he could teach kids how to read by replicating interactivity. We gave him a trailer at Universal Studios. He carefully watched the pacing that four-year-olds had in answering his questions so the program would simulate interactivity. *Blue's Clues* was based on the same premise. What great direct communications with little kids!

HJ: Why don't we shift to talk about Nick at Nite just a little bit? The notion of a television heritage crops up in the early ads as spoof but also, as a number of people in our field have noted, comes at the same moment television history is being introduced in universities. To some degree, Nick at Nite set the canon for our field's growth. There were few television archives, so programs on Nick at Nite provided the basic materials used in our television history classes. I wondered how serious you were about this concept of television's heritage when this programming started. Was it just a branding for reruns, or was there something deeper in your thinking?

GL: There was a lot in our thinking, but our criteria were we had to get something on the air within two months with $1 million. We had just aired *Lassie* and were receiving letters from parents saying, "Thank you so much for bringing back my childhood. This is really great!" and "I love watching it with my kids." We were primarily concerned with not closing the door on kids as we opened the door to adults. Debby Beece led the charge to give the nighttime its own identity without alienating kids. When I showed our first sales tape to my son at home, he said, "Mom, this is a lie. It says it's for adults, but this Nick at Nite is *my* network." So the kids never felt like we turned our backs on them. They felt welcomed, and they ran to their parents saying, "Mommy, there's this new show on TV, *Mr. Ed*." We loved it! We loved TV. We loved our TV heritage. We were very careful to have the best prints we could possibly have, and we spent a lot of money doing great promos to give this atmosphere of real reverence. I mean, yes, it was funny, but it was very reverential. We never made fun of television history. We said, let's put television history on a pedestal. We were also playing with our audience. The first thing we noticed was that our audience was sending detailed letters saying what they felt about these things and sending us their pictures. It was really wild. Nickelodeon's on-air group, led by Betty Cohen, created a campaign called, "The Nick at Nite Generation—TV for the TV generation." The campaign consisted of airing a viewer's picture while saying their favorite shows, and it was very personal. It was trying to get the audience to feel that they owned the network, the way we were getting kids to feel about Nickelodeon. At one point I remember being on a bus thinking, our program acquisitions person had just quit, and I thought, "I know . . . we'll offer the program acquisitions job on TV for Nick at Nite." So we had a big campaign, and it was hysterical! We hired Diane Robina, who saw the ad . . . but she actually was a television professional. Still, we really wanted to sell the idea that this was your network and you were a part of it.

HJ: You began by suggesting it was a political movement, and I'm wondering if you'd summarize what the politics were. Specifically, how was Nick at Nite as much a part of that politics at night as Nickelodeon was by day?

GL: It started with a real love of the audience, a love of the creative process, how we managed to find the most creative brains to work on behalf of the medium, and how we managed to be heard by the audience. We used an interesting statistical way of looking at the abundant TV history available at Nick at Nite, and Jules Haimowitz, who had been at Viacom, suggested we focus on the parents of the Nickelodeon viewership. We thought about the average age of parents of the average ten-year-old and aired shows that were popular when *they* were ten.

HJ: Well, if you want Nick to be remembered for one thing, what would it be?

GL: Taking its audience seriously. The commitment of the people at Nickelodeon was extraordinary. Everybody wanted to do something great, and it was amazing. And I think good television comes out of committed people. We weren't looking for formulas, and we weren't looking to repeat what others had done. We were looking for something that was fresh, new, and worthy of kids.

NOTES

1. "Sponsorship" is when a single company or product is associated with a program. "Advertising" refers to regular multiproduct sponsorship.

2. For background on Peggy Charren and Action for Children's Television, see Heather Hendershot, *Saturday Morning Censors: Television Regulation before the V-Chip* (Durham: Duke University Press, 1998).

3. For useful background and alternative perspectives on this debate, see Dale Kunkel, "From a Raised Eyebrow to a Turned Back: The FCC and Children's Product-Related Programming," *Journal of Communication* 38 (1988): 90–108; Tom Engelhardt, "The Shortcake Strategy," in Todd Gitlin, ed., *Watching Television* (New York: Pantheon Books, 1986), 68–110; Ellen Seiter, *Sold Separately: Children and Parents in Consumer Culture* (New Brunswick: Rutgers University Press, 1993); Marsha Kinder, *Playing with Power in Movies, Television and Video Games: From Muppet Babies to Teenage Mutant Ninja Turtles* (Berkeley: University of California Press, 1993); Steven Kline, *Out of the Garden: Toys, TV and Children's Culture* (New York: Verso, 1995).

4. For background on the debates about children's innocence and their desires, see Henry Jenkins, ed., *The Children's Culture Reader* (New York: NYU Press, 1998).

PART III

Programs and Politics

8

Ren & Stimpy
Fan Culture and Corporate Strategy

Mark Langer

One of the best publicized events related to animation and video during 1992 was the conflict between Nickelodeon and filmmaker John Kricfalusi over the cablecast animation series *The Ren & Stimpy Show*. Critics of the time hailed Kricfalusi as "a man of genius" and the series as "the best animated cartoon to come along since the glory days of the 1940s."[1] Nickelodeon owned the rights to the program and characters devised by Kricfalusi. The controversy arose when, despite the acclaim for the filmmaker and the series, Nickelodeon transferred production from Kricfalusi's Spumco studio to a new Games Productions studio, which used many former Spumco staff. At the time of this change, Nickelodeon maintained that it was forced into this position because of Kricfalusi's erratic performance. The filmmaker allegedly missed production deadlines and exceeded budgets on a regular basis. Kricfalusi claimed that Nickelodeon did not understand the series. Confronted with something that was too innovative and creative for pedestrian minds, averred the filmmaker, the company chose to remove Kricfalusi in order to produce a more conventional and low-budget series.

Much of the debate over this issue centered around time-honored myths of the artist in conflict with a corporate entity, and accusations of corporate philistinism on Nickelodeon's part or individual irresponsibility by Kricfalusi were fired back and forth. A paradigmatic comment on the situation was offered by Richard Gehr of the *Village Voice*, who maintained, "Wrenching Ren and Stimpy away from Kricfalusi is like taking *Twin Peaks* away from David Lynch and Mark Frost and handing it over to Quinn-Martin. . . . Or as John Kricfalusi says with utter seriousness, 'They didn't really deserve *The Ren & Stimpy Show.*'" *The Simpsons* creator Matt Groening observed, "It's like taking Dr. Frankenstein away from his monster."[2] Taking another approach than that popular at the time of the controversy, this study will not examine the Nickelodeon-Kricfalusi conflict from the point of view of artistic martyrdom, or of individuality versus corporatism. Instead, it will discuss this issue in terms of questions relating to the creation and marketing of products for different taste groups within a North American context, and in terms of the shifting position of animation within the cultural landscape. It will be argued that while Nickelodeon sought to provide a product for a juvenile or juvenile-oriented audience, Kricfalusi's product was influenced by his participation in a postmodernist young adult fan culture shaped by the changing status of animation as a social site.

Film historians traditionally have tended to regard their domain as the study of artists, art, or the corporate figures and institutions of the film industry. Alison Butler observes that among the basic strategies informing contemporary film histories is the treatment of cinema as an autonomous artistic-industrial practice separate from its sociocultural context.[3] Although cinema and television are overwhelmingly popular culture phenomena, until recently the influence of popular culture consumers as active agents in the shaping of cultural artifacts, rather than as passive dupes shaped by film or television artifacts, was frequently disregarded in historical considerations. Herbert Gans has described this problem, asking:

> Is popular culture something that is created in New York and Hollywood by skilled profit-seeking enterprises which have enough of a monopoly over the supply of entertainment and information that they can impose almost anything they think will sell on the American public, particularly on the television public—a captive audience to a handful of channels? Or are these enterprises themselves often unwitting agents of a culture in the anthropological sense, of a shared set of values or norms that they must try to express if they are to attract an audience and make their profits?[4]

This essay will examine *The Ren & Stimpy Show* with the assumption that both individual creators of cultural products and the larger cultural groups to which they may be allied are active agents of culture. Culture itself is not a monolithic institution, but is made up of many subcultures, which participate to varying degrees in the total culture. Individuals and creators can be agents of specific subcultures. It will be argued that much of the difficulty arising between Nickelodeon and Kricfalusi was due to the fact that they were agents of different cultural entities, and consequently did not share a congruent set of values or norms. Key to this is an appreciation of how steeped John Kricfalusi was in both the animation industry, and in animation fan culture. Many of the difficulties experienced by *The Ren & Stimpy Show* had to do with the placement of both the animation industry and the specialized fan culture of animation in the early 1990s. While Nickelodeon had its corporate agenda to provide a marketable product for a mass juvenile audience (subject to parental approval), Kricfalusi had a personal agenda shaped in large measure by his participation in an older taste group of animatophiles.

Animation—in particular commercial, studio animation—was for many years a marginalized form of expression with little cultural capital. Pierre Bourdieu has pointed out that capital is not solely a matter of economics. He defines capital as "the set of actually usable resources and powers." Capital can be either economic, cultural, or social. The total combined volume of these different kinds of capital varies according to social class. The dominant class, which includes members of the professions with high incomes and qualifications, has greater access to material and cultural goods. Unskilled workers and laborers have the lowest access to such resources. People who stem from these different classes will have access to different amounts of capital, based on the amount of economic, cultural, or social capital with which they begin life. Within different realms of society, the proportion of one's capital can vary. Thus, artists and industrialists may both be seen as belonging to an upper class, but will differ in the kinds of capital that they have acquired. An artist will have much cultural capital but less economic capital. The proportion may be quite the opposite for an industrialist. Each group often will give cultural legitimacy to different forms of cultural goods. For example, while theater may be patronized by artists and industrialists, more avant-garde works would be consumed by the former than by the latter, since the former depends on its specialized knowledge in this area as part of its cultural capital. Both these theatrical forms are legitimated by their association with this class.[5] Forms of theatrical practice patronized by the lower classes, such as wrestling, have little cultural capital.

Similarly, children's tastes tend to be regarded as lacking cultural capital by adults. One thinks of the extreme distaste expressed in hipper or more adult cultural forms for such children's shows as *Barney, Blue's Clues,* or, earlier, for *Mister Rogers' Neighborhood* (the latter frequently spoofed by the hipper, more adult *Saturday Night Live* as *Mister Robinson's Neighborhood*). Often, hipness within animated programming specifically directed at a juvenile audience has been expressed in a parallel text that few of the younger audience members could decipher, such as the Cold War references or allusions to adult television programming found in the *Rocky and Bullwinkle* television program. Of course, it must be noted parenthetically that children themselves form their own taste hierarchies that often take into account, or even reverse, legitimized adult tastes.

During the 1960s, when film became institutionalized as a form of intellectual discourse with academic journals and university programs, expressions of interest in animation were ignored at best. At worst, these expressions were dismissed on intellectual and aesthetic grounds. Due to the economics of theatrical distribution, animated shorts made for adult audiences were no longer distributed theatrically in North America. Because most animation—even animation originally produced in the 1930s and 1940s for general audiences—was now only available as children's programming on television (with the exception of the occasional child-oriented Disney theatrical feature), the juvenilization of the audience reduced animation's already low cultural capital. Affected by widespread misogelastic tendencies among arbiters of film culture, animation was relegated to reaches of a cultural limbo even beyond those occupied by other film forms with a touch of levity, such as the musical or comedy. Popular cultural discourse joined with intellectual discourse in its assessment of animation as incompatible with high or even middlebrow thought. Within mainstream culture and its organs of legitimation, animation was devoid of cultural capital.

This view began to change around the mid-1970s following such events as the Lincoln Center Disney retrospective in 1973, Jay Cocks's 1973 article on Chuck Jones in *Time,* the animation issue of *Film Comment* edited by Greg Ford in 1975, and the Whitney Museum Disney show in 1981.[6] In this period, institutions of higher learning began to introduce animation as part of general scholarly film curricula, rather than as ghettoized craft courses or programs in the Fine Arts. For example, in New York, the New School for Social Research introduced a course on the history of animation in 1973. By 1975, a similar course was being offered in the Film Division of the Graduate School of Arts at Columbia University.[7] These institutions began to validate animation as a worthy object of adult study. Having been reclaimed from the limbo of kiddie entertainment, animation could be taken seriously.

In the wake of this movement in academe in the 1970s, *Cinema Journal, Screen, The Velvet Light Trap,* and *Film History* now routinely publish articles on topics previously covered only in such underground animation periodicals or fan magazines as *Funnyworld, Film Fan Monthly, Starlog,* or *Mindrot.* Emulating the institutions of traditional art forms, the study of animation has created its own agents of cultural respectability. The discipline has been served by its own scholarly society since 1986 (the Society for Animation Studies), and by its own peer-reviewed academic publication since 1992 (*Animation Journal*).

The growing acceptance of animation by the institutions of high culture coincided with its acceptance by more broadly based social institutions. By the time John Kricfalusi began animating, certain areas of animation had been validated by mainstream culture as something other than simple-minded entertainment directed toward a juvenile audience. Now animation was art, which children might just happen to enjoy. Christopher Finch's *The Art of Walt Disney,* Thomas and Johnson's *Disney Animation: The Illusion of Life,* John Canemaker's *Treasures of Disney Animation Art* and Patrick Brion's *Tex Avery: les dessins* led a trend to produce expensive coffee-table art books presenting the work of the Disney, Warner Bros. and MGM studios in the same manner as that used to merchandise the Old Masters.[8] Mainstream publishers, such as St. Martin's Press and Farrar Straus Giroux, marketed memoirs of prominent animators like Shamus Culhane and Chuck Jones.[9] Cel art galleries operate in every major city. Through this cultural imprimatur, animation history was transformed into a variety of consumer goods that cater to a now-popular taste.

All this profoundly changed the position of animatophiles on the cultural terrain. Animatophiles are a taste group characterized by a high degree of knowledge about animation. Animatophiles consist of a tiny total culture, whose participants exist largely apart from the mainstream, and a bigger partial culture, whose participants exist mainly within the dominant total culture, but who function as animatophiles on a part-time basis. Animatophilia, as a total culture in itself, has participants who are animation company owners and employees, animation scholars, devoted fans, and obsessive consumers of animation and its ancillary products. This core is composed of those animatophiles with the highest degree of specialized knowledge about the subject and whose lives revolve around animation. As participants in a partial culture, animatophiles include buyers of animation art, casual fans, and other people with an interest in animation beyond that of the total culture. In other words, the culture of animatophiles has a core of people whose lives are completely devoted to animation, surrounded by a more diffuse but larger body of animation fans who more or less live predominantly within the broader mass culture. The member group of animatophiles may also intersect with the membership of other taste groups.[10]

The specialized knowledge of core animatophiles forms a different kind of cultural capital which is defined by its opposition to, or separateness from, the tastes of mainstream culture. Taste groups, as forms of social distinction, do not depend on traditional notions of class determination through economic ranking. Within a consumer society, people are confronted with an enormous range of goods. As they select and classify goods from all the possibilities offered, they position themselves within a particular social space which can be determined not only by economic position, but by taste.[11] Goods with low cultural status, like Liberace recordings, can cost as much as or more than goods with high cultural status, like Phillip Glass or Bach recordings. Consequently, taste can be more important than economics as a means of social positioning. As Bourdieu has stated, "nothing classifies somebody more than the way he or she classifies."[12]

Animatophiles share characteristics with other postindustrial marginalized taste groups (such as Trekkies, Transcendentalists, jazz 78 rpm recording collectors, or forms of both black and adolescent culture) in that they maintain a certain degree of hipness. Don Wallace has pointed out that hipness "differentiates through the discovery of the exotic, through the legitimation of the illegitimate, and therefore its power is not in knowledge *per se* but in the ability to confer on the otherwise forbidden the status of rarity and desirability." Wallace goes on to observe that "hip is a category that is always in motion: by increasing the desirability of a practice, there is the risk that it will be popularized and therefore devalued."[13] Hipness becomes a game of displaced authenticity that often derives its meaning and value from the exclusive nature of the code used by a particular taste group. Once the code is decipherable by the total culture, it ceases to be exclusive and loses its value to members of the group.[14] In other words, the cultural capital of this code depends on its ownership by a particular taste group.[15]

Adolescent obsessive fans and the creators of comics form another taste group similar to animatophiles. Like animatophiles, they grew in strength during the postwar baby boom period, and like their animation counterparts, they were considered to be an outlaw or fringe taste group. In response to a general condemnation of comics as trash, the late 1940s and early 1950s saw the emergence of artists such as Basil Wolverton and the team of Will Elder and Harvey Kurtzman of *Mad* magazine. These artists, and their readers (who were somewhat older than consumers of the comics often parodied in *Mad*), exemplify certain trends in this sort of cultural subgrouping. First of all, Wolverton, through the exaggerated grotesquery of his style, deliberately violated the aesthetic norms of graphic arts.[16] Will Elder and Harvey Kurtzman's satires of popular mainstream comics (including "Woman Wonder!" "Starchie," "Mickey Rodent!" "Outer Sanctum," and the *Classic Comics* takeoff of "Robinson Crusoe" [with Jack Webb as Friday]) relied on a reader's sophisticated level of knowledge about this manifestation of popular culture.[17] Forms and conventions of comic art were recombined to create new, and often ironic, meanings. Indeed, Kurtzman has been described by Art Spiegelman as America's "first post-modern humorist, laying the groundwork for such contemporary humor and satire as *Saturday Night Live, Monty Python,* and *Naked Gun.*" Spiegelman called Kurtzman "the spiritual godfather of underground comics."[18]

Mad catered to an adolescent taste group which asserted its cultural space through the appropriation of an illegitimate art form. Attacks on publications such as *Mad* for their bad taste and their inappropriateness for a juvenile audience resulted in the establishment of a Comics Code, which effectively suppressed such expression for a number of years.[19] Nevertheless, *Mad* prevailed and was finally accepted by mainstream culture during the 1960s, when the pop art phenomenon and growing acceptance of *Mad*'s trash parodies in such television programming as *Rowan and Martin's Laugh-In* made the *Mad* perspective more mainstream.

Through its popularity, the cultural capital of *Mad* was devalued among comic fans, even as its cultural capital rose within society as a whole. The specialized knowledge inherent among such fans of comic books as *Mad* readers became diffused throughout society. Once an outlaw form of culture, many comics became legitimized as they were popularized through the total culture.[20] Exhibitions of pop art based on comics became commonplace during the 1960s, when comic art visual and narrative conventions were appropriated by such artists as Roy Lichtenstein, Oyvind Fahlström, or Bernard Rancillac,[21] redefining comic art hipness in terms of the total culture's notion of more adult tastes in fine art. Hipness in the comic book taste group moved on to underground publications. These underground comics further pushed beyond the norms of legitimized tastes in narrative and visual aesthetics through their examination of such topics as black culture, drugs, sex, and new left politics, and through their abandonment of color images for the cheaper use of black and white.

Film history often deals with issues through analogy to other entertainment forms. For example, much scholarship on the subject of early cinema has examined the medium in relation to theater, vaudeville, magic lanterns, magic shows, and other nineteenth-century modes of performance.[22] Analogous patterns similar to the *Mad* phenomenon (and Kricfalusi's fondness for the work of early *Mad* artists is a factor here) can be observed in the social positioning of animatophiles. Mainstream culture valorized classical American studio animation into a system of taste norms. Within scholarship, the study of animation aped time-honored forms of academic practice. Long before the time of *The Ren & Stimpy Show*, there was a tradition of analyzing animated cartoons by attributing their characteristic features to the particular achievements of an individual, paralleling the auteurist approach to the study of live-action film. Scholars or enthusiasts in journals like *Funnyworld* or *Mindrot* identified unheralded artists of animation in emulation of the treatment of live-action counterparts identified by such publications as *Cahiers du cinéma, Movie,* and *Film Comment.* True artists of animation were seen as those who ran the institution (like Disney or Lantz) or they were seen as auteurial escape artists who wriggled out of studio straightjackets made by producers like Schlesinger at Warners or Quimby at MGM.[23]

Academic discourse established a hagiography of great animation artists as early as 1975. In the groundbreaking "Hollywood Cartoon" issue of *Film Comment,* Winsor McCay, Chuck Jones, Grim Natwick, Walt Disney, Tex Avery, Max and Dave Fleischer, as well as Bill Hanna and Joe Barbera (in their *Tom and Jerry* period) were singled out as artists. Television animation was dismissed in the same issue as "the

Muzak of animation," "an insistent assault of mediocrity," and as "assembly-line shorts grudgingly executed by cartoon veterans who hate what they're doing. What's missing here is not money, but imagination."[24] The critics and historians writing in *Film Comment* distinguished the earlier theatrical cartoons with easily identifiable directors, higher production values, and more "hand crafted" qualities consistent with traditional notions of "art" from television animation, which lacked many of these hallmarks.

A similar distinction may be noted in the reception of animation by the general public at the time. As knowledge of animation became commodified, it followed the "great man–great artist" model originally adopted in the scholarly treatment of animation. Artifacts and ephemera associated with important artists, such as Disney, Avery, or Hanna and Barbera had their status revised in terms of cultural capital. For example, before the reinscription of animation during this period, probably no one could have imagined a time when Annette Michelson, highbrow avatar of such auteurs as Eisenstein and Vertov, would translate a coffee-table art book that reproduced images from *Tom and Jerry* cartoons.[25]

One can track this revision through examination of the changing status of cels and other forms of animation artwork. Cels were once considered the detritus of the industry. Black and white cels were commonly washed of their images and reused. This was not possible to do with color cels, which were most commonly thrown away after use. The current practice of collecting animation artwork began in the late 1960s and early 1970s, but at first was strictly a low-budget affair restricted to animatophiles. Early ads in fanzines and other dealer offerings marketed original artwork for $10 to $20.[26] With the acceptance of certain figures as "masters of animation," the animation art market was in a boom phase at the time of the creation of the *Ren & Stimpy* series. In 1989, a black-and-white cel from *"Orphan's Benefit"* (1934) was sold for $286,000 at an auction at Christie's. Seventy-nine Disney drawings, watercolors, and cels were offered for sale at Sotheby's in New York on 27 June 1992. The firm estimated that this sale would realize $1.5 million.[27] Background art from Disney's *Beauty and the Beast* (1991), with gouache cel overlay replicas of characters from the film, were auctioned at estimates of $1,000 to $10,000 by Sotheby's in Los Angeles in October 1992. Seventeen thousand catalogs—a record for an auction house—were printed for the sale.[28] By the early 1990s, animation art was sold by the same institutions that dealt in high-culture art, or by specialist galleries that mimicked the behavior of major art dealers. Animation art attained the cultural respectability of an investment, albeit (in the words of one gallery), "An investment that makes you smile."[29] One straight-faced gallery owner at the time likened cel art to "the paintings off the ceiling of the Sistine Chapel."[30] What was once the pursuit of marginalized fan culture had been redefined into conventional notions of a commodity merchandised within fine art commerce.

This tendency toward absorption on the part of the dominant culture threatened the existence of animatophiles as a taste group distinct by the nature of its specialized knowledge. Consequently, animatophiles distinguished themselves as a taste group by resorting to strategies mapped out earlier in other comic media. Core animatophiles sought out more obscure sources to locate forms of expression that had not been legitimated by popular consumer culture. Since the 1970s, as "classical Hollywood" animation joined the mainstream and as its codes became the new norm of taste, the cutting edge of animatophilia moved from the cult of Disney and Warner Bros. products to such sources as early television animation, children's broadcasting, commercials, and other forms of expression that remained disenfranchised by both mass culture and the academic and art establishments. As Heather Hendershot has observed, "Notably, it was *vintage* television animation that was reclaimed. Through a deft juggling act, animatophiles discovered that *Crusader Rabbit* was actually sophisticated, but there was little interest in then-contemporary programming."[31] As the code of hipness was deciphered by the total culture, animatophiles created new codes from the detritus of animation. In this sense, animatophilia became a trash aesthetic (or perhaps more correctly, a trash practice), which examined the detritus of mass culture and recombined it to produce cultural capital. The violation of taste norms (a Kricfalusi specialty) became a key element of this animatophile practice.

By pushing further into the realm of cultural illegitimacy, animatophiles redefined themselves as a taste group more hip in terms of animation than the general Disney and Warner Bros.–loving public. A glance at a recent publication like the *Whole Toon Catalog* (whose very title conjured up the counterculture stance of the *Whole Earth Catalog*) testifies to the 1990s shift of interest to past series like *The Beany and Cecil Show*, which was marketed as, "Created by the great Bob Clampett . . . Brilliant and inventive, much of the adult-oriented punning will go over younger children's heads." Conventional criteria of quality, such as links to cartoon auteurs, now were applied to previously unvalued animated works like "classic Raid commercials, Shamus Culhane's Muriel Cigar commercials, the Hamm's Bear, EZ-Pop popcorn, and Westinghouse." Other entries in the *Whole Toon Catalog* testify to the popularity of such fifties and sixties "trash" as *Colonel Bleep, Clutch Cargo,* or vintage animated cereal commercials.[32] Within the cultural shift in animatophilia, certain graphic styles, limited animation, the use of public domain music or formulaic advertising jingles, and the like—still hallmarks of cheapness and bad taste within the total culture—now became icons of rarity and desirability among animatophiles.

Through the participation of Kricfalusi and many of his coworkers in this taste group, animatophilia had a profound effect on the production of Nickelodeon's *Ren & Stimpy* cartoon series. *The Ren & Stimpy Show* originally was conceived in terms of forms of children's broadcasting which had been legitimized by more mainstream animated films. According to Karen Flischel, vice president of Research at Nickelodeon, "It *The Ren & Stimpy Show*] is made for children. . . . *Ren & Stimpy* follows the 'Looney Tunes' or 'Bullwinkle' model, where there are two levels of appeal—the gross look for kids, and the zany humour for the older crowd."[33] In other words, the series was intended to appeal to the tastes of both children and their parents, who would watch television together in a family environment. Nickelodeon did not intend to serve adolescent animatophiles seeking postmodern kicks. An early press release described the series as family entertainment, being in "the tradition of Laurel and Hardy, Abbott and Costello and Flintstone and Rubble." *Ren & Stimpy* was announced as part of a ninety-minute block of new animation, following the highly conventional series *Rugrats* and *Doug,* both of which emphasized family life, nonviolence, and moral values.[34]

Since 1979, Nickelodeon had been cable television's only basic channel devoted solely to children's broadcasting. However, the high cost of animation prevented the network from developing its own original cartoon programming. But there was a corporate tradition, at least within other constituent parts of Viacom, to produce animation. Viacom's Columbia Broadcasting System had been deeply involved with animation production since its takeover of Terrytoons in the early 1960s. Fred Silverman, head of daytime programming for CBS, revolutionized animation broadcasting by devoting CBS's entire Saturday morning to animation in 1965, a move that was soon copied by the entire broadcast industry. Silverman's alliances with major animation companies resulted in such programs as *Scooby-Doo: Where Are You?* in 1969 and *The Banana*

Splits in 1970 with Hanna-Barbera, and *Superman* in 1965, *The Archies* in 1968, and *Fat Albert and the Cosby Kids* in 1971 with Filmation.

The takeover of Nickelodeon's parent company Viacom by media tycoon Sumner Redstone in 1987 and the restructuring of the company's debt over the next few years brought a massive infusion of new capital that allowed Nickelodeon to resume the policy of its corporate predecessor. Redstone invested $40 million in the development of new animated programs for Nickelodeon.[35] Drawing on the experience of other studios such as Disney and Warner Bros., whose work has entered the cultural pantheon, Nickelodeon executives realized that animation offers attractive long-term financial prospects. "We know that kids like animation, and that good quality animation lasts forever," said Nickelodeon president Geraldine Laybourne. "'Looney Tunes' are fifty years old and they still play today."[36] Elsewhere in this book, Linda Simensky stresses that Nickelodeon executives determined that the longevity of such animated films was due to their "creator-driven" nature. In other words, to make contemporary equivalents of classic animation, the company sought a new generation of Chuck Joneses and Shamus Culhanes.

Nickelodeon wanted what Todd Gitlin would call a "recombinant" animation series, where older forms are repackaged in slightly different variations from the originals.[37] In the tradition of the Disney and Warner Bros. studios, Nickelodeon sought to find styles and characters that would create a distinctive product identity in order to differentiate its programs from the programs of other companies.[38] *The Ren & Stimpy Show* was to become a mass-marketable form of cultural capital for Nickelodeon, following the model of other animated series, like Warner Bros.' "Looney Tunes" shorts, which had attained cultural capital within society at large. Hired in 1989, Nickelodeon's vice president of animation, Vanessa Coffey, was to develop new animated series for the network. Coffey, who had previously worked on CBS's successful recombinant series *Muppet Babies* (1984–92) and on the first few episodes of *Teenage Mutant Ninja Turtles* (1988–96), was no stranger to this kind of marketing strategy.

Kricfalusi's work on such projects as the Filmation *Droopy* series in 1980, and his later experience on the Ralph Bakshi and Jim Hyde–produced series *Mighty Mouse: The New Adventures*, beginning in 1987, must have seemed ideal for this corporate strategy. The *Droopy* cartoons were a bland retreading of the classic Tex Avery M-G-M cartoons, subject to all the limitations of Filmation's low-budget and dim imagination style. *Mighty Mouse: The New Adventures* drew on both the Paul Terry theatrical cartoons featuring this Superman parody as well as CBS's 1966 series from early in the Silverman era, *Mighty Mouse Playhouse*. *Mighty Mouse: The New Adventures,* in turn, inspired the new recombinant series *Tiny Toon Adventures* for which Warner Bros. in 1989 had hired away such Bakshi-Hyde Ventures staffers as Bruce Timm. John Kricfalusi, together with *Mighty Mouse* employees Lynne Naylor and Jim Smith, joined with *Tiny Toon* defector Bob Camp to form Spumco, which pitched *The Ren & Stimpy Show* to Nickelodeon. Given the background of the participants in Spumco, it is easy to understand why Nickelodeon entered into a production agreement with the new company.

But Nickelodeon, which had become the owner and distributor of *The Ren & Stimpy Show,* had an agenda that was not completely coherent with that of director John Kricfalusi and his colleagues at Spumco. Although Kricfalusi had come up in the industry working for traditional daytime animation providers like Hanna-Barbera and Filmation, his views on animation were not entirely aligned either with the decidedly unhip strategies of these companies or with those of Nickelodeon. Nickelodeon wanted to satisfy the requirements of children and their parents. As an animatophile, Kricfalusi's work was informed by the tastes of this young adult taste group. Central to an understanding of this was Kricfalusi's work on the *Mighty Mouse: The New Adventures* beginning in 1987. *Mighty Mouse: The New Adventures* was produced for CBS as a recombinant series that set the pattern for the later *Tiny Toon Adventures* by seeking to update an old Terrytoon classic.

But Kricfalusi's approach to the series was informed by his animatophilia. Paul Terry once said of his studio, "If Disney is the Tiffany of animation, we are the Woolworth's." This self-assessment has stood the test of time. By the late 1980s, Terry characters such as Mighty Mouse, Heckle and Jeckle, or Gandy Goose still lacked the cultural cachet of the Disney and Warner Bros. characters. *Mighty Mouse: The New Adventures* not only treated its subject matter as cultural detritus, but was filled with bad taste jokes revolving around udders, bad breath, excrement, and surreal references to comic and cartoon history through such characters as Bat-Bat and his companion The Bug Wonder. Although the series developed a cult following among animatophiles, it also provoked popular outrage when the American Family Association led an attack on the series. This conservative Christian pressure group averred that an episode of the series promoted cocaine use among children through its depiction of a character becoming invigorated by sniffing a flower. CBS had to censor the episode, and it was widely alleged that this is why the series was canceled.[39]

Within the *Ren & Stimpy* series, as in his earlier work on the ill-fated *Mighty Mouse: The New Adventures* or the more recent *New Beany & Cecil Show,* Kricfalusi constantly made reference to the detritus of American culture and deliberately violated norms of good taste. While some "gross-out" comedy is not unusual in children's broadcasting, a company like Nickelodeon has to engage in a difficult balancing act in which it is necessary to please children without offending parents. Kricfalusi was not similarly inclined. The first of the *Ren & Stimpy* episodes to be aired, "Stimpy's Big Day" (4 August 1991), serves as a useful example of this orientation.[40] The story of "Stimpy's Big Day" is fairly rudimentary. The program begins with Stimpson J. Cat watching television in a "fabulous '50s" decorated room. Although the viewer cannot see Stimpy's TV screen, one can hear the sound track, which consists exclusively of boings, crashes, and honks. Stimpy's partner Ren Hoek,[41] a demented chihuahua, enters and berates Stimpy for watching cartoons, stating, "Cartoons aren't real . . . they're *puppets*!" Their conversation is interrupted by the beginning of the *Muddy Mudskipper Show.* Stimpy, a devoted fan, turns from Ren to the screen. During the commercial break, Ren and Stimpy learn of a contest organized by the show's sponsor, Gritty Kitty Litter. The winner of the best poem praising the qualities of Gritty Kitty Litter's product will become eligible for prizes of up to $47 million, plus an appearance on the *Muddy Mudskipper Show.* Despite Ren's discouragement, Stimpy sends in his entry and wins.

In Hollywood, Stimpy meets Muddy Mudskipper and goes through makeup in preparation for his guest appearance on the show. The appearance is a sensation. At home, Ren's gradual deterioration parallels Stimpy's climb to stardom. Stimpy becomes the star of several television series, but he finally rejects fame and fortune to return home and live with Ren. Ren and Stimpy embrace in friendship, but the narrative ends with Ren berating Stimpy ("You filthy worm!") for giving away the $47 million.

The basic narrative of "Stimpy's Big Day" is unremarkable by children's show standards in many ways. It emphasizes loyalty between two childlike characters and reinforces popular myths about success and social mores. But the story of "Stimpy's Big Day" can also be seen as a postmodernist ironic commentary on the seminal 1950s film *A Star Is Born*

(1954) through its hip respinning of the high-budget "serious examination of show business" concerns of Cukor's film into the low-budget, cultural trash form of children's television animation. The relationship between Stimpy and Muddy Mudskipper recalls that between Esther Blodgett and Norman Main. Stimpy's preparation in the makeup room for his first television appearance seems to be modeled on the overly enthusiastic styling that Esther endures in *A Star Is Born*. Other filmic references include the use of the Hollywood sign and Kirk Douglas's face as icons introducing Hollywood.

Although Kricfalusi recombines elements of cinema for purposes of parody in "Stimpy's Big Day," he primarily foregrounds his debt to the cultural detritus of past television forms loved by animatophiles, like commercials and low-budget animation. "Stimpy's Big Day" not only uses public-domain music, which was common given the low budgets of early television animation, but it also recycles music from the television show *Truth or Consequences* (1950–58).[42] Stimpy's success on television is marked by his appearance in a string of programs, such as *Marshall Stimpy*, *Stimpy the Jungle Boy*, *Sergeant Stimpy of the Klondike*, *Ask Dr. Stupid*, and *I Love Stimpy*, which are derived from past television programming. The episode ends with a sequence in which Ren and Stimpy appear onstage before a curtain to bid the audience farewell, as was customary with the television comedy teams of Martin and Lewis on the *Colgate Comedy Hour* (1950–55), or Burns and Allen on *The George Burns and Gracie Allen Show* (1950–58).

But it is in the handling of narrative and other conventions that the influence of animatophilia becomes most obvious. The story of "Stimpy's Big Day" is preceded by an advertisement for a fictitious product called "Log." Log is a piece of merchandise in the tradition of the Slinky, Silly Putty, or the Frisbee, which were created for a juvenile market and widely advertised on television. Just as these products were fundamentally only a spring, a glob of malleable plastic, and a pie plate—Log is just a log. Its fictional manufacturer, Blammo, has a name reminiscent of Whammo, the manufacturer of the Frisbee. The "Log" song combines and spoofs advertising jingles for earlier products, with its children's chorus touting Log's ability to roll down stairs (as did the Slinky song), run over the neighbor's dog, or serve as a great snack. The central character in the "Log" advertisement bears an unmistakable resemblance in both design and petulance to John Hubley's Marky Maypo character used in the Maypo cereal advertising campaign of 1956. The interpolation of such references to past cultural artifacts continued throughout the series. For example, "Log" commercials were a recurring motif in many *Ren & Stimpy* episodes. Later "Log" ads included "Log for Girls," "High Fashion Log," "Action Log," "G.I. Log," "The Visible Log," and "Anatomically Correct Log."[43] Other Kricfalusi commercials included the breakfast cereal spoofs "Powdered Toast" and "Sugar Frosted Milk," which stays lumpy, even in cereal. Typical of the animatophile viewpoint, these mock commercials made fun of vintage children's television advertisements, while also celebrating them.

In "Stimpy's Big Day," a scene depicting Stimpy and Muddy on the *Stimpy and Muddy Show* further indicates Kricfalusi's concern with the cultural detritus of past children's television animated series. Muddy and Stimpy's dialogue consists almost entirely of old clichés and catch phrases from earlier cartoons produced for television, or vintage theatrical animation repackaged as TV kiddie fare during the 1950s and 1960s, including "Get your hand out of that pic-i-nic basket!" from *Yogi Bear,* "I hate meeses to pieces!" from *Pixie and Dixie,* "Well blow me down!" from *Popeye,* and Elmer Fudd's "I'm huntin' for a wabbit!" from the "Looney Tunes" and "Merrie Melodies" animated films.

While Nickelodeon press releases for *Ren & Stimpy* promised "the anarchic physical comedy of the great Warner Brothers [sic] cartoons of the '40s and '50s" with "lovable stars of animation,"[44] the reception of the product—both positive and negative—emphasized its appeal to animatophiles through the recycling of animation and pop-culture conventions. Richard Gehr, writing in the *Village Voice,* noted that the show was "preceded by *Doug* and *Rugrats,* two sensitive failures in a post-*Simpsons* mode," but noted that "*Ren & Stimpy* . . . is the first TV cartoon aimed at practically everyone *but* children. Underground comics' influence—especially Peter Bagge's *Hate* and Daniel Clowes's *Eightball*—is apparent in Ren's violent mood swings and the show's fabulous-'50s backgrounds. The music is nostalgic with generic library stock, bongos, and guitars alternating with DNA-embedded classics like Rossini's 'Thieving Magpie,' heard in 'Space Madness' as a nod to both *2001* and *A Clockwork Orange.*"[45]

Gehr may have been right. The show did seem to be for everyone but children. But children loved it. Early market research indicated that *Ren & Stimpy* doubled Nickelodeon's ratings among children aged two to eleven, increasing the total number of viewers to 1.2 million. It also had one of the largest adult concentrations of any Nickelodeon show. About

35 percent of *Ren & Stimpy*'s audience was eighteen or over. With an eye to increasing audience share, the animation department at Nickelodeon requested that Viacom, owner of Nickelodeon, run the series on Saturday nights on another Viacom network, MTV, which catered to adolescents and young adults. This was done in order to get the MTV audience and bring it to Nickelodeon for Sunday morning *Ren & Stimpy* cablecasts.[46] The result was a near-doubling of viewers to 2.2 million households, with 45 percent of the audience being eighteen or over.[47] Ren and Stimpy became icons of adolescent culture, with extensive coverage in such magazines as *Dirt* and *Film Threat*. The hip stance of the animatophile trash aesthetic suddenly was absorbed by the larger taste group of adolescent and young adult culture.[48]

Ratings were up, but Nickelodeon was not exactly delighted. Institutional and marketing considerations turned this demographic shift into a problem. The promised benefits of convergence and synergy, which propelled the media mergers of the 1980s and 1990s, were already presenting difficulties. The corporate cultures of Nickelodeon and MTV, which were highly competitive and occasionally noncooperative, resulted in *Ren & Stimpy*'s withdrawal from the rock music network.[49] From Nickelodeon's point of view, the eight weeks of MTV cablecast had served its purpose. The series was withdrawn, despite MTV's request to prolong it.

While Nickelodeon was committed to children's broadcasting, Kricfalusi and his coworkers increasingly created programming that catered to his cult following among young adult animatophiles and allied youth taste groups addicted to the show's hip references, deliberate bad taste, and trash aesthetic. Observed *Ren & Stimpy* writer Bob Camp, "Nickelodeon's target market is 10–12 year olds—but we're not aiming the stuff at little kids. . . . We want to really push the envelope—disembowelment gags and all."[50] Embarrassing for Nickelodeon was the fact that while children might love disembowelment gags, their parents could have a different view. The show wasn't necessarily too gross for kids, but it was too gross for Nickelodeon's idealized child viewer. Anything that offended this hypothetical viewer (or more importantly, its parents) jeopardized the corporate image. Nickelodeon looked toward Disney or Warner Bros. as models of what was fun and in good taste. Kricfalusi and his staff leaned toward the early *Mad* approach to culture. Spumco staff member Bill Wray maintained, "If we could find some budding Harvey Kurtzmans who could draw . . . they'd have a job here. That's what we're looking for."[51]

Nickelodeon story editors continually requested script and other modifications, which were resisted by Kricfalusi. Revisions to "Stimpy's Big Day" included the deletions of a character sniffing kitty litter and use of the word "Ragu." The original ending of this episode was to show Stimpy presenting himself for a smacking. Nickelodeon story editors deemed this to be "too masochistic for the younger viewers." Other suggestions for changes were resisted by the filmmaker. When Nickelodeon asked why the perspective on a car in "Stimpy's Big Day" looked as if it were from a second-story window, Kricfalusi retorted, "Because we can't draw cars, let alone perspective."[52] Kricfalusi removed his name from "Nurse Stimpy" because of changes that Nickelodeon urged him to make to the script. In "Stimpy's Big Day," a microphone that was inserted into Stimpy's mouth was deemed too phallic; in "Space Madness," lines emulating dialogue from *Night of the Hunter* ("You're not like the others, Johnnie, you hate the same things I hate . . . perfume-smelling things . . . lacy things, things with curly hair.") were altered; and in "Stimpy's Inventions," a scene where Ren licks Stimpy's armpit was cut.[53] Standards and Practices at Nickelodeon withheld network approval from such items as the episode titles "Ren and Stimpy Bugger Christmas" and "Stimpy's First Fart," and Kricfalusi strained harder and harder against these production constraints. Nickelodeon began to receive finished episodes that had to be censored in part.[54]

Eventually, two episodes featuring a new character named George Liquor (a sadistic middle-aged authority figure allegedly modeled after Kricfalusi's father) were deemed unsuitable for broadcast altogether. "Man's Best Friend" featured Ren clubbing George Liquor with an oar in a black-and-white slow motion parody of *Raging Bull* (1980).[55] In "Dog Show," George Liquor tormented Ren and Stimpy to make them competitive in a dog show. "Powdered Toast Man" (1992) did make it to air. This was a spoof of animated superhero conventions dating back to the *Superman* series of 1941–42 (and later returned to by Kricfalusi in his more recent *Ripping Friends* television series). The "Powdered Toast Man" episode featured the Pope clinging tenaciously to Powdered Toast Man's buttocks, and showed the hero using the Bill of Rights and the Constitution as kindling. When viewers complained to the FCC, Nickelodeon dropped the episode from replay on future airdates.[56] These shows presented real problems for the cable network. Children liked the show, and Nickelodeon was committed to serving children. But both finances and public relations were critical problems. With an investment of approximately $400,000 per episode, Nickelodeon could not pump money into a program that was, in its corporate view, inappropriate for the 55 percent of its audience that was under eighteen.

This consideration was particularly important in light of the marketing deal Nickelodeon signed with Mattel to license Ren and Stimpy products to children—a deal that *Variety* considered "one of the entertainment industry's major licenses this year."[57] The licensing of products based on animated characters has been a vital economic factor in the animation industry since the 1920s.[58] Positioning *Ren & Stimpy* outside a juvenile taste group might have jeopardized the popularity of the series among potential Mattel toy purchasers, adversely affecting the value of the license and the profitability of *Ren & Stimpy* to Nickelodeon. One can only imagine the reaction of Nickelodeon executives when Kricfalusi's partner Bob Camp told the press about Spumco's merchandising ideas. "We're gonna [*sic*] do great stuff! Enema bags, butt plugs . . . we want really stupid toys, not your regular G.I. Joe crap. We want toys that leak on you and explode in your face—*real* fun stuff!"[59]

The Nickelodeon-Spumco tensions were compounded by production problems. Spumco simply could not manage delivery of episodes on time or on budget. A Nickelodeon story editor observed that, "Nickelodeon have one of the hottest shows in the country right now, and a potential merchandising bonanza if they can get new shows to the public. And John is sitting on the shows."[60] The problems with production delays became so notorious that they were even spoofed in a *Simpsons* episode broadcast on the Fox network, where the presentation of a *Ren & Stimpy* episode at an awards ceremony resulted in an "episode not completed" message on the screen. Nickelodeon claimed that Kricfalusi was not only responsible for missing deadlines, but also for going over budget. Kricfalusi appeared intransigent about changing either program content or his working methods. Instead, the filmmaker blamed Nickelodeon for the missed deadlines through its delays on script approval and story comments.[61]

In light of these problems, Nickelodeon's parent company, Viacom, decided to end the relationship with Kricfalusi. Nickelodeon arranged for Kricfalusi's more compliant partner Bob Camp to take over production of the series by Games Productions, a studio reorganized for the manufacture of *Ren & Stimpy Nicktoons*. Linda Simensky of Nickelodeon observed that the firing of Kricfalusi was primarily a practical matter from the company's viewpoint. "If the problem were just one of taste and censorship, we probably could have solved it here. The decision to get John [Kricfalusi] off *Ren & Stimpy* was based in part on taste considerations, but mainly was motivated by problems with budget and schedules." On the other hand, Simensky added, "We *were* constantly confronted with all sorts of in-jokes and obscure references in *Ren & Stimpy* that staff at Nickelodeon didn't feel were funny or understandable by anyone."[62] Kricfalusi maintained that the problem was purely one of taste. In a statement given to *Variety* after he lost control of the series, the director disavowed the scatological humor that characterized *Ren & Stimpy*. A supposedly repentant Kricfalusi said, "Farts are behind me."[63]

It would be too much to claim that Kricfalusi's animatophilia was solely responsible for his removal from *Ren & Stimpy*. But it was certainly a strong contributing factor. As the aesthetic of a young adult group that continually redefines itself outside the taste norms of mainstream society, animatophilia was an aesthetic alternate to that of mainstream culture. Nickelodeon sought profit by mass-merchandising children's products to mainstream culture. Consequently, Kricfalusi's fate was probably inevitable.

NOTES

An earlier version of this chapter appeared in *Film History* Vol. 5 no. 1 (1993). Reprinted by permission of *Film History*. Preliminary versions of this chapter were given at the Society for Animation Studies Conference at the California Institute of the Arts in Valencia, California, on 24 October 1992. I am indebted to Don Wallace and Dave Marshall for their insights on taste groups and popular culture, and to Linda Simensky for her information about corporate strategies at Nickelodeon. This chapter was written at the instigation of Tom Knott, who drew my attention to the vitality of contemporary television animation, and was an excellent source of research material. Will Ryan's knowledge about *Mad* is rivaled only by Jerry Beck, who remains not only my guru on all things animated, but a valuable resource in seeing visual material crucial for this chapter. Further assistance was given by Karen Flischel and Bronwyn McElroy of Nickelodeon, Harvey Deneroff, Karl Cohen, Bill Mikulak, Susan Kelly, Hank Sartin, Myron Waldman, Sybil del Gaudio, Ron Magliozzi, Will Straw, and Janet Staiger. Finally, a note of gratitude is due to Heather Hendershot for her assistance in the adaptation of this article to its present form.

1. Wheeler Winston Dixon, "Interview with John Kricfalusi," *Film Criticism*, Vol. 17 no. 1 (Fall 1992), 39.

2. Richard Gehr, "You Filthy Worms! Ren and Stimpy's Creator Gives Hell to Nickelodeon," *Village Voice* (17 November 1992): 58. "Who, Where, Ren?" *Entertainment Weekly* (20 November 1992): 8. Other comments include, "It's like someone saying, 'We like this Little Tramp character, but let's get rid of that Chaplin guy.'" David Silverman, quoted in "Cheers 'n' Jeers," *TV Guide* (17 October 1992): 4. Elsewhere, Kricfalusi's loss of the series has been likened to a similar experience early in Walt Disney's career, with Nickelodeon, by implication, cast in the role of the odious producer Charles Mintz. Harvey Deneroff, "Of Bluth and Spumco," *Animation Report*, Vol. 1 no. 7 (September 1992): 2.

3. Alison Butler, "New Film Histories and the Politics of Location," *Screen*, Vol. 33 no. 4 (Winter 1992): 414.

4. Herbert J. Gans, *Popular Culture and High Culture* (New York: Basic Books, 1974), viii–ix.

5. Pierre Bourdieu, *Distinction: A Social Critique of the Judgement of Taste* (Cambridge, Mass.: Harvard University Press, 1984), 114–120.

6. Ford, a key figure in the legitimation of animation, curated the 1981 Whitney show and programmed the influential 1979 "Cartoonal Knowledge" series at New York's Thalia Theater. Jay Cocks, "The World Jones Made," *Time* (17 December 1973): 17; "The Hollywood Cartoon," special issue of *Film Comment*, Vol. 11 no. 1 (January–February 1975).

7. The former was taught by Leonard Maltin, the latter by the author.

8. Christopher Finch, *The Art of Walt Disney* (New York: Abrams, 1973); Frank Thomas and Ollie Johnston, *Disney Animation: The Illusion of Life* (New York: Abbeville, 1981); John Canemaker, *Treasures of Disney Animation* (New York: Abbeville, 1982); Patrick Brion, *Tex Avery: les dessins* (Paris: Éditions Nathan Image, 1988).

9. Shamus Culhane, *Talking Animals and Other People* (New York: St. Martin's Press, 1986); Chuck Jones, *Chuck Amuck* (New York: Farrar, Straus, Giroux, 1990). It should be noted that at this stage, art books and galleries privileged those who created theatrical cartoons over television animation. It was fine to praise Bill Hannah and Joe Barbera for creating Tom and Jerry, but it was as if Scooby Doo had never existed. Similarly, while Jones was hailed for his Warner Bros. films, little attention was paid to his ambitious television literary adaptations, such as *Ricky Ticky Tavy* or *The Grinch Who Stole Christmas*.

10. Gans, *Popular Culture and High Culture*, 94–100. Within this article, I will not explore the more politically charged notions of resistance or subversion employed in many cultural studies examinations of subculture.

11. I am indebted to Don Wallace for this insight. Ian Angus observes, "commodities are produced for 'individuals' who define themselves through their difference from other production groups." Ian H. Angus, "Circumscribing Postmodern Culture," in *Cultural Politics in Contemporary America*, eds. Ian Angus and Sut Jhally (New York: Routledge, 1989), 101.

12. Pierre Bourdieu, *In Other Words: Essays towards a Reflexive Sociology,* trans. Matthew Adamson (Stanford: Stanford University Press, 1990), 132.

13. Don Wallace, "Consumption, Class and Taste: The Construction of the Market for Popular Literature" (M.A. thesis, Carleton University, 1992), 57. It should be noted that one man's hipster is another man's nerd. Hipness or nerdness lie in the eye of the beholder. For example, the hippest of a youth taste group may appear as just another sulking adolescent to other taste groups. Hipness varies from one taste group to another. However, the hip are recognized as arbiters of taste norms within their particular taste group.

14. I am indebted to David Marshall for this insight.

15. While this essay deals with the importance of "hipness," other factors come into play in defining taste groups and similar social organizations. These will not be dealt with directly here. In a critique of this article, William Mikulak correctly observes:

> There are numerous specialized taste/consumption/fandom groups that overlap in today's popular culture landscape. . . . They each encompass a wide range of modes of relating to the shared interest beyond a mere knowledge gradient. . . . There are differing degrees of sincerity toward the subject ranging from zealous religiosity toward canonical texts to high campiness. Psychic immersion varies from passive spectatorship to intensive role-playing, complete with costumes. Fans may appropriate favorite characters for use in their own narratives and art objects, extending the fictive universe to suit their needs. Sometimes it seems as if rather than opposing the mainstream, they choose to ignore it while in their insular fan communities, focusing vast energies on arguing the fine points of each other's interpretation of the subject matter. Thus, while you are no doubt correct in arguing that taste groups respond to the mainstreaming of their marginal tastes by seeking even more marginal subjects, more insular groups may use esoterica as a means to make distinctions among group members. Here I see a parallel between animatophile taste groups and academic researchers intent on uncovering ever more obscure corners of filmdom on which to stake their claims as experts.

William Mikulak, letter to the author, 15 January 1993.

16. See, for example, Basil Wolverton, "Mad Hats," *Mad* #36 and "Mad Reader," *Mad* #11, reprinted in Maria Reidelbach, *Completely Mad: A History of the Comic Book and Magazine* (Boston: Little, Brown & Co., 1991), 190, 199.

17. Harvey Kurtzman and Will Elder, "Woman Wonder!" *Mad* #10 in Reidelbach, *Completely Mad,* 34–35; "Mickey Rodent!" *Mad* #13 in Reidelbach, *Completely Mad,* 29; "Outer Sanctum," in William Gaines, ed., *The Bedside Mad* (New York: Signet, 1959), 6–29; "Robinson Crusoe," in Gaines, *The Bedside Mad,* 158–178; Les Daniels, *Comix: A History of Comic Books in America* (New York: Bonanza Books, 1971), 61–70. Similar satires were done by Wally

Wood ("Batboy and Rubin" and "Flesh Garden"), Jack Davis ("High Noon"), and others.

18. Richard D. Lyons, "Harvey Kurtzman Is Dead at 68; Cartoonist Was Creator of *Mad*," *New York Times*, 23 February 1993: B7.

19. Daniels, *Comix*, 83–90; Frederic Wertham, *Seduction of the Innocent* (New York: Rinehart and Winston, 1954).

20. One indicator of this mass popularity can be seen in the increasing acceptance of American television series based on comics, beginning with *Dick Tracy* (1950–51), *The Adventures of Superman* (1952–57), *Flash Gordon* (1953–54), and *Steve Canyon* (1958–60). The proliferation and longevity of such shows peaked in the 1960s with *Dennis the Menace* (1959–63), *Hazel* (1961–66), *The Addams Family* (1964–66), *Batman* (1966–68), *Tarzan* (1966–69), and *My World and Welcome to It* (1969–72) before tapering off in the 1970s with *Wonder Woman* (1976–79) and *Buck Rogers in the 25th Century* (1979–81). Occasionally, these programs reinforced condescending attitudes toward their comic sources by emphasizing the "camp" nature of the work. This was particularly stressed in the *Batman* series.

21. Pierre Couperie and Maurice C. Horn, *Bande Dessinée et Figuration Narrative* (Paris: Société Civile d'Etudes et de Recherches des Littératures Dessinées, 1967), reprinted as *A History of the Comic Strip* (New York: Crown, 1968), 228–252.

22. See, for example, Robert C. Allen, *Vaudeville and Film 1895–1915: A Study in Media Interaction* (New York: Arno, 1980); Erik Barnouw, *The Magician and the Cinema* (New York: Oxford University Press, 1981), and C. W. Ceram, *The Archaeology of the Cinema* (New York: Harcourt, Brace & World, 1965).

23. Frank Tashlin embodied an important transitional point in the study of animation, largely because his career spanned live-action and animated films. His reputation spread as early as Jean-Luc Godard's appreciations in *Cahiers du cinéma*, reprinted in *Godard on Godard*, ed. Tom Milne (New York: Viking, 1972), 35–36, 57–59; the article by Roger Tailleur in *Positif* no. 29 (1958), translated by Paul Willemen as "Anything Goes" in *Frank Tashlin* (Edinburgh: Edinburgh Film Festival, 1973), 17–31; Ian Cameron, "Frank Tashlin and the New World," *Movie* no. 16 (Winter 1968–69): 38–39; Mike Barrier, "Interview," in *Frank Tashlin*, 45–53, etc. Similar consideration of other animation auteurs can be found in Mike Barrier, "Screenwriter for a Duck," *Funnyworld* no. 21: 9–14; Jeff Missine, "Walter Lantz: Cartune-ist," *Mindrot* no. 10 (20 April 1978): 13–21; Joe Adamson, *Tex Avery: King of Cartoons* (New York: Popular Library, 1975), and Joe Adamson, *The Walter Lantz Story with Woody Woodpecker and Friends* (New York: G. P. Putnam & Sons, 1985); and in many of the essays in *The American Animated Cartoon*, ed. Danny Peary and Gerald Peary (New York: Dutton, 1980).

24. Leonard Maltin, "TV Animation," *Film Comment,* Vol. 11 no. 1 (January–February 1975): 77. See also Greg Ford and Richard Thompson, "Chuck Jones"; John Canemaker, "Winsor McCay" and "Grim Natwick"; Mark Langer, "Max and Dave Fleischer"; Jonathan Rosenbaum, "Walt Disney" and "Tex Avery," and Mark Kausler, "Tom and Jerry," in *ibid.* 21–38, 44–47, 48–56, 57–61, 64–69, 70–73, 74–75.

25. Patrick Brion, *Tom and Jerry,* translated by Annette Michelson (New York: Crescent/Nathan, 1987).

26. This interest in cels parallels that of an earlier period when Disney's work was held in high regard by both critics and the public. A critic in the 1940s observed, "The original drawings and paintings for Walt Disney's *Dumbo* are already being shown in the Harlow, Keppel & Co. gallery and are interesting the usual public. This is 'art for the people' very distinctly and has been so from the beginning." With a lessening in interest by high culture critics for Disney films came a diminishment of the market for animation art. Cel art no longer was sold in galleries. For years, animation art was relatively valueless within the total culture, and became almost exclusively marketed within the animatophile taste group. For example, in the late 1970s, one dealer offered original animation drawings of Bugs and Elmer from *"What's Opera Doc?"* (1957) for $20 each, while Gallery Lainzberg offered cels and animation drawings from $20, including custom matting. Even taking inflation into account, these are bargains in terms of today's prices for such items. H. McB., "Attractions in the Galleries," *New York Sun* (31 October 1941): n.p.; Timothy White, "From Disney to Warner Bros.: The Critical Shift," unpublished paper, Society for Cinema Studies Conference, Washington D.C., 28 May 1990; Brian Tischler, letters to the author, 5 and 13 December 1978; Gallery Lainzberg advertisement, *Mindrot* no. 7 (15 June 1977), 19.

27. Rita Reif, "Are Cartoon Stills Still a Hot Ticket?" *New York Times* (12 April 1992): 33.

28. Rita Reif, "Animation Auction Is Questioned," *New York Times* (17 October 1992): 17.

29. Silver Stone Gallery advertisement, *StoryboarD/The Art of Laughter* (December–January 1992–93): 38.

30. Howard Lowery, quoted in Joanne Kirschner, "Collecting 'Toons for Fun & Profit," *Rapport,* Vol. 17 no. 2 (December 1992–January 1993): 9.

31. Heather Hendershot, note to the author, 12 August 2002.

32. "Animated Commercials #1," "Animated Commercials #5," "Beany and Cecil," "Clutch Cargo Vol. 1," and "Colonel Bleep Vol. 1," *Whole Toon Catalog* no. 8 (November 1992), 18, 20, 29.

33. Karen Flischel, interview with author, 6 September 1992.

34. "Nickelodeon to Debut Original Animation Block Sunday, August 11

Featuring: *Rugrats, The Ren & Stimpy Show* and *Doug,"* *Anymator* (May 1991): 2–3.

35. Viacom International owns MTV, VH-1, Showtime and a number of syndicated series such as *The Cosby Show* and *Roseanne.* Nickelodeon had 55 million subscribers and earned $169 million in revenue during 1991. Mark Langler and Geoffrey Smith, "The MTV Tycoon," *Business Week,* 21 September 1992: 56–62.

36. Daniel Cerone, "Eye on TV," *Star-Ledger* (10 August 1991): 23.

37. Todd Gitlin, *Inside Prime Time* (New York: Pantheon Books, 1983), 77–85.

38. "We were looking for a Nicktoons style with a Nicktoons identity." Linda Simensky, interview with the author, 16 October 1992.

39. Tasha Robinson, "John Kricfalusi: 'Anything That's Corporate and Large Is Doomed to Be Bad,'" *The Onion,* Vol. 37 no. 12 (4 April 2001), http://avclub.theonion.com/avclub3712/avfeature_3712html, Phyllis Pollack, "Censorship's New Wave," *Freedom Writer* (January–February 1989) http://www.ifas.org/fw/8901/censorship.html, Ron Kurer, "The End of Terrytoons," *The Toon Tracker,* http://www.toontracker.com/terry/terry4.htm.

40. "Stimpy's Big Day" and "The Big Shot!" will be treated as one episode in this chapter. Both were broadcast as consecutive halves of the same series episode. "The Big Shot!" is simply the concluding half of "Stimpy's Big Day's" narrative.

41. Terms for bodily exudates are common in Kricfalusi's series. Hoek is pronounced "hork," which is a slang term for the expectoration of phlegm. The first four letters of Kricfalusi's company name—Spumco—suggests a slang term for semen. Early in "Stimpy's Big Day," Ren eats the contents of Stimpy's kitty litter box in an act of caecophilia. At the end of "Stimpy's Big Day," Stimpy displays his collection of "magic nose goblins." "I picked them myself," he proudly says, displaying his nose to the viewer. Freud has observed that much humor "includes what is *common* to both sexes and to which the feeling of shame extends—that is to say, what is excremental in the most comprehensive sense. This is, however, the sense covered by sexuality in childhood, an age at which there is, as it were, a cloaca within which what is sexual and what is excremental are barely or not at all distinguished." Sigmund Freud, *Jokes and Their Relation to the Unconscious* (translated by James Strachey) (New York: W. W. Norton, 1963), 97–98. While *The Ren & Stimpy Show* serves as an excellent subject for psychoanalytic analysis, such analysis will only be suggested by this study.

42. Dave Mackey, "Sour Persimmons #1" *Apatoons* #63 (June–July 1992), n.p. Use of recycled material such as jingles or theme music from television is common in contemporary animation. Another example is the use of music from *The Price Is Right* in John Lasseter's "Tin Toy" (1988).

43. The Maypo commercials featured the characters Marky Maypo and his Uncle Ralph, and concerned the attempts by Uncle Ralph to get his nephew to eat a new maple-flavored breakfast cereal. Each commercial concluded with the line, "I want my Maypo!" which became one of the most successful advertising slogans of the 1950s. These spots were produced by John and Faith Hubley, directed by John Hubley, and animated by Emery Hawkins for the advertising agency of Fletcher Richards, Calkins & Holdin, Inc. and their client Heublin, Inc. At least four separate Maypo advertisements were created by Hubley's Storyboard Productions. Sybil del Gaudio, interview with the author, 1 February 1993; Alice C. Wolf, "The History of American Television Commercials 1947–1977," *Millimeter,* Vol. 5 no. 4 (April 1977): 22–24, 27, 46, 58–61.

44. Bronwyn Smith, "Animated Duo Takes to the Road on Nickelodeon for the Premiere of *The Ren & Stimpy Show,*" 25 July 1991: 2; Bronwyn McElroy, "Hey, Man, *The Ren & Stimpy Show* Premieres All-New Episodes When the Nicktoons Hit Begins Airing on 'Snick' August 15," 6 July 1992: 1.

45. Richard Gehr, "Maim That Toon," *Village Voice* (8 October 1991): 49.

46. Simensky interview, 16 October 1992.

47. Flischel interview; Stefan Kanfer, "Loonier Toon Tales," *Time* (13 April 1992): 79; Mark Robichaux, "For Nickelodeon, Crude 'Toon Is Big Hit," *Wall Street Journal* (27 January 1992): B1.

48. Ren and Stimpy were on the cover of *Utne Reader,* (October–November 1992); A. A. Perry, "The Great Unwritten Rules of Comedy," *Dirt* no. 2 (1992): 12; Christian Gore, "Celling Out," *Film Threat* no. 7 (December 1992): 22–25, 28–39; Alice Pinch and Stiffy Miller "The Screechin' Ren & Stimpy Episode Log," *ibid.*: 26–27. The series is used in the marketing of other adolescent culture products attempting to position themselves within changing parameters of hipness. Among the first signs of *Ren & Stimpy* losing hip status is the ad copy for Slave Labor Graphics: "Ren & Stimpy? Bah! Milk and Cheese. Dairy Products Gone Bad! They're Drunk! They're Violent! They're Dairy Products Gone Bad and They're rampaging their way across America! Get your copy of Milk & Cheese before they too become hip & trendy!" Slave Labor Graphics advertisement, *Film Threat* no. 8 (February 1993): 12.

49. Linda Simensky, interview with the author, 3 October 1992.

50. Pam Murray and Doug Murray, "Ren & Stimpy's Pals," *Comics Scene* no. 28 (August 1992): 10.

51. "Bill Wray Interview," *Pure Images* no. 5 (1992): n.p.

52. "Revisions Made," memo from Will McRobb to John Kricfalusi, 2 April 1991, and "Revisions in Contention," memo from Will McRobb to John Kricfalusi, with annotations by John Kricfalusi, 2 April 1991 (private collection).

53. The credits eventually read, "Directed by Raymond Spum." Cerone, "Toontown Terrors," 90.

54. Will McRobb, memo to Libby Simon, 22 October 1991 (private collection); Pinch and Miller, "The Screechin' Ren & Stimpy Episode Log," 26.

55. While I was writing the first version of this chapter, it was rumored in one trade publication that an edited and reanimated version of this episode was being prepared by Games Production. Karl Cohen, "Oh No, Not Another *Ren & Stimpy* Update!" *ASIFA—San Francisco Bulletin* (March 1993), 6.

56. Daniel Cerone, "Ren & Stimpy and Its Creator: A Parting of Ways," *Los Angeles Times* (28 September 1992): F12; Jennifer Pendleton, "Groening Sides with 'Ren' Artist," *Daily Variety* (25 September 1992): 22; Dan Persons, "Ren & Stimpy Massacre," *Cinefantastique,* Vol. 23 no. 5 (February 1993): 5.

57. Jennifer Pendleton, "Nick Faves Launch New Mattel Line," *Daily Variety* (12 June 1992): 3, 10.

58. Walt Disney and Pat Sullivan were particularly successful practitioners of product licensing. John Canemaker, *Felix the Cat: The Twisted Tale of the World's Most Famous Cat* (New York: Pantheon, 1991), 64–65, 71, 85, 88; *Annual Report Fiscal Year Ended September 28, 1940* (Burbank: Walt Disney Productions, 1940).

59. Murray and Murray, "Ren & Stimpy's Pals," 12.

60. Cerone, "*Ren & Stimpy* and Its Creator," F12.

61. Persons, "Ren & Stimpy Massacre," 60.

62. Linda Simensky, interview with the author, 14 October 1992.

63. Daniel Cerone, "*Ren & Stimpy* Creator Fired," *Los Angeles Times* (26 September 1992): D1; Jennifer Pendleton, "'Ren & Stimpy' Goes to Camp; Kricfalusi Sings New Toon," *Variety* (5 October 1992): 26.

9

Nickelodeon's Nautical Nonsense

The Intergenerational Appeal of SpongeBob SquarePants

Heather Hendershot

Who lives in a pineapple under the sea?
SpongeBob SquarePants!
Absorbent and yellow and porous is he . . .
SpongeBob SquarePants!
If nautical nonsense be something you wish . . .
SpongeBob SquarePants!
. . . then drop on the deck and flop like a fish!
SpongeBob SquarePants!
SpongeBob SquarePants!
SpongeBob SquarePants!
SpongeBob SquarePants!
SpongeBob SquarePaaaaaants!

—*SpongeBob SquarePants* theme song

In early 1999, *Pokémon* ruled the Saturday morning U.S. television ratings. The convoluted plotlines—and hundreds of characters—were indecipherable to adults, and utterly compelling to children. Kids were not only gaga over the show, they were also rapacious collectors of *Pokémon* toys and trading cards, and players of *Pokémon* video games. No other children's television show, it seemed, could compete with this kind of licensing synergy. The Pokémon phenomenon constituted nothing short of a national obsession. But children's television shows often fall as quickly as they rise. While adult hits like *Seinfeld* have a long shelf life, both originally and in syndication, children's shows often begin in syndication, saturating the market and the shelves of toy stores, before finally, and suddenly, fizzling out. It was not surprising, then, when the Pokémon fad finally crashed and burned. What was surprising was that the show that toppled *Pokémon* was not aligned with a hot toy or video game. The star of this new children's TV show was not a superhero from a hit movie. He was not even a mammal.

In July 1999, Nickelodeon premiered a new show about a geeky, naive, perpetually optimistic sea sponge. By August, *Pokémon* and *SpongeBob SquarePants* were neck-and-neck in the competition for viewers. Shortly thereafter, *SpongeBob* surpassed *Pokémon's* Saturday morning ratings. The show's ratings eventually even surpassed Nickelodeon's own champion, *Rugrats*. Was this a David and Goliath moment, or just another typical upheaval in the faddish world of children's television? This essay will examine the *SpongeBob* phenomenon, asking why this show has hit it big, and what this success means financially for Nickelodeon. I will also examine *SpongeBob* itself, a program which is disarmingly upbeat, aesthetically complex, and sporadically gender-bending.

What is perhaps most interesting about the show is its popularity among both children and adults. Nickelodeon's *Ren & Stimpy* was an adult cartoon show that brought along kids for the ride; that the network actually thought it was creating a kid's show indicates nothing less than a willful blindness, or, to put it more kindly, wishful thinking on its part. *SpongeBob* shares none of *Ren & Stimpy's* abrasive edge and scatological humor. It is, theoretically, designed only for children. That adults are also drawn to the show should not be surprising, though, for the paradox of children's television is that it is created by adults for children. "Children's" television, like children's literature in Jacqueline Rose's well-known formulation, is impossible. Like children's literature, children's TV is designed by adults to fulfill their conceptions of what childhood should be.[1]

Nickelodeon claims, however, to be different from other children's television providers. It doesn't give kids what adults *think* they want—except in its first few years of operation, for which it earned the nickname "the green vegetable channel"—it gives children what they *really* want. Grown-ups who work for Nickelodeon can, apparently, magically violate the sacrosanct division between adult and child, a division about which there is much cultural anxiety, in order to think like kids and create shows "just for kids." Marsha Kinder has argued that it is a current strategy of popular culture to both exaggerate generational differences and to profit from transgenerational address with products that are distinct from rival products by virtue of being "youthful."[2] Simply put, youthful products, which exaggerate the differences between adults and youths, and which both kids and grown-ups like, are highly profitable. Nick claims to produce kids' shows that an adult could not possible enjoy, because adults are stuffy, rational, and boring (until they watch Nick's adult nostalgia programming at night, which makes them fun and playful). Thus, according to the Nickelodeon logic, if adults are sometimes not stuffy, just as children are sometimes not innocent and naive, it proves (or disproves) nothing about the "essential nature" of adulthood or childhood; it proves only that adults and kids can play at being each other. *SpongeBob* illustrates the ways in which this play can work, the ways in which the boundaries between children and adults can, as David Buckingham has shown, be simultaneously blurred and reinforced.[3]

As Linda Simensky explains in this volume, Nickelodeon has been pursuing original cartoon production since the early 1990s. In 1996, Stephen Hillenburg pitched an idea for a show about a sea sponge to Nickelodeon. The idea was accepted, Hillenburg was made executive producer, and the show went into production under his supervision. The show reflects Hillenburg's vision, but is the property of Nickelodeon, and it was therefore Nick which reaped the most profit from the $700 million worth of SpongeBob toys, clothing, and trinkets that were sold in 2002.

SpongeBob was a new venture for the network; it was the first time it premiered a show on Saturday morning. Previously, Nick had put new shows on Sunday morning, when kids were underserved by other broadcasters; the cable network scheduled only reruns of its popular shows on Saturday mornings.[4] Even with reruns, Nick has scored number one in the Saturday morning ratings since 1997, although the "Kids WB!" block persistently beats out Nick when it comes to one key subdemographic of viewers: boys aged six to eleven.[5] The reason is clear: WB programs rock-'em-sock-'em action shows like *X-Men: Evolution,* while Nickelodeon's policy is to avoid representations of violent or sexist behavior. Like all Nick programming, *SpongeBob* was practically devoid of violence and was designed to appeal to both boys and girls.[6] That adults would also become such a large audience for the program was, apparently, an unexpected surprise.

Officially, the target audience for *SpongeBob* was six- to eleven-year-olds, but by the summer of 2000 Nick realized that the adult audience for *SpongeBob* was quite large, and it began to air the show on weekdays at 8:00 P.M. In this way, Nick encouraged increased adult viewing, and in June 2002 viewers between the ages of eighteen and forty-nine constituted almost one-third of the program's total prime-time audience.[7]

SpongeBob's high ratings have, naturally, meant that Nickelodeon could raise its advertising rates; *SpongeBob* increased the cable network's prime-time viewership by 13 percent.[8] The network generally does not sell advertising to go with specific programs, which shows how strong Nickelodeon itself is as a brand. Companies buy ad time to be associated not with a particular show but rather with Nickelodeon itself. When *SpongeBob* succeeds, then, it strengthens the whole Nickelodeon brand, and people will pay higher advertising rates, even if they don't know whether their ad will be shown during *SpongeBob*.

In addition to selling advertising time, Nickelodeon brings in tremendous income from licensing characters from its successful shows. Its first big licensing hit was *Rugrats*. Once *SpongeBob* was a confirmed hit, Nickelodeon started a licensing campaign, and SpongeBob appeared on kids' products such as Game Boy and PlayStation games, Cheese Nips, Wendy's Kids' Meals, macaroni and cheese, bandages, coloring books, ice cream, stickers, school supplies, and Jell-o. When Mattel introduced Babbling SpongeBob dolls in 2002, it sold seventy-five thousand per week, outpacing sales of Tickle Me Elmo dolls, which until then had been "the industry standard for hot sellers."[9] Good Humor-Breyer's SpongeBob ice cream bar even outsold all other "face bars" in 2002.[10] The key to *SpongeBob*'s profitability as a licensed product is that its fans are of all ages. *Blue's Clues* products may be very popular and profitable, but adults buy them for their kids, not for themselves, and this inherently limits the amount of merchandise that can be sold. SpongeBob's likeness, by contrast, has been sold to adults on T-shirts, license-plate frames, flip-flops, and air fresheners. College students have been specifically targeted with products such as boxers, dorm room memo boards, navel rings, and soap-on-a-rope. Even bra-and-panty sets are now available, emblazoned with the smiling sponge. Thong panties picture SpongeBob's home town, "Bikini Bottom," on the front.

Adult fans of *SpongeBob* include Bruce Willis, Ellen DeGeneres, Tom Waits, Jackie Chan, Dr. Dre, Sigourney Weaver, the Violent Femmes, Tony Bennett, and, significantly, as Hillenburg often cites him as an inspiration for the character, Jerry Lewis. That this "children's" show is widely embraced by adult viewers may seem strange, but there are numerous precedents of kids' shows with grown-up fans. Jason Mittell, for example, has shown that 1960s "children's" shows such as *Huckleberry Hound, Quick Draw McGraw,* and *Yogi Bear* were praised for their satirical content and adult wit. In fact, "the most vital effect of establishing

Saturday morning cartoons as a cultural category," Mittell argues, "was filing the entire genre under a 'kid-only' label. This was accomplished less through targeting a children's audience and more by driving away the adult audience."[11] *Sesame Street* has cultivated an adult viewership since it first went on the air in 1969. The Children's Television Workshop felt that the show's lessons would work best if parents (or, to be precise, mothers) watched along with their kids. Like *The Electric Company* later, *Sesame Street* also could be used in classrooms, where teachers could watch with kids and incorporate the program into lesson plans. To attract adults, the Workshop featured celebrities known to adults but unknown to young viewers, and, likewise, it offered clever parodies of genres and personalities that children would enjoy but wouldn't get ("Allistair Cookie" hosting "Monsterpiece Theater," for example).[12] The puppet show *Kukla, Fran, and Ollie* was also immensely popular with adults, and, as Lynn Spigel has explained, in 1951 the adult protest was tremendous when NBC tried to split the program into two fifteen-minute shows, a children's programming format. An angry insurance executive wrote to the network, "Who ever got the idea that *Kukla, Fran, and Ollie* is a juvenile show? It's an adult program, pure and simple, and contains too many subtleties to be successful completely except with that [adult] mind."[13] More recently, *Pee Wee's Playhouse* was enjoyed by many adults for its camp sensibility, wild creativity, and sly sexual jokes. As Constance Penley observes, "the dialogue and visuals of *Pee-Wee's Playhouse* abound with weenie jokes, for the most part of the size variety."[14] In sum, we should not be surprised that *SpongeBob SquarePants* has an adult following. In spite of our culture's insistent separation of childhood and adulthood, adult fans of kids' shows are not at all uncommon. What is surprising, then, is not so much the phenomenon of "children's" shows that appeal to adults but rather the fact that we continue to be surprised by this phenomenon.

What is it that draws adults to kids' shows? Sophisticated dialogue, ironic humor, and parody are often key, as in *Pinky and the Brain*, *Animaniacs*, and *Tiny-Toons*, all "children's" shows with enormous adult fan bases. It would seem that a superior (and certainly misguided) feeling that you understand references that children would not get is often key to enjoyment. This requires quite a bit of disavowal on the part of adults, who labor in particular under the assumption that children are oblivious to sexual innuendo. (In one episode of *SpongeBob*, for example, a snow sculpture of a mermaid lacks cleavage, which seems very chaste until you

notice that each of the two fish constructing her is holding a big ball destined to be a breast; many adults will expect children to miss this detail.)
Children's shows that adults enjoy often offer winks to their grown-up
viewers and include "edgy" (as the industry puts it) material, material
that is slightly mean or off-color, the kind of jokes that fly on *Roseanne,*
in contrast to the unedgy humor of *The Donna Reed Show.*[15] *SpongeBob,*
conversely, is just about the least ironic or edgy show on television.

Indeed, what is perhaps most striking about *SpongeBob* is its sincerity.
This is not to say that there are never moments when adults are expected
to get jokes that children will miss. For example, a subtle moment of
adult humor occurs when SpongeBob pummels his best friend Patrick
with snowballs, in rapid-fire, and the image goes slow-mo like in a Sam
Peckinpah movie. But notwithstanding such winks to adult viewers,
SpongeBob is stunningly straightforward. When the program references
the outside world of popular culture, it usually references *types* rather
than specific films or personalities that some viewers might not get.[16]
When SpongeBob engages in a pencil-sword fight with a menacing animated doodle, he breaks the doodle's pencil and says, in a mock-serious
voice, "Looks like it's a draw." The doodle sharpens its pencil, and
SpongeBob says, "I see your point." Here, he is using the silly verbal
strategies of James Bond, or action heroes like Bruce Willis, but he's not
actually *doing* imitations of Bond or Willis, imitations which only viewers "in the know" would catch. Instead, he does a *type* of character recognizable from pop culture. At the end of the "Frankendoodle" episode,
when the doodle has been contained on a piece of paper, Patrick refers to
him as evil. "No, no, not evil," SpongeBob responds in a pseudoserious
voice, immediately donning a pair of glasses and smoking a large (bubble) pipe, "he was just a two-dimensional creature lost in our three-di-
mensional aquatic world, longing for a purpose." Here again, SpongeBob
enacts a pop culture type, the narrator or scientist or detective who au-
thoritatively sums things up. Such references are clever, but they are not
ironic or edgy. As one journalist explains, an "apparent lack of sardonic
self-awareness in a culture defined by wiseguy knowingness may be exactly what works for SpongeBob. Adults—and even kids—know the
wink-and-nudge routine all too well."[17] One might even say "*especially*
kids," since the wink-and-nudge ironic routine is so pervasive in children's shows.

While viewers may appreciate the sincerity of *SpongeBob,* the central appeal of the show, of course, is its eponymous star. SpongeBob is

With bubble pipe and monacle, SpongeBob
enacts the adult detective character-type.
Frame grab from *SpongeBob SquarePants*. © 2002
Viacom International Inc.

described by Hillenburg as a man-child. He works, like an adult, but
plays like a child. One episode in particular highlights SpongeBob's indeterminate status as neither adult nor child. SpongeBob is embarrassed
when everyone calls him a baby because he lets his grandmother lavish
him with kisses and homemade cookies. He is fed up, and Patrick offers
to teach him how to be an adult. All he has to do is: (1) puff out his chest,
(2) say "tax exemption," and (3) develop a taste for free-form jazz.
(Number three proves to be the hardest.) To test his new status as a
grown-up, SpongeBob goes to visit his grandmother, but first he pulls out
something he has been growing in a box for some time, "icing on the maturity cake . . . sideburns." After affixing his facial hair, he informs his
grandmother that he is an adult. She treats him like one, giving him tech-
nical manuals to read, feeding him steamed coral for dinner, and, as a special gift, presenting him with office supplies. This is too much for Sponge-
Bob, who finally drops his sideburns, bawls like a baby, grabs a teddy
bear, and generally acts the part of the infant, which is substantially
younger than his usual self. Grandma informs him that even an adult can
still get kisses from his grandma, and presents him with his sideburns *and*
a cookie. With these two props, SpongeBob can act his proper role as
adult-child.

The adult-child is a figure that has a long history in children's television. As Spigel argues, the children's shows of postwar America "engaged
the hearts of children (and often adults as well) by presenting a topsy-
turvy world where the lines between young and old were blurred and literally represented by clowns, fairies, and cowboys who functioned as
modern-day Peter Pans. Indeed . . . the narrative pleasure these programs
offered was based in large part on the transgression of generational roles
that were idealized in the child rearing advice literature of the period."[18]
Yet such generational transgression is not always pleasurable. The adult
actors on *Sesame Street* have a gentle delivery that adult viewers do not
find irritating. Mr. Rogers is, on the other hand, too soft and saccharine,
not adult (or "man") enough for many adults. And, notwithstanding all
his adult fans, PeeWee was simply too childish and irritating for many
grown-ups.

PeeWee was played by an actual adult man, Paul Reubens, who was
putting on an excessive childhood act. Reubens knew exactly what he
was doing when PeeWee flirted with Tito, the buff bodyguard who wore
only swim trunks and a whistle. Similarly, the genie character Jambi was
deliberately performed as a "raging queen in a box."[19] SpongeBob is different, because there is no body propping up his character, winking at
viewers.[20] In other words, the very fact that SpongeBob is animated, in a
visually kid-friendly "cartoony" style, I would argue, makes a difference.
With its bright colors, fun music, and goofy sound effects, this cartoon
feels "childish" and, by extension, "innocent." That the characters are
animated and have no life outside the show helps matters; if a slightly off-
color potty reference is made, the joke is tempered by the fact that this is
a cartoon, without adult actors pretending to be childish. Hillenburg may
call him a man-child, but SpongeBob is technically neither, "underneath
it all." When Paul Reubens, the PeeWee actor, was arrested for mastur-
bating in an adult movie theater, adults were uncomfortably reminded
that this man-child was a man. The animated SpongeBob, by contrast,
will never tip his hand about whether he is "really" boy or man. His animated status thus makes him fundamentally different from the classic
man-child of children's television, the children's television host (such as
Buffalo Bob from *Howdy Doody*, or, more recently, Steve and Joe from
Blue's Clues)[21] who playfully performs in a childlike manner.

What does it mean to perform age? I would argue that in children's
television age can be understood to be much like gender, as articulated
by queer theory: like gender, age is enacted. Both are requirements of

society—you must be one of two genders, you must have a level of maturity that "matches" your physical age—that may appear to have some biological basis, yet which have no essential, transhistorical nature. Obviously, there are biological differences among differently aged children, such that a three-year-old, for example, is dramatically different from a one-year-old. Yet it is clear that the parameters defining what it means to be a child or an adult are not transhistorical and have, on the contrary, endured constant change over time. Just as "proper" ways to enact femininity and masculinity are subject to revision, the definitions of what constitutes adulthood or childhood—indeed, to what extent these categories even exist—are frequently destabilized and revised. Whether children engage in labor or not, whether or when they can legally engage in sexual activity (and with whom), whether they can drink liquor or smoke, at what age they are considered self-sufficient, whether they attend school (and for how long)—these are all historically shifting parameters defining childhood. Learning how to "act your age" was very different a hundred years ago from what it is now.[22]

Failure to act one's age properly, like the transgression of cross-dressing, produces what Marjorie Garber calls a "category crisis." Garber argues for confronting "the extraordinary power of transvestism to disrupt, expose, and challenge, putting in question the very notion of the 'original' and of stable identity."[23] There is, of course, much cultural resistance to this kind of disruption, and rather than acknowledging the challenge of transvestism, it is easier to see the transvestite "as a figure of development, progress, or a 'stage of life.'"[24] Transgression of age roles can be justified similarly. But whereas the adultlike child can be "fixed" by growing up, the childish adult is more culturally jarring. The "natural" process of development will make precocious children eventually play their age roles properly; some day they will not be children, so their adult behavior will be appropriate. The childish adult, on the other hand, has done the impossible, taken a developmental step backward.

Children's cartoons are often populated by characters acting the part of the child. These characters are designed and voiced (for the most part) by adults who want to convey a certain idea of childhood. For example, the children of *Rugrats* are, with the partial exception of Angelica, naive innocents, and jokes center on their misunderstandings of the adult world. There is no attempt to convey a developmental idea of childhood; the infants and toddlers all physically appear to be of different ages, but they are performed at the same cognitive level of understanding, a level invented by their adult creators. Although these animated characters have no autonomous existence or agency, we might say that they, like Sponge-Bob, perform a certain idea of age. Lacking the biological referent of a "real, adult" body, though, the animated childish character's performance is invisible. It's a different story with live-action performances. Like Stella Dallas putting on her excessive masquerade of femininity, in the well-known example from feminist film theory,[25] the flesh-and-bones adult-children of children's television often push their childish drag so far that one cannot help but see it as performance. Steve on *Blue's Clues* seemed to be putting on an act in a way that SpongeBob does not, because SpongeBob seems to "really" be young. This is, of course, an illusion. Both Steve and SpongeBob perform age, even if SpongeBob has no biological age against which we can judge whether he is "really" young or old.

Like an idealized child, *SpongeBob* appears wholesome. As a typical journalist notes, "The tenor of *SpongeBob SquarePants* is distinctly sweet and silly. It lacks most of the blatant scatology of recent crossover hits like *Ren & Stimpy,* and avoids the acerbic social commentary of adults-only [*sic*] cartoons like *The Simpsons* and *South Park.*"[26] With this program, we see a reversal in the way children's shows that adults like are usually discussed. *PeeWee* and *Kukla, Fran, and Ollie* were "over kid's heads," according to popular wisdom. Sure, kids liked them, but these shows were "wasted on them," their adult fans asserted. Many adults claim to watch *SpongeBob,* conversely, to be less adult.[27] These adults may pretend just to be along for the ride, watching *SpongeBob* "as if" they were kids, but, to reiterate, "children's" television is impossible. Although some shows seem to succeed in offering absolutely nothing of interest to adults (*Barney and Friends* being a particularly striking example), kids' shows are nonetheless the product of adult minds. This fact can be a bit uncomfortable to acknowledge in a culture that invests so much in the concept of childhood innocence. Such innocence is often seen as being endangered by popular culture such as rap music, violent films, or bawdy sitcoms. Even if media directed to teens is "contaminated," though, adults at least expect *children's* television to be free of corruption. That's why the industry's children's television censors stay in business.

The popularity of *SpongeBob* among adults is an interesting example of the paedocratization (as Kinder puts it, following John Hartley) of adult consumers of popular culture. To reiterate, it is increasingly common for American pop culture artifacts, such as "teen" television shows like *Buffy the Vampire Slayer* and *Dawson's Creek,* to stress generational difference, thereby increasing transgenerational appeal and fostering huge adult fan bases. David Buckingham argues that "'youth' has become an extremely elastic category, that seems to extend ever further upwards. In their shared enthusiasm for Britpop, Nike sportswear, Nintendo, or *South Park,* for example, ten-year-olds and forty-year-olds can be seen as members of a 'youth' market that is quite self-consciously distinct from a family market."[28] From the industry's standpoint, "youthful" programming has little to do with biological age. As Buckingham says, "in this environment, 'youth' has come to be perceived as a kind of lifestyle choice, defined by its relationship to specific brands and commodities, and also available to those who fall well outside its biological limits (which are fluid in any case)."[29] Although one might posit that Viacom has a whole life trajectory plotted out for viewers—they start out as Nickelodeon viewers, graduate to MTV as teenagers, and finally settle into VH1 and TV Land as adults—in practice all age groups are interested in all these kinds of programming.

South Park is a particularly striking instance of "childish" entertainment, and it offers an interesting contrast to the more clean-cut *Sponge-Bob*. *South Park,* which is shown late at night and is not intended for young children, is hardly devoid of sophisticated content, yet part of its appeal is its "childishness." Like a naughty child, the show embraces the taboo, seemingly unfettered by superego. This cartoon would appear to challenge the mythical idea of child innocence. Yet, at the same time, the program upholds this very ideal. The children on the show swear frequently, and seem cynical and jaded, but the crux of the program's humor is often the fact that the kids don't really understand the adult world. Cartman, for example, explains in one episode that his grandfather was a lesbian, so he is one quarter lesbian. In another episode, Cartman becomes poster boy for the North American Man Boy Love Association (NAMBLA), thrilled that he has finally found mature friends who can appreciate him. Cartman may be a potty-mouth, but he is in many ways as naive as SpongeBob.

Even as adult interest in an "immature," racy cartoon like *South Park* would seem to indicate a breakdown in the childhood-adulthood opposition, the program itself often plays with this very opposition in sophisticated ways. These inappropriately "adult" children have no idea what Chef's racy love songs mean; they are gullible enough to believe that you can become a lesbian by licking cardboard; and given a million bucks, they would blow it all on buying an amusement park, not on stocks and bonds. As Buckingham explains succinctly, childhood is a "shifting, relational term, whose meaning is defined primarily through its opposition to another shifting term, 'adulthood.'"[30] The children of *South Park* are funny precisely because they are children who sometimes act like adults; this naughty play with the relational terms of child and adult can be enjoyed by adult viewers, who, in getting the jokes that the kids on the show don't understand, affirm that they, the viewers, actually are adults. At the same time that the cartoon confirms the sophistication of the viewer, it allows him or her—perhaps more likely "him," since Comedy Central targets a male demographic, and the show's "immaturity" is often of the boyish variety—the childish naughtiness of vicarious taboo-breaking. The thrill, then, comes from the simultaneous dissolution and reinforcement of the boundaries between childhood and adulthood.

It's one thing for adults to enjoy *South Park,* or even *Beavis and Butthead,* which was designed for an audience of disaffected MTV teens, but what are we to make of adult interest in popular culture designed for much younger children? *SpongeBob SquarePants* is not the only example of this. Buckingham, for example, notes the cult success of *Teletubbies* among young adults in the United Kingdom. As the program was created for infants, this seems to take the paedocratization phenomenon to quite an extreme. "While some of this interest," Buckingham explains, "was perhaps merely nostalgic, some of it was undoubtedly ironic and subversively 'childish.'"[31] The BBC was less than thrilled by the news that club kids were doing ecstasy and dancing to *Teletubbies* tunes at raves. Such activity further tainted a children's product that was already somewhat controversial.[32] The BBC aside, Buckingham's observation that interest in the show was ironic is, I believe, key. The fun in enjoying a kids' show lies in liking something that you are not supposed to like. Irony allows an appropriate distance, so that the "inappropriate" fan does not feel like an idiot. It's sort of like enjoying a low-budget horror film precisely because "it's so bad." You enjoy it because (you claim) you don't enjoy it. *Teletubbies* is extremely slowly paced, with minimal narrative, and would seem to offer little to appeal to adults, but the show's style is vaguely psychedelic and weird, enabling adults (or teens) to playfully enjoy the program at a distance.

It would be more difficult, I would argue, to enjoy *SpongeBob* at an ironic distance. SpongeBob may be naive, but the program rarely encourages viewers to laugh at him. In fact, the only character whom viewers are

ever allowed to laugh at is the ridiculously stupid Patrick. When Squidward asks everyone who has ever played a musical instrument to raise
their hand, for example, Patrick raises his hand and asks, "Is mayonnaise
an instrument?" When Squidward says no, Patrick raises his hand to indicate that, in that case, he *has* played a musical instrument. Familiar
with Patrick's thought processes, Squidward immediately says, "Horse-
radish is not an instrument either," and the disappointed Patrick lowers
his hand. Everyone knows Patrick is stupid, but no one, except maybe the
grumpy Squidward, would ever cruelly mock him. The show has com-
passion for its characters and asks viewers to empathize with them. Even
the most die-hard cynic would find it difficult to step back and laugh at a
show that is so good-natured and clever.

The show is perhaps most clever on the aesthetic level. In fact, *Sponge-
Bob*'s sophisticated design is another key element of its appeal to adults.
Visually, it is one of the most creative programs currently on the air. One
key aesthetic factor, in terms of its adult appeal, is that the show is not
cheap looking. The children's shows that adults hate most, such as
Mighty Morphin' Power Rangers, My Little Pony, or *The Care Bears,* are
often those with a low-budget appearance that violates middle-class
adult taste norms.[33] As Buckingham argues, it is the regulation of children's taste—not simply their protection from harm—that is at stake in
keeping them away from certain kinds of programming. To the despair
of self-professed tasteful adults, Buckingham et al. note, audience data
reveal that children are particularly drawn to "lavatory humor . . . ritu-
alized violence . . . and vulgar sexual innuendo."[34] Adults may like the
same things, but most would claim these things to be distasteful and inappropriate for children. Lacking both the aesthetic and the narrative
"vulgarity" of the typical toy-promoting action cartoon, *SpongeBob* is a
show that adults can enjoy without feeling like they are slumming it aesthetically. The show is even lightly peppered with references to classical
art, as when Squidward accidentally crafts an exact replica of Michelan-
gelo's David, or when SpongeBob emerges from a trash can covered with
food and looking exactly like an Archimbaldo painting. In one episode,
Squidward is trying to find a perfect spot to sit in: the first spot is "too
hot," the second "too wet," and the third "too-louse Lautrec." Here, the
background briefly metamorphoses into a pastiche of a Lautrec poster
with fish Cancan dancers. *SpongeBob*'s appeal to adults is clearly indebted to such "sophisticated" allusions, which confirm the validity of
adult tastes.

SpongeBob and Patrick carry Squidward
through terrain that is "Too-Louse Lautrec."
Frame grab from *SpongeBob SquarePants.* © 2002
Viacom International Inc.

Journalists are quick to observe that Hillenburg has an advanced degree in marine biology, but it is his degree in experimental animation that
is more germane to understanding the show. The backgrounds are abstract "Polynesian" designs, with a vaguely kitschy sixties look. It is
somewhat reminiscent of the design of Chuck Jones's Coyote-Roadrun-
ner cartoons, where the backgrounds were mostly sky and rock, criss-
crossed with roads, all with more or less accurate perspective lines, but
vaguely abstract looking nonetheless. *SpongeBob* takes place in a similarly spare terrain. The characters themselves have a traditionally squishy
cartoony look, more like Warner Bros. theatrical cartoons than the
harsher, more angular, primary color look that predominates in many
television cartoons, especially the action-superhero ones targeted to boys.
What makes the cartoon truly distinctive is its mix of cel animation (or,
at least, computer-produced material that has a traditional cel look) with
live-action images.

Mixed cel and live-action images come when you least expect them
and, at times, seem indebted to the Fleischer Brothers' Koko the Clown
theatrical cartoons of the 1920s. As in the Koko cartoons, when live action is used in *SpongeBob* it is most frequently a still photograph. Koko
cartoons often opened with Max Fleischer's hand, as a photo cutout,
quickly drawing the character. The fingers didn't really move, and it was

"primitive" by today's standards. A similar giant human photographic hand is used in the *SpongeBob* opening credits. The show opens with a portrait of Painty the Pirate; his lips are live action, and he sings. (A singing painting was a typical Fleischer gag after the coming of sound.) From him, there is a cut to the live-action "ocean" (which looks phony, a bit like a set from an ad for boys' action figures), and a simulated camera movement under the ocean, which brings us into the animated world. SpongeBob emerges from his pineapple house, but—oops!—he's only wearing tighty-whitey underpants. A giant photographic human hand slides in from the right at this point, a Fleischer-style cutout, and deposits square pants on the surprised SpongeBob. At the end of "Squidward the Unfriendly Ghost" there is another Fleischer-inspired moment, when Squidward is trapped in a giant bubble and floats out of the animated ocean and into the live-action air. This sequence is evocative of a common Fleischer scenario, where Koko would escape his drawing board and enter the world, often causing havoc. Some of the show's more visually bizarre, almost surrealist moments, also have a Fleischer feeling to them. In "The Graveyard Shift," for example, SpongeBob screams bloody murder, first with his mouth, and then with his pupils, which suddenly turn into little mouths with teeth. This is reminiscent of similarly grotesque moments in Fleischer cartoons, such as "Bimbo's Initiation," where Bimbo is so frightened he vomits his own heart.[35]

Less indebted to Fleischer are the cutaways to live-action images that serve as joke punch lines. In "Fry Cook Games," boiling oil is accidentally thrown on a crowd of fish, who immediately turn into a photograph of fish sticks. The announcer of the Fry Cook Games is a photo of a dead stuffed fish, named "Realistic Fish Head." In this episode Patrick high-dives into chocolate syrup, with an ice cream cone attached to his butt, and emerges, briefly, as an actual still photo of a strawberry ice cream cone with syrup on top. In "Band Geeks," the residents of Bikini Bottom perform a musical number at the Bubble Bowl. They are raised on a platform under a glass dome filled with water, and viewers are suddenly treated to an aerial live-action shot (this time with motion) of a football field and hysterical screaming fans.[36] At the end of a show in which Squidward and SpongeBob think they are being haunted, it turns out that the person who has been turning out the lights is . . . Nosferatu! The last shot is a cut to Murnau's silent film vampire, in a photo, grinning, and, with a deliberately awkwardly animated arm, playing with the light switch. Most hilariously, in one episode SpongeBob tells Sandy Cheeks (a squirrel who wears an underwater suit so as not to drown) that he has been working out. She asks him if he wants to have muscles like hers, and there is an immediate cut to a close-up photo of a superpumped, veiny, huge, human weight lifter's arm. What is funny here, obviously, is not simply the photo but the fact that Sandy is a girl squirrel, who wears a flower on her air helmet and lounges in her giant air dome home in a miniskirt and bikini top, and yet who also has freakishly huge "masculine" muscles.

Although *SpongeBob* is low on violence and devoid of salty language, it is not devoid of sexual dynamics. In fact, if there is anything "adult" about this world, it is the recurrence of the question of sexuality and sexual difference. The show parodies masculinity and features the most "out" gay character on children's television. Of course, none of this is inherently "adult." "Our prevailing conception of childhood innocence excludes children from the realm of adult sexuality,"[37] but children are intensely curious about sexuality, the very thing that adults fear will corrupt them. As a former director of the United Kingdom's Broadcasting Standards Commission explains, "tits and bums are natural fare for children."[38] *SpongeBob* is loved by adults for its "childlike" naiveté, but the show is also quite "childlike" in its playful interest in bums (tits are of less interest) and, more generally, in the performance of gender.

The eternally infantile SpongeBob and his best friend Patrick, for example, are coded as a couple in several episodes. In "Rock-A-Bye Bivalve," they adopt a foundling baby mollusk. In a montage sequence of family bonding, SpongeBob, Patrick, and baby pass a fish family, and the adult fish, who are confused by the implications of the mollusk in the baby carriage, conjure a curious thought bubble showing a pictorial equation: sponge + starfish = mollusk? After the joyous montage sequence, the realities of conjugal life sink in. Adopting the stereotypical female role, SpongeBob stays home changing stinky diapers, slaving over a hot stove, and, inexplicably, wearing rollers (he has no hair), while Patrick goes to "the office" every day and refuses to help around the house. They play the couple with utter earnestness, never intimating that it is play. Most cartoon drag—the classic example being Bugs Bunny with lipstick and falsies—is played at the expense of women.[39] "The feminine or feminized man is always the butt of the joke."[40] Here, conversely, the episode makes a feminist statement about sharing in domestic work. Although the two characters are male, the scene is strikingly reminiscent of the gags in the lesbian sitcoms that Alexander Doty has described, shows such as *I Love Lucy, Laverne and Shirley,* and *Designing Women,* in which "women marrying women" and raising babies together are leit-motifs.[41]

In "Fry Cook Games," SpongeBob and Patrick are pitted against each other in a wrestling match. They sprout grotesquely huge bodybuilder arms and torsos, à la Rambo, beat each other up, and end up locked head to head, hurling insults at each other. The yellow SpongeBob calls Patrick "pink!" while the pink Patrick calls SpongeBob "yellow!" As they strain their enormous bodies, a loud ripping noise is heard. Their pants fall to the floor, and we see that SpongeBob is wearing pink underpants, while Patrick is wearing yellow underpants. Having thus revealed their true feelings for each other, they quit fighting and walk into the sunset, their arms around each other. Patrick confesses, "You know, these were white when I bought them."

Notwithstanding these two episodes, in most shows SpongeBob and Patrick are portrayed as just good friends, without overt romantic over-tones. In fact, overt romantic couples are few and far between in Bikini Bottom. Although the very name might make this sound like a sexy spot (Hillenburg coyly suggests that his reference is to the Bikini Atoll), there is little reproduction going on. Mr. Krabs has a daughter (a whale, which hints at a rather interesting act of copulation on Krabs's part), and Patrick and SpongeBob have parents, but, as usual on children's shows, sex is both there and not there.[42] While we can speculate that SpongeBob could reproduce on his own, since he is a sponge and is often shown regenerat-ing his body at will, the idea that the infantile SpongeBob could actually be a father is far-fetched not only because of his indeterminate age, but also because he is comically lacking in masculinity. SpongeBob's lack is often parodied, as when Mr. Krabs tells him that his novelty soda-drink-ing cap makes him "look like a girl," and SpongeBob is flattered, coyly asking, "Am I a preeeety giiiirl?" In "No Weenies Allowed," SpongeBob wants to get into a tough club, but only mean-looking fish with tattoos are allowed inside. SpongeBob insists that he is worthy of entry; in fact, he explains, when he stubbed his toe while watering his spice garden, he only cried for twenty minutes! Rejected and dejected, SpongeBob ends up at Weenie Hut Junior's, a soda fountain for nerds, with a bright Candy Land look that clearly parodies old girls' cartoons like *Rainbow Brite.*

SpongeBob has a high-pitched voice and no secondary sex characteris-tics. He is "male" simply because other characters assume him to be so, and because he wears pants and a tie. He also wears male underwear. In

Squidward confronts SpongeBob, who has left his underpants on Squidward's front yard.
Frame grab from *SpongeBob SquarePants.* © 2002 Viacom International Inc.

fact, SpongeBob's last name might as well be "UnderPants" not "SquarePants," since he truly delights in his tighty-whities. He is frequently seen lounging or jumping around in his underpants, as in the title sequence. The underpants seem rather unnecessary: since his whole body is porous and often sends fluid in every direction, can't he pee from any opening? Why the underpants? One might speculate that he must have a weenie after all. One episode opens with SpongeBob watching a sea anemone on TV gyrating to mod sixties music. He is clearly turned on and is terribly embarrassed when his pet snail Gary enters the room. This scene is our biggest clue that SpongeBob has some kind of a sex life. And that several key scenes in the series take place in bathroom stalls would seem to confirm that SpongeBob does pee, and therefore has a you-know-what. Or does he? In "Nature Pants," our hero decides to abandon civilization and live in natural harmony with the jellyfish. He throws off his clothes, and we see him naked: a yellow square, with no "privates." To parody this very lack, SpongeBob repeatedly appears with seaweed or other obstructions strategically placed in front of his groin, like in a silly 1960s sex farce, as if there were actually something to hide.

If SpongeBob is lacking his private muscle, he is short on public ones as well. Whereas many children's shows feature hyper-masculine super-hero types, this show laughs at a character who completely lacks muscles, and, by implication, masculinity. Although he was able to sprout spectacular muscles for the boxing match with Patrick, SpongeBob's arms regularly tear off when he attempts any strenuous activity. One episode in particular establishes SpongeBob's complete lack of physical strength. Incapable of the simplest workout, he sends off for massive inflatable muscles, which he proudly wears to "Mussel Beach," where macho fish and lobsters do their lifting. SpongeBob's muscles are so big that he walks on his dragging knuckles, as his feet swing through the air. When the virile weight lifters inquire about his workout, he claims to have acquired his muscles through squeezing his hand in his armpit to make fartlike noises. Even when SpongeBob seems most masculine and, at least physically, adult in appearance, his true childlike persona shines through. And his put-on masculinity is short-lived. During a climactic anchor-throwing contest, SpongeBob blows and blows on his muscles, making them grotesquely huge and veiny, until they explode.[43] Sandy Cheeks, his buff squirrel friend, punishes him by making him operate the TV remote control for her. Having lost his fake arms, he now loses his real arms, which fall off from the channel-surfing effort. In sum, SpongeBob is a total washout as a masculine figure, and the show delights in this.

In fact, SpongeBob's favorite sport is not football or basketball but rather jelly-fishing, which he does with a net, wearing geeky safety glasses. As a *New York Times* reporter puts it, "He la-la's happily like PeeWee Herman as he flits about with a butterfly net chasing jellyfish."[44] It's rather like catching butterflies for sport (except that SpongeBob squeezes his catches for jelly and then lets them go), a very old-fashioned sissy-boy caricature. It is *fun*, the show insists, to be a sissy-boy, and, occasionally, parodically masculine or feminine, and, at other times, seemingly asexual. It is also fun to dance to technomusic with jellyfish, blow bubbles, hunt for treasure, fry Krabby Patties on a grill, and celebrate the funnest holiday of the year, April Fool's Day. In other words, SpongeBob is polymorphously perverse, filled with joy in every direction, whether an episode focuses on the shortcomings of his body or his aptitude for driving Squidward nuts.

If any single character on *SpongeBob SquarePants* epitomizes the program's successful efforts to balance intergenerational appeal, it is Squidward Tentacles, whose sarcasm and resistance to fun symbolize all that is dreary about being an adult. Squidward offers the lone voice of pessimism on the show and seems to be the opposite of SpongeBob in every way. SpongeBob is always happy, delights in being a fry-cook (even com-

Squidward beds down with the only thing he loves as much as himself—his clarinet.
Frame grab from *SpongeBob SquarePants.* © 2002 Viacom International Inc.

ing in every morning at 3 A.M. to count the sesame seeds on the patty buns), lives in a whimsical pineapple home, and spends his spare time playing silly games with Patrick. Squidward, on the other hand, is perennially glum, does not enjoy his cashier job at the Krusty Krab, lives in a stern house shaped like an Easter Island head, seems to have no friends, and spends his spare time engaged in "constructive" activities—making art (always representing himself), practicing the clarinet (which he plays very badly), and reading *Frown Digest.* If SpongeBob is a man-child, Squidward would seem to be a man, embodying all that is stultifying about the adult world. Or so it appears at first glance. Ultimately, of course, it is impossible to determine the ages of SpongeBob or Squidward. Both perform age, as I have argued. Both live alone in homes, have jobs, and are often childish. In fact, one might see them as two sides of one coin, SpongeBob embodying all that is mythologically good about childhood (innocence, carefreeness, cheerfulness) and Squidward embodying the mythically corrupted child (self-absorbed, prone to tantrums, incapable of empathy). While SpongeBob most often performs childhood, and Squidward most often performs adulthood, both seem to exist in limbo in between these theoretical opposites.

Squidward combines, according to one reviewer, "the nasal bitchiness of Paul Lynde and the artistic pretensions of Felix Unger."[45] The show provides endless clues that Squidward is gay, but his one true love is . . . himself. A typical scenario shows Squidward making declarations of love to a mirror reflection or to one of his many self-portraits. ("Squidward, if you had some hair, you'd be the most gorgeous creature in the sea!") In "Squidward the Unfriendly Ghost," he creates a full-sized wax sculpture of himself, thrilled to have finally mastered himself in every medium. Around him we see portrayals in oils, pencils, mosaic tiles, neon, and on an Egyptian-style carved urn. There is even a version of DaVinci's famous sketch of "Vitruvian Man," but now featuring Squidward. While Squidward takes a bath, SpongeBob and Patrick accidentally "kill" the wax sculpture, which they think is Squidward. Meanwhile, Squidward emerges from the tub, uses a powder puff to cover himself with talc, and dons a robe and turban-like towel on his head. Parading into the room like Norma Desmond, he terrifies SpongeBob and Patrick, who think that he is Squidward's ghost. Sensing that he can benefit from the situation, Squidward plays the role of imperious queen, telling them that they must obey his every command, "tickle his every fancy." SpongeBob asks, "Does that include—" but is cut off by Squidward, who makes the boys carry him around on a Nefertiti-like divan. Alas, like Daffy Duck—his closest cartoon progenitor in terms of vanity, misplaced self-assurance, and, ultimately, haplessness—Squidward cannot win at this game. Squidward and SpongeBob try to "put his soul to rest" by burying him and sending him to heaven. But while it lasts, Squidward puts on quite a show.

In classic drama queen fashion, Squidward is obsessed with performance. In one episode, he longingly reads a book, *Dance Now!* We cut in to a POV shot of the illustration he is sighing over, a live-action photo of a male ballet dancer in tights posing with a female dancer. Squidward's cartoon head is cut onto the male dancer's body, though, in Squidward's fevered fantasy. By the end of this episode, Squidward has put on a talent show, but the audience does not appreciate his modern dance routine and pummels him with tomatoes. In another episode, Squidward sports a full Carman Miranda fruit headpiece and sings show tunes while playing the piano on a desert island—a dream, it turns out, from which SpongeBob rudely awakens him. In "Jellyfish Hunter," SpongeBob treats a Krusty Krab customer to some jellyfish jelly, which, it turns out, is delicious on Krabby Patties. The customer immediately breaks into a showtune medley, and Mr. Krabs cries, "SpongeBob, who's playin' Squidward's records again?!" Squidward twice has pseudoheterosexual moments. Once, he delightedly exclaims, "I've got a date with a lovely lady tonight, and her

Squidward suffers from male-pattern-baldness.
Note the self-portraits on the wall.
Frame grab from *SpongeBob SquarePants*. © 2002
Viacom International Inc.

name is clarinet!" He is going home to practice. In "Just One Bite" Squidward has his first Krabby Patty, but is embarrassed to admit how much he likes it. In a dream sequence, however, a giant patty arrives at his door. They marry, sire a junior patty, and grow old together. Although it is perhaps implied that this is a female patty (it wears a veil at the wedding), the patty is missing the usual obvious markers of cartoon drag (lipstick, high heels, falsies).

Squidward's appeal to adults works, I think, on several levels. There is a childish delight in seeing a campy gay character on a children's show because one knows that this is a little bit naughty. Children's television is *supposed* to be sex-free, and network censors are particularly wary of gay content. As I've observed elsewhere, it seems that the producers of children's television believe that children are both nonsexual and heterosexual.[46] Adults not attuned to Squidward's gayness may be drawn to his crankiness, a relative anomaly in children's TV, and one that will certainly be appreciated by parents who have endured endless hours of their children's *Barney* videos. One adult viewer who avows a strong identification with Squidward explains, "I love Squidward because he's so grumpy and he's clearly very, very intelligent, and yet he's working this menial job that's well below his skill level, sort of this underappreciated artist."[47]

(Squidward is also tormented by male-pattern-baldness, surely not a phenomenon alien to many of his grown-up fans.)

Further cementing his own identification with Squidward, this viewer adds, "I consider *SpongeBob* up there with *The Sopranos* in terms of quality and writing." In other words, this show is the kind of thing Squidward likes—art, not kid's stuff. An icon of proper adult tastes, Squidward is both mocked and embraced by the show. He thus appeals to the tastes of both children and adults and functions as a character who mediates between the adult-child binary. If his implied sexual orientation may make him seem more adult than child, it is not because children aren't gay or interested in gayness but rather because children are falsely assumed to be uninterested in such issues. Both children and adults may pick up on Squidward's queerness, but adults will enjoy it, in part, under the assumption that this is something that is over kids' heads. Childhood innocence is thus affirmed not in spite of but because children are viewing material with potential to "corrupt" them.

Adult fans of kids' shows are nothing new. Yet *SpongeBob*'s intergenerational appeal is, I believe, particularly strong. There is one episode, "Sailor Mouth," which perhaps best encapsulates how *SpongeBob* craftily gives adults and children exactly what they want. Taking out the trash at the Krabby Patty one day, SpongeBob notices the graffiti on the dumpster: "Nematodes are people too"; "Up with bubbles, down with air"; and "Squidward smells." SpongeBob is so naive, he thinks that the writer forgot to complete this last graffito, and he adds a third word so that it reads, "Squidward smells good." Then SpongeBob reads aloud, "Krabs is a ———." Where the dirty word goes, he makes a dolphin noise. Is this how you really swear in Bikini Bottom, or are we to take this as a playfully censorious bleep? Patrick arrives, and SpongeBob explains his confusion. What does this mystery word mean? Patrick says it must be a "sentence enhancer," something you throw into a sentence whenever you want to sound "fancy." Needless to say, they start using the enhancer in every sentence, and they get in big trouble with Mr. Krabs, who informs them that this is a bad word, one of thirteen bad words, in fact. Squidward objects that there are only seven bad words, implicitly referencing the famous George Carlin "Seven Dirty Words" routine, which led to the FCC decision that would require broadcasters to bleep a bad word, exactly as *SpongeBob*'s creators have done. Only seven words? "Not if you're a sailor!" Mr. Krabs retorts. SpongeBob and Patrick are horrified that they have said a bad word, but now that they have been introduced to the word, they can't stop using it. Mr. Krabs eventually stubs his toe and uses all thirteen words (all represented by different sounds, like bells, whistles, and horns). SpongeBob and Patrick report Krabs to his mother, repeating all thirteen words. She is appalled, and shortly afterward stubs her toe, making a bad noise. But it turns out it was a real horn on a boat-car, and everybody laughs. The end.

This episode brilliantly speaks to both parents and children. Parents want to prevent their children from hearing bad language, which would corrupt them, just like Patrick and SpongeBob, who don't understand their sentence enhancer but cannot stop using it. Child viewers will be familiar with the prohibition on bad words, as well as, no doubt, the hypocrisy that underpins such censorship; they know very well that adults use the very words that are not supposed to be used. The bleeping, of course, makes everyone happy. If you know the f-word, you can mentally fill it in. If you don't know it, you can try to imagine what this porpoise noise really means, and will probably come up with stuff just about as bad as the f-word. The bleeping allows everyone to be in on the joke by censoring and expressing naughtiness at the same time. Eager to believe that their children remain untainted by the corrupt adult world, parents may imagine that their children don't get the double-edged joke. If that's what they think, the joke's on them.

NOTES

1. Jacqueline Rose, *The Case of Peter Pan: On the Impossibility of Children's Fiction* (London: Falmer, 1984).

2. Marsha Kinder, "Home Alone in the 90s: Generational War and Transgenerational Address in American Movies, Television and Presidential Politics," in David Buckingham, ed., *In Front of the Children* (London: British Film Institute, 1995), 75–91.

3. David Buckingham, *After the Death of Childhood: Growing Up in the Age of Electronic Media* (Cambridge: Polity Press, 2000).

4. Jefferson Graham, "As Nick Soaks up Kids, Rivals Revamp Saturdays," *USA Today*, July 12, 1999, Life Section, 3D.

5. Lily Oei, "Nick Still Rules Saturday AM," *Daily Variety*, May 29, 2002, 5.

6. Stylistically, "nonviolence" often translates as a lack of hard edges and loud music, the use of pastels instead of primary colors, and a general bounciness (or "squash and stretch") in the way characters move.

7. John Dempsey, "Nick's Toon Hits Its Target," *Variety,* June 3–June 9 2002, Television sec., 15.

8. Gary Strauss, "Life's Good for SpongeBob," *USA Today,* May 17, 2002, sec. B, 1.

9. Ibid.

10. Ibid.

11. Jason Mittell, "The Great Saturday Morning Exile: Scheduling Cartoons on Television's Periphery in the 1960s," in Carole A. Stabile and Mark Harrison, eds., *Prime Time Animation: Television Animation and American Culture* (New York: Routledge, 2003), 50.

12. Heather Hendershot, *Saturday Morning Censors: Television Regulation before the V-Chip* (Durham: Duke UP, 1998).

13. Lynn Spigel, "Seducing the Innocent," in Henry Jenkins, ed., *The Children's Culture Reader* (New York: NYU Press, 1998), 122. Spigel argues that the imparting of adult tastes onto children was a goal of the media in the 1950s, and that *Parents Magazine* instructed readers to "elevate" their children's taste standards.

14. Constance Penley, *The Future of an Illusion: Film, Feminism, and Psychoanalysis* (Minneapolis: U of Minnesota P, 1989), 141.

15. On "edge," see the interview "David Kendall Warner Bros. Television," in Richard Ohmann, ed., *Making and Selling Culture* (Hanover: Wesleyan UP, 1996), 62.

16. Avoiding topical references is, it should be noted, a smart tactic for a show that Nickelodeon hopes to endlessly syndicate, as it has done with *Rugrats.* By not referencing contemporary films, television, and so on, *SpongeBob* can theoretically avoid ever appearing dated.

17. Tom Zeller, "Cleaning Up: How to Succeed without Attitude," *New York Times,* July 21, 2002.

18. Spigel, "Seducing the Innocent," 111.

19. Penley, *The Future of an Illusion,* 153.

20. One might argue that Tom Kenny, the voice of SpongeBob, constitutes the body behind the character. While Kenny's brilliant characterization cannot be underestimated, a voice-artist can be replaced, and most people will consider the old character with the new voice to be authentic. When John Kricfalusi was fired from *Ren & Stimpy,* some fans complained that the show had lost its edge, but Ren, even without Kricfalusi's voice, continued to "exist."

21. For a U.K. example, see Buckingham, "On the Impossibility of Children's Television: The Case of Timmy Mallett," in Buckingham, ed., *In Front of the Children,* 47–61.

22. See Karin Calvert, "Children in the House: The Material Culture of Early Childhood," in Henry Jenkins, ed., *The Children's Culture Reader,* 67–80.

23. Marjorie Garber, *Vested Interests: Cross-Dressing and Cultural Anxiety* (New York: Routledge, 1992), 16.

24. Ibid.

25. Linda Williams, "'Something Else Besides a Mother': *Stella Dallas* and the Maternal Melodrama," *Cinema Journal* 24.1: 2–27.

26. Zeller, "Cleaning Up."

27. Nickelodeon president Herb Scannell believes that adults watch the program as an alternative to "vulgar" (sexual or violent) entertainment: "Adults are watching it because many of them are fed up with the vulgarization of comedy represented by everything from *South Park* to *There's Something about Mary*. Sponge-Bob is counter-intuitive to that trend: He's innocent, naive and Chaplinesque." Cited in Dempsey, "Nick's Toon Hits Its Target."

28. Buckingham, *After the Death of Childhood*, 99.

29. Ibid., 99.

30. Ibid., 7.

31. Ibid., 100

32. Heather Hendershot, "Teletubby Trouble: How Justified Were Rev. Falwell's Attacks?" *Television Quarterly* 31.1 (Spring 2000), 19–25.

33. In the case of *My Little Pony*, Ellen Seiter has argued that middle-class parents are offended by the excessive, pink and frilly femininity of the ponies, which they perceive as low-class. Such an aesthetic classifies (in French sociologist Pierre Bourdieu's use of the word) young fans as less-than-middle-class. Ellen Seiter, *Sold Separately: Children and Parents in Consumer Culture* (New Brunswick: Rutgers UP, 1993).

34. Hannah Davies, David Buckingham, and Peter Kelley, "In the Worst Possible Taste: Children, Television and Cultural Value," www.ccsonline.org.uk/mediacentre/Research_Projects/cmc_taste.html. A slightly different version of the essay has been published in the *International Journal of Cultural Studies* 3.1 (1 January 2000), 5–25.

35. I am focusing on visual aesthetics here, but one could also examine Hillenburg's audio experiments, as when he directly borrows music from Fleischer cartoons.

36. SpongeBob then performs as a rock star with a big, Michael Bolton–style voice. The joke here lies in his sudden adult, masculine performance.

37. Henry Jenkins, "The Sensuous Child: Benjamin Spock and the Sexual Revolution," in Henry Jenkins, ed., *The Children's Culture Reader*, 211.

38. Cited in Davies, Buckingham, and Kelley, "In the Worst Possible Taste," on-line version.

39. Sybil DelGaudio, "Seduced and Reduced: Female Animated Characters in Some Warners Cartoons," in Danny Peary and Gerald Peary, eds., *The American Animated Cartoon: A Critical Anthology* (New York: E. P. Dutton, 1980), 211–216.

40. Kevin S. Sandler, "Gendered Evasion: Bugs Bunny in Drag," in Kevin S. Sandler, ed., *Reading the Rabbit: Explorations in Warner Bros. Animation* (New Brunswick: Rutgers UP, 1998), 164.

41. Alexander Doty, "I Love *Laverne and Shirley*: Lesbian Narratives, Queer Pleasures, and Television Sitcoms," in his book *Making Things Perfectly Queer: Interpreting Mass Culture* (Minneapolis: U of Minnesota P, 1993), 39–62.

42. See my discussion of reproduction on *Strawberry Shortcake,* in Hendershot, *Saturday Morning Censors.*

43. As a figure comically lacking in masculinity, SpongeBob makes an interesting comparison to Jerry Lewis. In fact, this scene evokes the classic moment in *The Nutty Professor* when Lewis, as Juluis Kelp, works out at the gym and ends up with grotesquely stretched out arms. Ultimately, neither Kelp nor SpongeBob can "get it up." As Peter Lehman and Susan Hunt put it, "'Real men' get harder at the gym; in contrast, Kelp's limpness becomes a spectacle." Peter Lehman and Susan Hunt, "'The Inner Man': Mind, Body, and Transformations of Masculinity in *The Nutty Professor,*" in Murray Pomerance, ed., *Enfant Terrible: Jerry Lewis in American Film* (New York, NYU Press, 2002), 203.

44. Joyce Millman, "Television/Radio: The Gentle World of a Joyful Sponge," *New York Times,* July 8, 2001, sec. 2, 30.

45. Ibid.

46. Hendershot, *Saturday Morning Censors.* See also Hendershot, "Teletubby Trouble."

47. L. A. Johnson, "Nick's 'SpongeBob' Floats, Attracting Adult and Child Viewers," *Pittsburgh Post-Gazette,* July 2, 2002, sec. D, 3.

10

"We Pledge Allegiance to Kids"
Nickelodeon and Citizenship

Sarah Banet-Weiser

Within two weeks of the September 11, 2001, terrorist attacks on the World Trade Center and the Pentagon, Nickelodeon released a special episode of its children's news program, *Nick News.* "Kids, Terrorism, and the American Spirit" featured host Linda Ellerbee discussing the attacks with a group of children of various ages, genders, nationalities, and religions. The greater part of this *Nick News* episode was dedicated to defining the "American Spirit" for its audience through a mélange of patriotic images, liberal platitudes, and messages of "hope for the future." Then, in October 2001, Nickelodeon featured another special episode of another popular program. This program, the animated series, *Rugrats,* was aired in honor of Columbus Day, and was entitled "Rugrats Discover America." Unlike the *Nick News* special, *Rugrats* represented "America" through a variety of popular cultural and commercial references: Hollywood films, rock-and-roll music, and tourist souvenirs. These cultural artifacts were situated as "symbols" of America that were purchased on a cross-country vacation.

Both these programs contribute to a general discourse regarding children and citizenship, and both address, albeit in very different registers, questions about what it means to be an American. What I find particularly interesting about these two programs is that they are very good examples of Nickelodeon programming that attend to the tensions about citizenship within their narratives. The *Nick News* special attends to the various ways in which Americans unified around traditional liberal terms after September 11: individual displays of heroism, community mourning rituals, candlelight vigils for the victims, and melodramatic sequences of the flag and other national symbols. *Rugrats,* while also focusing on issues of patriotism, interprets the sentiment within a slightly different frame of reference: patriotism is defined through a collection of consumer items or *products* that symbolize national identity, commitment, and community. In both these programs, political empowerment is referenced as a key component of citizenship, represented on one end of a continuum as a commitment to liberal ideals of individual agency and on the other end, as a kind of "market patriotism" or consumer freedom.

As these two examples illustrate, the definition of citizenship (both its construction in popular cultural texts and our own experience as "citizens") is characterized above all else by tensions in existing dominant beliefs and ideologies. Perhaps the sharpest contradiction in dominant understandings of citizenship is represented in the tensions between political subjectivity and consumerism. These tensions revolve around the conventional notion that citizenship is a *political* category, represented and constituted not within the world of commerce, but rather in direct opposition to those kinds of material interests and situated in contrast to the world of "official" state politics. In other words, despite what seems to be a steadily increasing disaffection with the state of "politics as usual," when it comes to defining citizenship, themes of a Habermasian liberal democracy characterized by such ideals as rational discourse, rights and liberties, and political freedom still seem to find their way in as necessary conditions of this definition. This kind of *civil citizenship* is in tension with another, progressively more visible kind of citizenship, that of *consumer citizenship.*

The commercial realm is increasingly the place in which many of the questions that are distinctive of citizenship, questions of belonging, community, and representation, are both posed and answered. *Consumer citizenship* situates politics and agency not within an idealized public sphere, but rather within ideologies of consumer choices. In the last few decades, the notion that commercial media are not simply low culture without redeeming value, but are rather an important cultural site in which adults negotiate and struggle over meanings of identity (including the identity of citizenship), has been largely accepted, even while the extent and nature of the commercial media's influence is continually debated. Cultural scholar Nestor Garcia Canclini, for example, argues that consumption can be "good for thinking," and can allow for a reimagining of the public, as well as a relocation of the market within that public.[1]

Thus, when "empowerment" is invoked as crucial to an American sense of citizenship, we need to ask: what kind of empowerment are we talking about? Do individuals constitute their political identity—their "empowerment" as citizens—through the traditional channels, through actions like voting, becoming politically informed, engaging in Habermasian forms of rational debate? Or are these "political" actions themselves part of a larger world divided not by state loyalties but rather by the vagaries of the market? Determining a modern sense of citizenship entails understanding the relationship between these two tensions. Is it realistic, or simply nostalgic, to assume that there is a direct connection between civil citizenship and politically progressive behavior? Or do we need to look to the category of consumer citizenship for political agency? Despite their seemingly obvious differences, these definitions of citizenship are not binary opposites. Rather, they work in conjunction with each other, demonstrating a different emphasis depending on the context. Within the Nickelodeon universe, these two definitions of citizenship intermix and represent a broader tension in recent debates framing discussions of children, media, and citizenship. In the following pages, I examine the way Nickelodeon balances these seemingly contradictory ideals of citizenship through its use of audience empowerment rhetoric and its cross-generational address that insists that "Nick Is for Kids!"

Children, Media, and Political Empowerment

During the last several decades in the United States the question of whether, and how, children are politically empowered has developed into an increasingly complicated public, mass-mediated debate. More specifically, a public focus on children and empowerment frequently includes a discussion of technology and the potential "effects" (either positive or negative) of technologies such as television, the movies, and most recently the Internet on the political empowerment of children. The perceived connection between technology and empowerment is certainly not a novel discovery; as many scholars have noted, public opinion about new developments in technologies throughout the twentieth century has been both optimistic and pessimistic about the influence of technology on individual agency.[2] And when the discourse involves children and their relation with technology, the stakes become even higher and the debate that much more hotly contested.

Although mass-mediated debates around the question of technology's influence on children have heightened in recent years as school shootings in Colorado, Kentucky, and Arkansas have been "connected" to violent television, video games, music, and the Internet, the relation between children and technology has historically been fraught with conflict and contradiction. For example, as Lynn Spigel has astutely documented, in postwar American culture television was popularly understood as being both an important factor in "family togetherness" and the primary culprit in the creation of the "juvenile delinquent."[3] Later in the twentieth century, television advertising and the apparent excessive influence it had on children generated other debates over the problems of the "commercialization of childhood," while at the same time child development specialists were advocating the purchase of *particular* products to aid in the intellectual development of children.[4] And most recently, while new technologies and the Internet have been widely recognized by corporate culture and politicians as offering an enormous potential in terms of democracy, tolerance, and most importantly, commerce, the "dark side" of technologies such as the Internet are often understood in terms of the influence and control they seemingly have over children.

Part of the reason the debate over children and technology is so fraught with tension is because the definition of the child is characterized by different emphases depending on the context. Is the child an innocent victim of the corporate giants of mass media, or is the child an active citizen, involved in the negotiation and struggle over meaning in a productive, identity-making manner? Or, as I hope to demonstrate in this essay, are these two positions *not* oppositional, but rather in constant tension and conversation with each other in the construction of citizenship? Indeed, as Marsha Kinder, Henry Jenkins, and others have argued, although popular debate on the issue of children and the media has been largely formulated around these two oppositional extremes, it would be misleading to characterize scholarly debates around this issue as a simple binary opposition.[5] The "child as innocent victim" camp primarily understands the relationship between children and the media as one that needs to be continually supervised and protected (because of increasing violence, sexual activity among young adults, and so on). The "child as active player" camp challenges this cultural construction of the "innocence" of children and rather situates the child as a citizen who actively uses the media as a means to gain empowerment. Both sides, however, stipulate that the relationship between children and media is a complicated and contradictory set of historical arrangements, one that resists either a simple definition or a simple solution.

Thus, in order to theorize the complex relationship between children, empowerment, and media, we need to more sharply imagine the sense of contradiction that characterizes this relationship. By focusing on the instabilities and competing interests that permeate discussions of children and media, we witness how the category of "child" or, more broadly, "youth," operates as not only a social and political category but also as an important agenda for public debate about the broader concern of citizenship and empowerment. As Joe Austin and Michael Nevin Willard put it, "'Youth' becomes a metaphor for perceived social change and its projected consequences, and as such it is an enduring locus for displaced social anxieties."[6] These anxieties reflect the tensions within the paradoxical constructions of young people, tensions that "highlight the bifurcated social identity of youth as a vicious, threatening sign of social decay and our best hope for the future."[7] Perhaps one of the most dynamic cultural sites for both the representation of and the struggle over these tensions is within entertainment and commercial culture.

Thus, I would like to shift the question of political empowerment to a commercial media audience of children. What, really, does it mean to invoke the idea of the "empowerment" of children? Can we, or how do we, take seriously the notion that a young media audience is "active" politically in the current political and commercial climate? Does conceptualizing children as "citizens" allow us to think of how and in what ways children are empowered politically? Children *are* in fact outside political life in the way that adults understand politics—they are not rights-bearing citizens of a nation in the way that adults are, they cannot vote, they do not have "free choice" as this is legally defined. However, to say that children are outside political life is not to say that they are outside relations of power. Indeed, the development of identity is *already* to be situated in relations of power, and children are developing their identities in part through their relationship to commercial media culture.

It is more productive, then, to theorize about the tensions represented within children's identity in a way that situates them within relations of power. This means in part to situate them within media and entertainment, and for the purposes of this essay, within the commercial world of Nickelodeon. How does Nickelodeon respond to the tensions between politics and consumerism in definitions of citizenship? How does this response by the network in turn create contradictions of its own? To clearly

Nickelodeon makes an overt connection between patriotism, citizenship, and the network's
claim to be a "kids only zone."
Frame grab from *How to Nickelodeon* video. © 1992
MTV Networks.

see the role that Nickelodeon plays in this dynamic, we first need to regard the self-conscious definition of the network as a "different" media
site, one that places the "rights" of kids above all else, and uses the
rhetoric of empowerment as a means through which children can potentially realize agency.

Nick's for Kids! Nickelodeon's Mission

The early history of Nickelodeon is largely one of failure in the television
market. The early programming itself is identified by Nickelodeon as
"green vegetable" television, primarily understood as beneficial for children by parents, but not by the children themselves. Regardless of
parental desire, however, from 1979 to 1984, Nickelodeon's subscription
rates were too low for the network to sustain itself financially. In 1984,
Geraldine Laybourne became general manager and transformed the network in two crucial and interrelated ways: the network began accepting
commercial sponsorship, and thus advertising became a key element in its
programming, and it adopted a new mission statement and overall philosophy that has since become its unique signature and contribution to

children's television, a promise that Nickelodeon is a "kids first" or a "kids only" network.[8]

The result of these changes was the creation of a network that self-consciously and aggressively identifies as a "safe" place for children, a place that understands children *as* children, and somehow understands them differently than the rest of the world. As Laybourne puts it: "For kids, it is 'us versus them' in the grown-up world: you're either for kids or against them. Either you think kids should be quiet and behave or you believe kids should stand up for themselves and be free to play around, explore, and be who they really are. We were on the kids' side and we wanted them to know it."[9] Despite both the hyperbole and the arrogance of this statement, Nickelodeon has been unusually successful with its claim that it just "lets kids be kids," as well as with its apparent dedication to empowering children. The network self-consciously constructs itself as a "haven" for children in an otherwise confusing and scary world.

Nickelodeon consistently attributes its unusual success in an oversaturated children's market to its emphasis on the cultural divide between children and adults, and to its privileging of children as a separate, unique audience. Aside from commercial success, the use of a generational address is also an interesting challenge to dominant definitions of childhood as specifically adult-generated. In other words, many scholars have examined the ways in which the cultural construction of childhood as clearly separate from adulthood functions as a kind of strategy that supports the affirmation of adult identity. As Spigel puts it: "Childhood is the difference against which adults define themselves. It is a time of innocence, a time that refers back to a fantasy world where the painful realities and social constraints of adult culture no longer exist. Childhood has less to do with what children experience (since they too are subject to the evils of our social world) than with what adults want to believe."[10] Nickelodeon's challenge to this position is evident in the myriad pledges to children from the network, including: "Nickelodeon is what kids want, not just what adults think kids want," and "Nickelodeon is always there, from breakfast to bedtime, everyday, whenever kids want to watch. Nick is their home base, a place kids can count on and trust."[11] Clearly, Nickelodeon's claim that it allows children to explore their own self-agency, a specific identity construction that stands in contrast to childhood innocence that has served adults so well in the twentieth century, is one that we need to take seriously as an important element in the construction of citizenship. In line with this, Laybourne uses a kind of "liberal citizen" rhetoric profusely in describing Nickelodeon's mission:

> We are here to accept kids, to help them feel good about themselves. It's a philosophy that impacts everything we do. It impacts casting: we don't look for gorgeous kids, we cast kids who are fat and who are skinny, kids of all colors and nationalities, every kind of kid. We don't give out the message, this is what a cool kid should look or be like. The philosophy impacts our marketing: we don't market based on gender, because that implies exclusion, which is not what we are about. If we want to make kids feel good, we have to embrace them all.[12]

The notion of inclusion, and the implied claim of equal opportunity, that permeates Laybourne's vocabulary is part of the overall political address that hails Nickelodeon kids as particular kinds of citizens. Indeed, the construction of childhood as a discrete realm, not only separate from adults but situated oppositionally, has allowed Nickelodeon to claim that it escapes the dynamic that Spigel discusses, where childhood is both defined and supported as a specific means to affirm *adult* identity. Insisting upon childhood as an identity construction that is created *by* kids *for* kids is an important part of the way in which Nickelodeon constructs citizenship. This has resulted in the active self-construction of Nickelodeon as a champion and defender of kids' "rights": "The company's battle cry became that Nickelodeon stood with kids against anyone who found them 'unbearably loathsome' or sought to condescend to or undermine them. This voice gave the network a means to develop a style of comedy built on opposition to pompous or mean authority figures—bus drivers who yell at kids, anyone who treats them unfairly. In this regard, Nickelodeon's distinctive voice has not been uncontroversial, for some critics have viewed it as undermining the respect children should show adults."[13] The very element that has been seen as "controversial" is the one that allows Nickelodeon to set itself apart from other children's networks. And, although clearly Nickelodeon does construct children as citizens in relation to adults, the oppositional nature of this dynamic has permitted Nickelodeon to claim that it recognizes children as autonomous political subjects.

Part of the way in which Nickelodeon makes this claim about citizenship is through its original programming itself. Nickelodeon cartoons, game shows, and news programs challenge conventional understandings of what is "good" television for children by insisting not only that adults understand children's media on its own terms (not through an adult lens or viewpoint of what constitutes good or bad media), but also that *children themselves* understand that they are being addressed as an important group outside adult culture. Indeed, Nickelodeon has occupied an interesting position in the children's media market precisely because it has challenged the traditional adult-produced dichotomies that constitute the debate about "good" and "bad" TV, a debate that, as cultural theorist David Buckingham has argued, "rests on a series of binary oppositions that are routinely taken for granted: British is good, American is bad; public service is good, commercial is bad; live action is good, animation is bad; education is good, entertainment is bad; and so on. In the process, certain genres—game shows, action-adventure, teenage romance—are deemed to be simply incompatible with quality."[14] In resisting these kinds of conventional oppositions, Nickelodeon deliberately uses a generational divide to challenge the assumptions that structure the children and media debate, and in so doing, also challenges key cultural assumptions about childhood in general. Specifically, Nickelodeon challenges the assumption that children are not capable of making informed choices about not only what they like to watch on television, but also about the larger world in general. Through an examination of Nickelodeon's news program, *Nick News,* we can see at least one way in which the commercial network constructs its audience in these kinds of terms, as a group of political or civil citizens.

Kids' Empowerment: Political Citizenship

Despite an increasingly negative public opinion in the United States about the corruption of "official" politics and growing frustrations with the intimate workings of the democratic process, the notion that citizenship is formed *via* the democratic process continues to have both social and political currency. A Habermasian notion of a public sphere is still invoked as the site in and through which citizenship is formed.[15] As Bruce Robbins has argued, "One of the reasons why we 'need' a public sphere is because it, at least utopically, is a place that is outside of the state on the one hand (therefore not subject to state regulatory and disciplinary practices) and outside of commercial culture—the 'official economy'—on the other (therefore not subject to the vagaries of the market, or commercial competition)."[16] These boundaries purportedly allocate a place "where we can address real social concerns," and a place in which an ideal sense of citizenship is formed. The mass media, especially news journalism, or what Benedict Anderson calls "print capitalism," function as a facilitator for this ideal space and offer the means through which one can become politically informed.[17]

News journalism, then, often has been situated as an essential part of democracy, and as the key to an informed citizenry. Buckingham theorizes the significance of news journalism for a young audience, attempting to determine what role the media plays in "extending and developing young people's sense of their own political agency."[18] Conventional wisdom (frequently supported by academic studies) increasingly maintains that modern children and youth are remarkably uninterested in reading and watching the news. This lack of interest is often attributed to either a postmodern citizenry comprised of a disaffected and cynical generation, or to a general understanding that children are politically "innocent" and thus incompetent to make informed decisions. Suggesting that both these positions are a kind of cop-out, Buckingham argues that "children will only be likely to become 'active citizens,' capable of exercising thoughtful choice in political matters, if they are presumed to be capable of doing so."[19] Within these terms, news programs for children are recognized as an important means through which young audiences can construct themselves as citizens. News programs for children (the few that are produced) offer factual information about current events and politics, and are considered "educational" television by the Children's Television Act of 1990. Nickelodeon produces perhaps the most successful U.S. children's news program, Nick News.[20] The program airs once a week, and is hosted by former network newscaster Linda Ellerbee (and is produced by her production company, Lucky Duck Productions). While most Nick News programs typically include four or five segments, Ellerbee also produces "news specials" which are entire programs dedicated to a particular cultural event, such as the aforementioned special on the terrorist attacks of September 11, "Kids, Terrorism, and the American Spirit."

In this episode, Ellerbee begins by addressing the audience, asking children to make sure their parents believe it to be appropriate for them to watch a television program about terrorism. Aesthetically, the setup of the news program, unlike most news shows, is quite casual: Ellerbee wears jeans and tennis shoes and addresses a diverse group of children from a cross-legged position on the floor. She begins the discussion by saying to the kids in the studio and the national audience: "We will not lie to you, and so we begin with the facts." The "facts" include not only a description of the September 11 attacks on the World Trade Center and the Pentagon but also a definition of terrorism itself. The episode is interspersed with video segments portraying displays of mourning and patriotism: candlelight vigils, flags, firefighters, and so on. Together with a child psychiatrist, Ellerbee questions the children in the studio, two of whom are wearing traditional Muslim clothing and headdress. She asks the children if they had watched television since the attacks, querying: "Do you think that kids should have been forbidden to watch television?" The children unanimously answered "No" to that question, with one child claiming, "We have a right to know." Ellerbee also asks the children what the response of the United States should be to the terrorist attacks, and asks specifically if "we" should bomb "them." The kids' answers to this question consisted primarily of proactive suggestions, for example, that children write letters, give blood, or help other kids. One of the children suggested that the United States rebuild the Twin Towers, but even higher than they were originally, "to prove that it's not going to let us down."

An important part of this special *Nick News* is a segment called "American Spirit." In this segment, Ellerbee narrates a mélange of images showing people helping victims of the attacks, giving blood, firefighters volunteering, people embracing around national images such as flags, candles, and other icons. These jingoistic displays of patriotism represented, for *Nick News,* the "American Spirit." Ellerbee says, "What we were seeing was the American spirit, and more important than anything else, it is that spirit that defines us as a nation, and no act of terrorism can take that from us." She also informs the audience that there is a message board on the Nickelodeon website that includes discussions about patriotism and the uniting of America during this crisis. From the moment Ellerbee began the program by informing the audience that she would "not lie" to them, it was clear that Ellerbee was taking her audience seriously as citizens.

Children's culture is fraught with conflict, contradiction, and power dynamics, despite the efforts of politicians, educators, academics, and parents to insist on childhood as a place that is innocent of the politics and power struggles that characterize adult culture. Occasionally, events within children's culture challenge both the construction of childhood "innocence" as a moralizing strategy that functions to obscure a more overt political agenda, and the notion that children themselves are out-side the political world. Cultural scholar Henry Jenkins sees Ellerbee's *Nick News* as one of these events. As he argues, Ellerbee confronts the as-sumption that children are outside power dynamics "when she creates television programs that encourage children's awareness of real-world problems, such as the Los Angeles riots, and enable children to find their own critical voice to speak back against the adult world. She trusts chil-dren to confront realities from which other adults might shield them, of-fering them the facts needed to form their own opinions and the air time to discuss issues."[21] Aside from the episode on September 11, *Nick News* has also had special shows on the Clinton-Lewinsky scandal (the program won a Peabody award for that episode), as well as a special episode on the fate of children in Afghanistan since the United States declared war on that country, "Faces of Hope: The Kids of Afghanistan."

However, like all media productions, *Nick News* is situated within the children's television market in ways marked by tension. In other words, *Nick News* is not immune from the pressures to be more entertaining and sensational that often inhibit "adult" news programs from functioning as a public sphere.[22] On Nickelodeon's message board, which Ellerbee en-courages children to visit, users exchange e-mails discussing program-ming. On the link for *Nick News*, there are many messages that claim the show is boring and unnecessary. For example, in one message titled "NickNews is sooooo lame," the child writes: "Nick News is so lame be-cause of the way the peoples [*sic*] set it up. Instead of talking about news that adults care about in kid form, they should talk about things that mat-ter to us (a.k.a. bands, the singer from TLC dying)."[23] This kind of senti-ment reflects the way in which "traditional" news formats such as *Nick News* can also work to alienate viewers by refusing to "talk about things that matter to us."

But the website itself is an interesting example of political debate. For example, although the majority of the messages seem to claim that *Nick News* is boring, others challenged this position. One child responded to the above e-mail message in the following way:

> So you don't care that Saddam Huessuen [*sic*] has nukes and could blow us up? Or that he is giving 25 grand to families that send their kids out to blow up other kids? Or that women in Afghanistan get beaten be-cause their clothes slipped down? Or because they laughed in public? Or

what about 911? Did you care about that? Or should Nick News talk about "Holy Fishpaste, News Flash! The guy from some boy band broke up with britney Spears!" This is whats goin on in the world today, people, and theres no denying it. As sad as it is that a singer is dying, there's millions of other people that live lives that are worse than being dead. Nick news tells us whats goin on without the graphic images of reality thats on NBC.[24]

The message boards on the Nickelodeon website seem to confront the conventional wisdom that children are "innocent" and outside the political world by insisting that at least *some* kids are invested in traditional politics; as another website visitor argued: "I like Nick News because it shows alot of interesting things I never knew before. I also watch CNN too. Kids should watch the new[s] so they know what is going on around the world."[25]

But the message board also reveals another contradiction within Nickelodeon's rhetorical address: when *Nick News* is situated within the context of the network's claim that "kids should just be kids," the national news becomes, for some kids, part of that boring world of adults, and current events and political issues are understood as "things that adults care about." While this could be read as mere political disaffection on the part of children, it could also be seen as a challenge to conceive of citizenship in a realm outside that of "official" politics. The child who complained about the way *Nick News* was "set up" argued that within the commercial and entertainment realm (bands, popular musicians) events occur that kids *do* care about. There are tensions involved, then, in maintaining the "kids only zone" as more than mere rhetoric. Constructing an active audience which is treated not as beings in constant need of protection from the "adult" world, but rather as agents in this world, requires more than simply an acknowledgment that children can think for themselves. Constructing this audience also requires providing children with the active *means to* think for themselves. *Nick News* seems to provide these means for some children by encouraging them to be informed about the world, or to take an active role in their communities. However, providing the means to think for oneself not only involves this kind of political action, but also engages the balancing of the tension between insisting that children are *citizens* and addressing them as *consumers.*

Kids' Empowerment: Consumers as Citizens

The construction of any modern audience, including children, as citizens is a process marked by tension and conflict, primarily because the category of citizenship itself seems increasingly murky and ill-defined. On the one hand, assuming that "politics" and "empowerment" are actions that most significantly emerge from a Habermasian framework that privileges news journalism as the key to an informed citizenry essentializes both these categories as real and authentic. For example, Buckingham argues: "Traditional notions of citizenship are, it is argued, no longer relevant as viewers zap distractedly between commercial messages and superficial entertainment, substituting vicarious experience for *authentic* social interaction and community life."[26] Buckingham does attempt to "turn this argument around," and he makes a good case that young people's lack of interest in "real" politics may be due not to their own ignorance or laziness, but rather to the fact that they have been excluded from "the domain of politics, and from dominant forms of political discourse."

However, this notion that young people are not apathetic but rather disenfranchised continues to privilege a particular view of politics as official and real (a Habermasian view of politics and the public sphere), and romanticizes the news media as the best source for the construction of this kind of political identity.[27] It seems clear that in order to understand the complexities of citizenship, we need to broaden this framework to include other, more contemporary processes and practices of political agency. Forms of popular culture and, more specifically, commercial entertainment, are not outside the realm of "official" politics; on the contrary, it is often within these realms that our understanding, resistance, and acquiescence to "official" politics are constituted.[28]

For example, the generational address of Nickelodeon is not only dedicated to recognizing children's *political* agency as it has been traditionally defined. It also recognizes the politics involved in recognizing children as a powerful consumer market in their own right, separate from adults. As Laybourne argues, "Nick empowers kids by saying to them, 'You're important—important enough to have a network of your own.'"[29] Indeed, it is clear that in the current cultural climate, visibility (whether on television, music, or other media outlets) does equal power—especially for children. In other words, being recognized as a "demographic" indicates a certain kind of power, and Nickelodeon certainly picks up on this dynamic. The unproblematic collapse that Laybourne makes between the realization of children as an important consumer group and perceived political power—"you're important enough to have a network of your own"—is certainly not a new phenomenon with adults, but the steadily increasing purchasing power of children ages four to eleven (American companies spend more than twenty times what they spent ten years ago on advertising for children, approximately $2 billion each year) should be a reason to pause and consider how these issues of citizenship, perceived political power, and consumer power are crucially intertwined.[30] Consumption habits code individuals as members of particular communities, and grant individuals a kind of power that accompanies such membership. Thus, citizenship is increasingly defined within consumer culture—indeed, as a *process* of consumption itself. Nickelodeon's self-conscious address about kids "as kids" is as much about the *purchasing* power of kids as it is about the *political* power of kids; in fact, these two discourses inform and constitute each other.

It seems, then, that the grandiose claim made by Nickelodeon that they "pledge allegiance to kids" is about both these discourses simultaneously. Simply claiming that children are separate from adults, and have their own agendas, needs, and desires is not quite enough to make a claim of political agency, because political agency is not necessarily defined within terms such as autonomy, independence, and "rights-bearing" citizens any longer (if it ever truly was). But we *do* define citizenship (and thus political agency) in terms of our consumption habits, and we *are* recognized as meaningful citizens depending on both an economic and a cultural recognition of our purchasing power (hence the political power of boycotts). The ability to consume, and thus constitute a "market," has everything to do with one's perceived political power. Nickelodeon's claim to be a network "just for kids" is one of the ways in which it acknowledges the connection between political subjectivity and consumer identity: it is not simply a place defined exclusively for kids; it also capitalizes on the enormous commercial potential of its child audience.

But, because conventional politics and commercialism *are* in tension with each other, Nickelodeon's approach involves a more complicated arrangement than simply constituting its child audience as a new market. Although the snappy do-wop/rap medleys that promoted Nickelodeon's recent campaign of "Nickelodeon Nation" may seem a bit obvious in their efforts to collapse citizenship with consumerism, there are other ways in which Nickelodeon does encourage an active political participation within the bounds of its commercial structure. Thus, Nickelodeon

Nickelodeon's promotional campaign "Nickelodeon Nation" appropriated the language of political rights and freedoms to drive home the point that the network had only kids' best interests in mind.

represents an example of children's media that authorizes children as both consumer-citizens and as civil citizens. And indeed, this often indicates the exact same process. Children are enjoying a constantly increasing recognition in both the commercial world and the world of civic responsibility. Although media scholars such as Buckingham seem to hold onto a more "authentic" politics as constitutive of citizenship, the civil-citizen and consumer-citizen are not binary opposites, but rather are situated as different points on a continuum of citizenship. Thus, when Buckingham asks, "Children may indeed have acquired a new status within the private sphere of consumption, but how far has this extended to the public sphere of social institutions and of politics? Children may have become 'sovereign consumers,' but to what extent have they also been recognized as *citizens* in their own right?" one potential reply is that to be a "sovereign consumer" *is* to be a citizen.[31]

Indeed, the notion that citizenship is an identity both constituted and affirmed within consumer culture is one that emerges from the shifting demographic, technological, and global terrain that characterized the United States in the later half of the twentieth century. As traditional rituals of citizenship and patriotism seem increasingly esoteric and inclusive of only particular "Americans," more and more citizens are structuring their identities along lines defined by markets rather than the nation-state. As cultural scholar Nestor Garcia Canclini points out, "Men and women increasingly feel that many of the questions proper to citizenship—where do I belong, what rights accrue to me, how can I get information, who represents my interests?—are being answered in the private realm of commodity consumption and the mass media more than in the abstract rules of democracy or collective participation in public spaces."[32] Canclini argues that our sense of social belonging, a crucial element of meaningful citizenship, is steeped in our consumption habits and routines, and that it thus makes sense to theorize citizenship and consumption as crucially connected practices. Indeed, legitimating only a traditional definition of political participation (such as voting or the rational debate of "ideas") as a necessary condition for citizenship misses a whole range of experiences that comprise national belonging: "When we select goods and appropriate them, we define what we consider publicly valuable, the ways we integrate and distinguish ourselves in society, and the ways to combine pragmatism with pleasure."[33] And not only are traditional definitions of political participation limited for most people, but an emphasis on voting and rational debate *necessarily* excludes children from the category of citizenship (simply because of the legal and educational boundaries of these practices). Yet the purchase and use of consumer products as ways to construct identity are practices in which children actively participate. Thus, if citizenship is defined by a sense of belonging, then belonging itself needs to be redefined as shaped by participation in what Canclini calls "communities of consumers," such as youth and rock music, or children and Nickelodeon.

As I've discussed, an important element of Nickelodeon's self-construction is its insistence that kids are an active audience in their own right, separate from the world of adults. Indeed, as much of Nickelodeon's programming demonstrates, "adults just don't get it." Part of what adults "just don't get" are the consumption habits of youth, which are important markers of identity and ways of distinguishing one social group from another.[34] The boundary between the worlds of children and adults that is implied by the idea that adults "don't get" the world of children is important to the self-construction of children as particular kinds of citizens. Indeed, Allison James has argued that the deliberate mystification of children's culture by children is crucial for the self-conscious construction of the child as an individual: "The true nature of the culture of childhood frequently remains hidden from adults, for the semantic cues which permit social recognition have been manipulated and disguised by children in terms of their alternative society. . . . By confusing the adult order children create for themselves considerable room for movement with the limits imposed upon them by adult society."[35] A successful way of manipulating adult authority as a means to create a separate children's culture has been to select consumer goods that are distinctly outside the adult world, whether these choices be situated in popular music, fashion, or television programming. However, this strategy does not simply establish "an alternative system of meanings which adults cannot perceive"; it also constructs children as a very important demographic.[36] In fact, according to marketing specialist James McNeal, "tweens," children between the ages of eight and twelve have "become the 'powerhouse' of the kids' market, spending close to $14 billion a year" and thus becoming a "retailer's dream."[37] The children's media market is especially attractive because of its multidimensional appeal: children have money of their own (and more and more each year), they have influence over the purchasing power of their parents, and they are considered a market for the future.[38] The relatively newfound (or at least, newly energized) recognition of children as a lucrative market has re-

Here, the network uses the playful conventions
of animation to connect traditional symbols of
citizenship—George Washington—with the consumer context of Nickelodeon to appeal to kids.
Frame grab from *How to Nickelodeon* video. © 1992
MTV Networks.

sulted in their increased visibility in the mass media—after all, part of targeting the tween market means that corporate culture needs to provide a
kind of representation that is both appealing and inclusive.

Nickelodeon's claim of being a "kids only zone," then, is not simply
about acknowledging youth as an audience in their own right, but also
about the specific recognition of this audience as an important group of
consumers. However, the construction of children as consumers has historically been formulated as a relationship characterized by *dependence*
and manipulation rather than *independence* and individual agency. For
example, media scholar Marsha Kinder argues that Nickelodeon's persis-
tence in claiming that the network is a place just for kids relies upon an
overt strategy of dividing children from adults as two very different consumer groups. In fact, she reads Nickelodeon's emphasis on generational
conflict as a strategy that actually functions commercially as *transgenerational*.[39] The issue of media inclusion—a "network of your own"—is
thus inseparable from other corporate and commercial interests and
points to Nickelodeon's transgenerational address as a slippery strategy
to target the kid market, rather than a means to empower kids as citizens.

In so doing, Nickelodeon's exploitation of generational differences works as a "site of displacement," in which other, important issues are rendered invisible through the clever, divisive strategy of separating children from adults as an audience. Kinder sees Nick's empowerment rhetoric, then, as a kind of political or moral agenda that works as an alibi for a sophisticated marketing strategy which invokes "empowerment" in order to sell commercial products to kids through advertising, "a marketing strategy that masquerades as a moral or political issue." This strategy itself privileges generational conflict between children and adults as a crucial social problem, effectively eclipsing other concerns, including conflicts of race, gender, and ethnicity.[40]

However, the fact that empowerment here means *consumer* empowerment does not necessarily mean that politics are not at work in this dynamic. On the contrary, the marketing strategy that Kinder criticizes *is* the political agenda, not a cover-up, and this relationship is one of dynamic (and often reflexive) *tension,* rather than of direct opposition. Although Kinder's argument about the generational address functioning in commercial terms is well taken, the notion that this marketing strategy is "masquerading" as a political issue reveals a privileging of politics as a realm that exists somehow outside the market. In other words, the marketing strategy of Nickelodeon *is* a political issue; defining the child as a free liberal subject, as Nickelodeon claims it does, implies in turn the freedom of consumer choice. Thus, it is true, as Kinder suggests, that Nickelodeon's focus on generational conflict obscures other forms of identification for children (as well as larger social concerns). It is also the case, however, that the concentration on the cultural divide between generations is an important modification to most research findings on media effects that insist that children are simply brainwashed by television programming. The assumption that children exist not simply in a cultural realm separate from adults, but in a social world that actively contradicts adult norms and boundaries (and thus adult authority) challenges a dominant argument that children are innocent and impressionable, and thus at the mercy of particular kinds of damaging media.[41] In other words, the recognition of kids as an important consumer market is a form of empowerment in the current political climate, where media representation and purchasing power are key allies in determining citizenship.

It is not merely the advertising that supports Nickelodeon that constructs its audience as consumer-citizens. This address is also present in the tensions and ironies of much of the programming. For example, consider "Rugrats Discover America." Ostensibly in honor of Columbus Day (although neither the historical figure nor the federal holiday is mentioned in the special), the program was aired about a month after the World Trade Center and Pentagon attacks, and took a different tack at representing American citizenship from the *Nick News* special discussed earlier. The program is a widely popular animated series that features four babies who constantly get into trouble and a group of parents who are generally clueless about what their children are "really" up to, a direct reference to Nickelodeon's rhetoric of generational conflict. "Rugrats Discover America" opens with the grandparents of some of the characters distributing souvenirs to the children from their recent trip across America. The souvenirs include a Native American artifact and a toy Statue of Liberty. These souvenirs prompt a fantasy by the main characters involving a vacation across America in a tour bus, with stops at particular places of interest. These include the Grand Canyon, the American West, and New York City. A side story features two older child characters taking a motorcycle trip across the same terrain, complete with Easy Rider outfits and a version of "Born to Be Wild" playing on the soundtrack (a visual trope that assumes a transgenerational audience).

The *Rugrats* special offers a pointed and specific version of citizenship; focusing on popular culture and tourism, this program defines citizenship in terms of the consumer who acquires "national" knowledge at different tourist stops around the country that are then represented in souvenirs. This definition of citizenship, as an American consumer spirit represented in popular film references and commercial souvenirs (a kind of "cultural capital" that seems to be a specific prerequisite for citizenship), is offered alongside the broader, idealist American "spirit" represented in more jingoistic displays of patriotism such as the *Nick News* special. The two definitions of citizenship inform and constitute each other, and in so doing, help to form the social construction of the child-citizen for Nickelodeon's audience. This then combines with the recent marketing campaign for the network that celebrates the "Nickelodeon Nation," as well as the promises to "pledge allegiance to kids," the encouragement of its young audience to "exercise those choice muscles," and the insistence that "You have more power than you think!" As Heather Hendershot has pointed out, Nickelodeon's emphasis on the "rights" of kids places in bold relief the connection *and* the tension between rights and modern citizenship, where rights for kids who watch Nickelodeon are most crucially the "right" to make purchases, and the "choices" that are exercised are consumer choices.[42]

Finally, then, it is this *tension*, between political and consumer rights, that most profoundly characterizes a modern sense of citizenship for both adults and children. For children, who are culturally situated outside formal, legal political rights, consumption habits take on perhaps even added significance in the construction of citizenship. In other words, while it is certainly true that political rights remain an important democratic freedom in the construction of citizenship, it is also the case that these older forms of understanding oneself as a citizen have been reformulated in the context of modern consumer culture. Rather, it is the *intermingling* of political rights and consumption habits that most profoundly characterizes citizenship. Indeed, political participation and consumption are mutually constitutive practices; they rely upon each other for their logic. That is to say, freedom of choice is still a relevant social category, but situated within consumer culture this kind of freedom encompasses more than simply private, political choices within the public sphere. It also indicates the freedom to choose one particular commodity over others, or the choice to belong to a specific community of consumers. As Canclini argues in regard to the relationship of political participation with consumer behavior: "The definition of a nation . . . is given less at this stage [in history] by its territorial limits or its political history. It survives, rather, as an *interpretive community of consumers,* whose traditional—alimentary, linguistic—habits induce them to relate in a peculiar way with the objects and information that circulate in international networks."[43] The community of consumers that comprises the Nickelodeon audience "provide[s] a sense of belonging where national loyalties have eroded"—indeed, in the modern context, national loyalty and citizenship make sense only *within* the confines of the commercial network. Consumption, then, for many children (as well as adults) becomes "the principal criterion of identification."[44]

Thus, Nickelodeon's philosophy of "let kids just be kids" distinguishes the network in the marketplace as a new voice. At the same time, this marks yet another tension in the network's rhetoric of citizenship. In order to be recognized in the marketplace, the network relies on its mission statement that implicitly situates its audience *outside* the market: "Just being a kid" has historically meant that children are situated outside the crass politics of the market, and are thus shielded from certain corruption.[45] Economist Viviana Zelizer traces this history as one in which the "social value" of children changed through various child labor reforms in the late eighteenth and early nineteenth centuries in the United States. This process of shifting the social value of children, motivated in large part by changing labor laws so as to prohibit children from working for wages outside the home, encouraged what Zelizer calls "the sacralization of children," a process whereby adults invest children, and childhood, with sentimental or religious meaning.[46] Children were thus newly thought to be easily "corruptible" by the consumer world and were ideologically situated as outside this realm.

Yet, as Ellen Seiter has argued, to be "just a kid" means in part to establish an imagined community with other children based on goods and commercial items. Seiter points out that "Toys, commercials, and animated programs are the lingua franca of young children at babysitters' and grandmothers' houses, day-care centers, and preschools across the United States."[47] Seiter argues that commercial goods provide children with "a shared repository of images," and this in turn allows for processes of identification based on race, class, and citizenship. Nickelodeon's vast empire of programming, toys, clothing, and other commercial goods clearly establishes a "shared repository of images" for its audience, which in turn organizes an imagined community based on a sense of belonging and membership.

In fact, according to Geraldine Laybourne, Nickelodeon's licensing agreement with the toy company Mattel is based on creating "the ideal citizen" through the particular marketing of toys. According to Laybourne, Nickelodeon was faced with a dilemma when it began working with Mattel because of Mattel's obvious gender-specific marketing. Since Nickelodeon was committed to banning gender-specific programming from its lineup (in an effort to be more inclusive of girls, a severely neglected demographic in children's programming), and since Mattel designs most of its products specifically for boys or girls, Nickelodeon worked with Mattel to design toys with empowerment in mind: "We hold to a philosophy of quality, of variety, of self-discovery for kids. We believe that boys and girls should be treated as equals. We expect the unexpected. And we seek to build a bridge for kids with the past, with what their parents did, that connects them to the whole history of American childhood."[48] Laybourne also argues that Nickelodeon's use of focus groups in its toy design is about recognizing the agency of children: "Surveys and research are the first steps in empowering kids—Nickelodeon's central mission. As part of the Nickelodeon Experience, when kids are given self-esteem and a voice, they are encouraged to make choices."[49] Again, the "choices" that Nickelodeon's audience are encouraged to make are consumer choices, and the network's "central mission" of empowerment is as much about authorizing kids as consumers as it is about empowering them in a more traditional political sense.

Conclusion: Children as Citizens

I really like nick news sometimes they have good topics sometimes and yes sometimes it makes me wanna go out and help others

Nick News Message Board
RE: nick news rocks
Date: 06/18/02

kids need to hear about what's going on in the world now, so they'll be better prepared to face and deal with it when they step out of their homes, and into the real world. Yes, it might be boring at times, but it is a necessary evil—and one which we must acknowledge . . .

Nick News Message Board
RE: No kids care about this stuff? oh really!?!
Date: 06/26/02

This is a club for everyone!!!!!!!! As long as you like rugrats you can gone [join] my club!!!!!! All you have to do is tell me why you like the rugrats and then you can join!!!!!! bye

Rugrats Message Board
RE: a rugrats club
Date: 04/16/02

It seems clear that in the contemporary political economy of the United States, citizens identify as much (if not more) in and through their consumption habits than through the processes that construct what Michael Schudson calls the "good citizen": voting, becoming politically informed, participating in the political process.[50] As Canclini argues, the traditional model of the public sphere needs to be reformulated to take into account the market as a site of meaningful social activity. Yet the market is not enough to produce a community of informed, empowered citizens. As citizenship is formed in and through a relationship with the commercial media, the category of citizenship itself is defined by a set of tensions about what Americans are and what they should be.

Certainly children have been addressed historically as citizens-in-the-making or as potential citizens. Many patriotic rituals—the Pledge of Allegiance, the school textbook, or student government—are about the education of young children to be citizens. Much of children's television has also approached children through this education angle. But to be considered "in-process" is to deny a particular power dynamic involved in identity making. In other words, it is difficult to exercise empowered and informed choices when always considered in a state of becoming. Nickelodeon seems to challenge this by addressing children as *citizens already,* and attending to their needs accordingly. If citizenship is both something that is ideologically "imposed" upon a member of society, and something that one creates and produces through activity, interaction, and identity construction, then Nickelodeon's strategy of addressing kids "as kids" is to consider its audience as citizens. The commercial structure of the network allows for even more coherence to this community, and allows children to politically connect with their own needs and desires rather than those defined by adults.

But, as Canclini argues, consumption habits need to be combined with political action to elevate the status of consumers to that of citizens. Among other things, this means requiring "democratic participation by the principal sectors of civil society in material, symbolic, juridical, and political decisions that organize consumption."[51] It is unclear whether Nickelodeon truly fosters this kind of intermixing of democratic participation and consumption. For the one child who wrote to the website claiming that watching *Nick News* made him "wanna go out and help others," there are even more children who demonstrate a much more cynical and disaffected view toward reflexive political action. Nickelodeon, like citizenship itself, is characterized by tension. The empowerment rhetoric of the network is at times connected to a more traditional material politics, such as the *Nick News* specials and other social outreach programs developed by Nickelodeon. At the same time, this empowerment rhetoric must be read through the lens of consumer culture. Thus, Nickelodeon's insistence that kids "exercise their choice muscles" often indicates a kind of empowerment that emerges through the recognition that children are a lucrative market. Either way, children are constructed as citizens. Whether citizenship is formulated in a meaningful way *within* consumer culture, a way that allows for the production of the social and political life of youth as a specific *function* of consumption, remains to be seen.

NOTES

1. Nestor Garcia Canclini, *Consumers and Citizens: Globalization and Multicultural Conflicts,* translated by George Yudice (Minneapolis: University of Minnesota Press, 2001), 47. I'm grateful to Dana Polan and Marita Sturken for their helpful comments regarding consumer citizenship and civil citizenship.

2. See Carolyn Marvin, *When Old Technologies Were New: Thinking about Electric Communication in the Late Nineteenth Century* (London: Oxford University Press, 1990); Lynn Spigel, *Make Room for TV: Television and the Family Ideal in Postwar America* (Chicago: University of Chicago Press, 1992), Michele Hilmes, *Radio Voices: American Broadcasting, 1922–1952* (Minneapolis: University of Minnesota Press, 1997); and George Lipsitz, *Time Passages: Collective Memory and American Popular Culture* (Minneapolis: University of Minnesota Press, 1990), among others.

3. Spigel, *Make Room for TV,* 53–55.

4. Ellen Seiter, *Sold Separately: Children and Parents in Consumer Culture* (New Brunswick: Rutgers University Press, 1993); and Stephen Kline, "The Making of Children's Culture," in Henry Jenkins, ed., *The Children's Culture Reader* (New York: NYU Press, 1998).

5. Henry Jenkins, "Introduction," in Jenkins, ed., *Children's Culture Reader*; and Marsha Kinder, "Kids' Media Culture: An Introduction," in Marsha Kinder, ed., *Kids' Media Culture* (Durham: Duke University Press, 1999).

6. Joe Austin and Michael Nevin Willard, "Introduction: Angels of History, Demons of Culture," in Joe Austin and Michael Nevin, eds., *Generations of Youth: Youth Cultures and History in Twentieth-Century America* (New York: NYU Press, 1998), 1.

7. Ibid., 2.

8. Geraldine Laybourne, "The Nickelodeon Experience," in G. L. Berry and J. K. Asamen, eds., *Children and Television* (London: Sage, 1993). See also Sally Helgesen, *The Web of Inclusion* (New York: Doubleday), 1995.

9. Laybourne, "Nickelodeon Experience," 304.

10. Lynn Spigel, "Seducing the Innocent: Childhood and Television in Postwar America," in Jenkins, ed., *Children's Culture Reader,* 110.

11. Laybourne, "Nickelodeon Experience," 305.

12. Laybourne, cited in Helgesen, *Web of Inclusion,* 222.

13. Helgesen, *Web of Inclusion,* 222.

14. David Buckingham, *After the Death of Childhood: Growing Up in the Age of Electronic Media* (Cambridge: Polity Press, 2000), 163.

15. Jurgen Habermas, *The Structural Transformation of the Public Sphere: An Inquiry into a Category of Bourgeois Society* (Cambridge: MIT Press, 1989). Habermas argues that a bourgeois public sphere emerged in eighteenth-century Europe through a newly organized civil society. This public sphere is, according to Habermas, a "domain of private autonomy . . . opposed to the state." He continues: "It is a forum in which the private people come together to form a public, readied themselves to compel public authority to legitimate itself before public opinion" (25–26). The public sphere is occupied by what he calls "educated" citizens (generally white, property-owning men), and serves as an important forum in which "rational critical public debate" over a variety of cultural and political issues takes place. Habermas argues that within the public sphere, debate provides an important mediating tool to negotiate the interests of potentially conflicting social groups, and allows for the social construction of oneself as a political subject, or citizen.

16. Bruce Robbins, ed., *The Phantom Public Sphere* (Minneapolis: University of Minnesota Press, 1993), xxiv.

17. See Robbins, *Phantom Public Sphere;* David Buckingham, *The Making of Citizens: Young People, News and Politics* (London: Routledge, 2000); and Benedict Richard O'G. Anderson, *Imagined Communities: Reflections on the Origin and Spread of Nationalism* (London: Verso, 1983).

18. Buckingham, *After the Death of Childhood,* 168.

19. Ibid., 169.

20. Another U.S. children's news program, *Channel One News,* is arguably the least successful news program currently aired, at least in terms of the interests of its child audience. *Channel One News* is transmitted to U.S. schools, with the ostensible purpose of using the show as a kind of tutorial. According to David Buckingham, schools receive around $50,000 in equipment when they subscribe to the show, but part of the deal is to broadcast the programming to 90 percent of the students, including the two minutes of advertising that accompanies every ten-minute segment. Because of this, it has been extremely controversial in the United States, and as Buckingham points out, there is little evidence that the news show is actively used by either teachers or students. Buckingham, *Making of Citizens,* and David Buckingham, "News and Advertising in the Classroom: Some Lessons from the Channel One Controversy," *International Journal of Media and Communication Studies* (1997, vol. 1).

21. Jenkins, "Introduction," 32.

22. Dana Polan, "The Public's Fear; or, Media as Monster in Habermas, Negt, and Kluge," in Robbins, *Phantom Public Sphere.*

23. Nickelodeon website, Message Board, *Nick News.* http://www.nick.com. Accessed June 2002.

24. Ibid.

25. Ibid.

26. Buckingham, *After the Death of Childhood*, 171, my emphasis.

27. Ibid., 175–182.

28. For more on this, see Robbins, *Phantom Public Sphere.*

29. Laybourne, "Nickelodeon Experience," 304.

30. Edward Cohn, "Marketwatch: Consuming Kids," *The American Prospect* 11:6 (June 28, 2002).

31. Buckingham, *After the Death of Childhood*, 168.

32. Canclini, *Citizens and Consumers*, 15.

33. Ibid., 20.

34. For more on this, see, for example, Dick Hebdige, *Subculture: The Meaning of Style* (London: Methuen, 1979); John Fiske, *Reading the Popular* (London: Unwyn Hyman, 1989); and Angela McRobbie, *Feminism and Youth Culture* (New York: Routledge, 1991).

35. Allison James, "Confections, Concoctions, and Conceptions," in Jenkins, ed., *Children's Culture Reader*, 394–395.

36. Ibid., 404.

37. Barbara Kantrowitz and Pat Wingert, "Tweens," *Newsweek* (October 18, 1999).

38. This point was made by Ellen Seiter in a talk given to the Annenberg School for Communication, University of Southern California, April 2001.

39. Marsha Kinder, "Home Alone in the 90s: Generational War and Transgenerational Address in American Movies, Television, and Presidential Politics" in Cary Bazalgette and David Buckingham, eds., *In Front of the Children: Screen Entertainment and Young Audiences* (London: British Film Institute, 1995), 75–91.

40. Ibid., 88–89.

41. For more on the critique of media effects research, see, for example, Buckingham, *After the Death of Childhood*; and Marjorie Heins, *Not in Front of the Children: "Indecency," Censorship, and the Innocence of Youth* (New York: Hill and Wang, 2001).

42. Heather Hendershot, *Saturday Morning Censors: Television Regulation before the V-Chip* (Durham: Duke University Press, 1998), 217–218.

43. Canclini, *Consumers and Citizens*, 43.

44. Ibid., 44.

45. For an excellent economic history of the construction of children as specifically outside the market, see Viviana Zelizer, *Pricing the Priceless Child: The Changing Social Value of Children* (Princeton: Princeton University Press, 1985).

46. Ibid., 59.

47. Ellen Seiter, "Children's Desires/Mothers' Dilemmas: The Social Contexts of Consumption," in Jenkins, ed., *Children's Culture Reader,* 297.

48. Laybourne, cited in Helgesen, *Web of Inclusion,* 230–231. Of course, this desire to "build a bridge for kids with the past," thus connecting kids with their parents, reveals a contradiction in Laybourne's idealist philosophy, for surely the parents of the current generation played with gender-specific toys.

49. Ibid., 228.

50. Michael Schudson, *The Good Citizen: A History of American Civic Life* (Cambridge: Harvard University Press, 1998).

51. Canclini, *Consumers and Citizens,* 46.

PART IV

Viewers

11

Watching Children Watch Television and the Creation of *Blue's Clues*

Daniel R. Anderson

In 1993 I was invited by Nickelodeon to advise on the development of the Nick Jr. block of preschool programs. Because Nickelodeon was interested in providing programs that would actually benefit preschoolers rather than merely entertain them, I jumped at the chance. In the course of my twenty years of academic research on children's television viewing and the impact of television on cognitive and educational development, I had become convinced that television had a huge unrealized potential to benefit children. This was a chance to put theory into action. I subsequently provided advice on many programs and on the Nick Jr. interstitials (the short content between programs) including the signature Nick Jr. character, Face.

A young researcher, Angela Santomero, frequently received my notes by telephone and always made a point of chatting with me during meetings in New York. She had read most of my published research and theoretical articles (she has a bachelor's degree in psychology and a master's degree in child development) and made it clear that she was intensely interested in developing her own program for Nick Jr., a program that would be innovative and educational and that would be based on a modern understanding of children's television viewing. She eventually persuaded Nickelodeon to fund her efforts, and I became a formal advisor to her project. In part from our discussions, in part from my own and others' research and theory, and in part from the prior examples of *Sesame Street* and *Mister Rogers' Neighborhood*, Santomero created *Blue's Clues* in collaboration with Tracie Paige Johnson and Todd Kessler. In this essay I summarize my research and theory as it relates to advice I gave for the development of *Blue's Clues*.

The Passive Theory of Television Viewing

The design of *Blue's Clues* makes the fundamental assumption that preschool children are intellectually active when they watch television. This assumption flies in the face of what many consider the commonsense notion that television is a passive medium of communication. I started my research career making the same assumption.

In the spring of 1972, as a young assistant professor, I delivered a lecture on the development of attention to my undergraduate class on Child Development and Behavior. After the lecture a student asked me, if young children are distractible and have trouble sustaining attention, why could they just sit and stare at *Sesame Street*? Glibly, and with the aplomb of a person who is deeply ignorant, I replied that the child's sustained attention was illusory, the TV was just a distractor that remained in place. A movement or visual change on the TV screen would attract the child's attention, and before she could look away, another movement or change would occur and so she would keep looking. In fact I knew nothing about children's attention to television. Subsequently, and with some intellectual guilt, I asked a graduate student, Stephen Levin, to review the research on children's attention to television. After a few weeks he reported that there was none. Sensing an interesting opportunity, I wrote a grant proposal to the National Science Foundation and soon launched a program of research into children's attention to television. Perhaps, to a later generation of students, I would be able to answer the question knowledgeably.

My glib answer fit perfectly with the intellectual zeitgeist of the 1970s and the 1980s. Within a few years Marie Winn would launch a major attack on children's television in general and *Sesame Street* in particular in her book *The Plug-In Drug*,[1] soon to be followed by Gerry Mander's *Four Arguments for the Elimination of Television*,[2] and many other anti-TV diatribes, culminating in Jane Healy's *Endangered Minds: Why Our Children Can't Think*.[3] A common argument underlying all these attacks is that television viewing is fundamentally and deeply passive, inducing a passivity of intellect. This passivity of intellect is said to be so harmful to development that educational television can only be an oxymoron.

According to these critics the passivity stems from the edited, visual nature of television. Visual movement or a scene change produces an orienting reaction in the child so that the child drops any other ongoing activity, turns toward the TV set, and begins to pay attention at a superficial level of cognitive processing. Such orienting reactions involve not only changes in visual attention but also heart rate changes and other physiological responses to visual novelty. Before the child can fully understand what he or she is seeing, however, the scene changes, and a new orienting reaction is produced that further maintains attention, but disrupts cognition and thought. Over time, the argument goes, the child appears to be paying sustained attention, but is really suffering a series of distractions in place, much as I hypothesized to my student. From this perspective, television leaves no opportunity for reflection or thought; the child merely absorbs a series of disconnected images, failing to gain any connected comprehension of the content.[4] The long-term consequences to children are said to be passivity of thought, inability to follow extended arguments, short attention spans, hyperactivity, inattention to language, and a lack of interest in reading and school.[5] According to this line of argument, *Sesame Street,* with its lively editing and brief segments, takes advantage of the orienting reaction to hold the attention of the audience, producing a fragmented comprehension of the program. As Jane Healy put it: "The worst thing about *Sesame Street* is that people believe it is educationally valuable."[6] These ideas have led many to claim that television, in and of itself, is harmful to children. The antitelevision contingent has undertaken widespread efforts to have TV-free weeks, and even created a TV-free America movement.

It should be noted that the passivity critique was based on little evidence. The substantive research and theory of the early 1970s was almost exclusively focused on the issue of television violence.[7] There was evidence then, and much more now, that TV violence does in fact foster aggression and other problems in children. But researchers had not yet turned their attention to the impact of television on intellectual development, on content that is not violent, or on content that is educational. Was *Sesame Street,* despite good intentions, really harming and not helping children? When I began my research there was a great deal of speculation, but little knowledge.

The Research Showing That
Television Viewing Is Cognitively Active

While the creation of *Blue's Clues* owed a debt of gratitude to *Sesame Street*, it also raised the bar for what educational television could be. After more than thirty years of production, it is easy to forget how radical *Sesame Street* was compared to the children's programs that came before. It was the first program to be designed with the best of contemporary child development research and theory for guidance. It was the first program to be designed based on extensive formative research with children. It was the first educational program to incorporate high production standards.

Sesame Street was the focus of much of my early research on children's television. The research was encouraged in part by my frequent interactions with Children's Television Workshop, producers of *Sesame Street*. CTW provided some of my research funding (although most came from the National Science Foundation, the National Institute of Mental Health, the Spencer Foundation, and the Markle Foundation).

A major feature of *Sesame Street* in its early years was its magazine format. Programs consisted of about forty segments ranging from ten seconds to about seven minutes in length, averaging about ninety seconds. The segments ranged from live-action "street scenes" and films, to puppet segments, to animations. Special visual effects, such as pixilation, were common. Live-action segments included standard video editing techniques ranging from cuts between cameras, giving varying visual perspectives, to transitions representing movements both forward and back in time, as well as point-of-view shots. Content varied widely across segments. Because the segments were so varied in form and content, the show was in many respects ideal for basic studies of young children's attention and comprehension.

My initial research focused on children's patterns of looking at *Sesame Street*. My students and I were surprised to find that at no age did the children just sit and stare at the TV. Rather, they would look at the TV for a while, look away, and eventually look back again. As long as there was something else to do in the viewing room, looking at the TV was highly variable. We then saw that our task was to understand in detail why a child initiated a look at the TV, maintained a look for some variable period of time, and then looked away.

Initially, we studied features of television such as movement and visual change. These features, known as "formal features" by TV researchers, are those that were hypothesized to passively control attention. Some of our findings were in fact consistent with the passive view of television viewing. For example, looking was clearly triggered and enhanced by visual changes and movement.[8] But these effects, while consistent, were fairly small, given the large variations of attention that we observed. We found other, much bigger, determinants of attention.

Consider changes linked to the age of television viewers. If visual changes and movement passively control young children's viewing, then it is reasonable to suppose that even infants will have high levels of attention to TV. This follows because the orienting reaction is well established in infants by a few months of age. In our first major study with *Sesame Street* we videotaped children ranging in age from twelve to forty-eight months in a comfortably furnished viewing room with toys available. We found that looking at *Sesame Street* steadily increased with age from about 10 percent of program time in twelve-month-olds to about 50 percent in forty-eight-month olds.[9] In a later study with three-, four-, and five-year-olds, using a variety of different children's programs, we again found a great increase in looking with age.[10] Subsequently, we verified these observations in ten-day time-lapse videotapes of children recorded in their homes.[11] There was no theory of orienting reactions that predicted such huge changes in attention with development.

What changes during the preschool years could account for this increase in attention to television? It began to dawn on us that the most obvious changes are cognitive. From one to five years of age, children have enormous growth in language and nearly all other cognitive capabilities. It is reasonable to suppose that this growth would be linked to their patterns of attention. Preschool children know very little and understand relatively little about the world around them, and consequently there should be the greatest developmental benefit for them to pay attention at those times when attention can be rewarded with understanding. This raised a series of questions. Could it be that children paid more attention to TV as they got older simply because they were able to understand more of what they saw and heard? If so, were children actually making comprehensibility judgments, paying attention to those parts of programs that were understandable and ignoring the TV when it was largely incomprehensible? On what basis were they making these comprehensibility judgments?

We undertook a series of studies to answer these questions. In the first experiment, we studied the relationship between comprehension of *Sesame Street* and looking at *Sesame Street*. We manipulated looking at the program by either having toys in the room, so that the five-year-olds in the experiment had alternative options to just watching TV, or having no toys. Not surprisingly, when there were no toys, the children looked much more, doubling their attention. The question we wanted to answer was whether the children's memory and comprehension of the program would increase as their attention increased. If understanding is passively controlled by attention to the screen, then the children with no toys would remember and understand substantially more of the program than children with toys would. On the other hand, if the children with toys selectively ignored those parts of the program they found incomprehensible, then they would understand about as much as the group who watched without toys available.

After the *Sesame Street* tape had finished, we tested the children's understanding of the program, using detailed probing. The results were straightforward: There was no difference in comprehension between the groups despite the fact that the group with no toys looked at the program twice as much as the group with toys. When we looked at the items the children in both groups got right and wrong, we found a clear pattern. The children that watched with toys available, when they got a question right, had been looking at the screen when the information necessary to answer a question was presented. They had generally been looking away if they had gotten the question wrong. On the other hand, the children without toys got the same questions right and wrong even though they looked at the TV nearly all the time. It appeared that when the children had toys with which they could play, they strategically divided their attention between the toy play and the TV show, giving full attention to the TV at those times when full attention would be rewarded with understandable content.[12]

If, by age five, children have developed a strategic approach to watching TV in order to selectively pay full attention at those points in the program that are most critical for understanding, we should be able to predict attention on the basis of program comprehensibility. We focused on the abstractness of dialogue. Preschool children should find concrete dialogue more understandable than abstract dialogue, and they should therefore attend more when the dialogue is concrete. We examined three- and five-year-olds looking at fifteen different *Sesame Street* programs and identified each utterance in each program (dialogue and narrative) as either having an immediate or nonimmediate referent. An utterance with an immediate referent refers to an object or event that is concretely present either visually or on the audio track. An utterance with a nonimmediate referent refers to all other utterances. The referents in these latter utterances were usually abstractions or events from past or future experience. Of the 70 percent of *Sesame Street* program time containing language, 20 percent contained immediate utterances. We found that the children at both ages looked more at the TV when the utterances had immediate referents. Even three-year-olds paid selective attention to those parts of the programs that were most likely to be understood.[13]

What about even younger children? Our prior research indicated that children began to pay substantial amounts of attention to *Sesame Street* between twenty-four and thirty months of age. Were children as young as twenty-four months sensitive to the comprehensibility of the program or did they just watch because of visual change, movement, sound effects, and the like? We were interested in directly manipulating the comprehensibility of *Sesame Street* without changing any visual or auditory features that might passively recruit attention along the lines claimed by the program's critics. One way we did this was by reediting segments so that the shots in the segments came in random order. These random shot segments had the same dialogue, the same number of shots, the same amount of visual change, and so on. Events just occurred in nonsensical order. In a second group of segments we edited each utterance of the audio so that it occupied the same video frames but ran backward. A character that said the word "fan" in a normal segment about the letter F, said something that sounds like "naf" when the utterance was reversed. We obtained a third group of segments from the international division of Children's Television Workshop. The dialogue in these segments was Greek. We showed two-, three-and-a-half-, and five-year-olds both the normal and distorted segments. If comprehensibility matters to the children, we argued, they should pay less attention to the distorted segments, even though those segments had all the same formal features of the normal segments.

The results were straightforward. At all ages the children looked less at the segments with reduced comprehensibility, and many of the children complained that something was wrong with the TV. The effect was biggest for the language distortions, indicating the importance of dialogue in driving young children's attention to *Sesame Street*. Importantly, even the twenty-four-month-olds paid less attention if the shots were in a nonsensical order, if the dialogue was backward, or if the dialogue was in a foreign language.[14]

Our work showed that preschool children do not merely passively react to the changing images on television. Rather, they strategically pay attention when that attention is most likely to lead them to content that is most important for understanding. This last point is illustrated by an experiment I conducted with Diane Field.[15] If children are firmly in control of their own attention to television, we reasoned, they should watch differently if they are told they will be tested on their understanding of the content. Half the children in an experiment (five- and nine-year-olds) were so told, and then both groups were shown an array of children's programs with toys present. The children did in fact adjust their viewing. The instructed children rated themselves as investing more effort in watching the programs, and looked at the screen more than the uninstructed group. Importantly, the increased looking occurred primarily for content that was visual in nature and where the content could not be understood simply by listening. Again, we found that the children were quite capable of strategically adjusting their attention to television. When the situation demands it, children appropriately modify their attention to television; this would not be expected if children only reflexively and passively orient themselves to television's formal features.

It became clear to us that young children preferentially seek out and pay attention to content that they believe they can understand and that they can adjust their attentional strategies if the situation demands it. But how do children know when to pay attention? My students and I argued that children use the audio to provide the primary cues as to when content is most likely to be comprehensible and interesting. We do not believe that children ordinarily pay full attention to the audio when they are not actually looking at the TV screen. We believe this because we repeatedly found that memory for auditory information was substantially reduced if the child was not looking at the screen at the time the audio information was given. In preschoolers, this linkage between looking and listening is quite strong, but it grows weaker in older children.[16] That said, even adults are less likely to remember audio content if they are not looking at the time the audio content is imparted. This auditory inattention grows deeper the longer it has been since the adult viewer last looked at the TV.[17]

If child viewers are generally not listening when they are not looking, then how do they know when to pay full attention? We hypothesized that the answer comes from consideration of levels of auditory attention. When not looking, we suggested that children listen at the level of audio quality, but not necessarily at the level of linguistic meaning. The children's viewing strategy is to initiate full attention, including looking, when the audio changes to a sound feature that is associated with comprehensible and interesting content. They continue to ignore the TV when the audio feature is associated with uninteresting, incomprehensible, adult content. The voice quality that is most associated with incomprehensible, uninteresting, and adult content is adult men's voices. Men were and still are ubiquitous on television, compared to women, and especially compared to children.[18] Men's voices, moreover, are most likely to be found in content least interesting to young children (such as news and documentaries). We found that adult men and men's voices are consistently (in nearly every child) associated with less looking at the screen.[19] Note that the hosts of *Blue's Clues*, Steve, and later Joe, are men. This choice seemingly flies in the face of our research and will be discussed later.

The audio qualities most associated with comprehensible children's content, on the other hand, are children's voices and peculiar voices (such as Bugs Bunny); these are associated with increased looking for almost every child. Women's voices are more or less neutral; they neither elicit nor inhibit looking. Also, and not surprisingly, any major abrupt change in sound quality elicits at least a brief look at the TV. In general, children are quite sensitive to auditory features and use them to guide their attention to TV. Once they are paying attention, however, the content has to be comprehensible and interesting for attention to be maintained.

At least as young as twenty-four months (and perhaps younger),[20] children look at television primarily because of its content and only secondarily because of its forms (such as movement and visual change). This has profound implications for preschool program design. The most obvious is that program structure and script development must respect the limited cognitive and language competencies of preschoolers, and, in every aspect, be designed to enhance children's ability to understand the content. Program structure and script development must also very carefully consider the audio aspects of the show. In particular, the producers must understand that children's attention is very strongly cued by the audio.

Comprehension of Video Montage

Naively, many people believe that the task of comprehending television is akin to looking through a window; the problem of comprehension, thus, is more perceptual than cognitive. Television and movies, however, are edited media. Shots are connected by a variety of transitions: cuts, fades, dissolves, wipes, and so on, with simple cuts being the most common. Many transitions are introduced merely to provide visual variation, such as cutting between cameras to provide a changed camera angle on the current scene. Many others, on the other hand, are used to convey meaning. Shot sequences may convey the layout of space within which the action is occurring, may provide the illusion of continuity of action when the action is actually filmed in numerous separate parts, may delete redundant or predictable parts of actions, may convey simultaneous actions in two or more places, may convey change of place of the action, may convey jumps forward or backward in time, may convey a character's visual point of view, or may convey a character's internal state, such as being drunk, or in the process of remembering, and the like. On American television, visual transitions of one kind or another tend to occur about every six seconds, on average.[21]

Even though it seems effortless to an adult, comprehension of filmic montage requires an extraordinary amount of cognitive computation and neural activity. Consider the following activities a viewer must go through as he or she watches a movie or TV show. Within shots, attention is moved to the most informative part of the shot, faces must be identified as familiar or new, objects must be identified, the setting must be identified, actions must be followed and interpreted (with respect to the ongoing narrative or argument), pertinence or overall meaning of the shot must be encoded, and the information must be stored in memory. When there is a transition to another shot, the viewer must compare many things to the immediately prior shot: faces, objects, setting, and action. The viewer must then make an implicit judgment about whether the action is continuous, and if not, what the transition signifies in terms of place, time, and meaning to the ongoing narrative or exposition.

Using the technique of functional magnetic resonance imaging, my colleagues and I have imaged adults' brain activity as they watched coherent filmic montage taken from Hollywood movies. Their brain activity was compared to their brain activity when they watched random sequences of shots taken from movies. By looking at brain areas that were uniquely activated by the coherent montage, we were able to get a sense of which brain areas are used to process and make sense of the transitions between shots (as opposed to those areas used to make sense of the individual shots). We found unique activation in numerous cortical brain areas, predominantly in the right hemisphere, and in all four lobes of the hemisphere. When we analyzed the research literature on the known functions of those brain areas, a sensible picture emerged. The areas are involved in face recognition, object recognition, perception of intentional actions, perception of the layout of space, interpretation of event sequences, and interpretation of the emotional significance of events.[22] Interpretation of montage clearly requires coordinated activity of a large number of brain areas.

Children start regularly watching TV programs and videos of films at around two years of age. Nearly all these TV shows and movies incorporate multiple elements of montage. How do preschoolers interpret filmic montage? Early theory, based on Piaget's theory of cognitive development, held that preschoolers were largely incapable of comprehending filmic montage. The preschoolers' problem, theoretically, is that they tend to perceive the world as a succession of events or states of being, with little comprehension of the intervening transformational events that connect one state to the next. In addition, the preschooler, by virtue of being deeply egocentric, would have great difficulty interpreting point-of-view shots. If these preschool shortcomings were true, then preschoolers would have enormous difficulty interpreting cinematic transitions representing space, time, implied intervening events, and character point of view. All but the simplest video would be incomprehensible except as a series of disconnected events and scenes.

I have already noted, however, that children as young as twenty-four months discriminate between *Sesame Street* segments with shots put in random order as compared to the normal versions of those segments. They pay more attention to the normal segments. They could not do so unless they recognized, at least to some extent, that the canonical order of shots makes more sense. This observation indicated to us that children might be able to comprehend filmic montage at an earlier age than Piagetian theory predicts.

We studied filmic montage comprehension by showing children experimental stop-animation segments that we had produced ourselves.[23] The segments showed Fisher-Price Little People dolls moving about Fisher-Price dollhouse-type environments. In our first study we showed three- and five-year-olds segments that incorporated montage requiring little inference for comprehension. These segments had cuts to different camera angles or close-ups, zooms, and camera pans. Other children saw the same segments but shot with a still camera as one long uninterrupted shot. After seeing a segment on a video monitor, an experimenter pulled aside a curtain that revealed the same set used in filming the segment. The dolls were in the same positions that they were in at the start of the segment. The children were asked to reconstruct the segment by showing and telling us what happened. The children would then move the dolls around the set and repeat the dialogue. We found that the children reconstructed the two types of segments equally well. While, not surprisingly, the five-year-olds reconstructed the segments better than the three-year-olds, the cuts, pans, and zooms did not interfere with reconstruction at either age.

In a second study,[24] we produced segments that required inference for comprehension. Each segment incorporated a cinematic transition requiring a more or less complex inference to comprehend the segment. For example, one segment opened with a long shot of two buildings with four windows in each building. The shot zoomed to the upper-right-hand window at which a doll was placed. A cut provided a transition to an interior shot showing the doll (from the rear) at the window. The doll turned, faced the camera, and said: "It's time to go to bed now." The doll moved to the bed in the room and lay on the bed. After the child viewer saw the video segment, a curtain opened to reveal the set as seen in the opening shot. We handed the child the doll and asked the child to show us and tell us what had happened in the segment. In this particular segment, placement of the doll in the correct room of the set was essential to demonstrate understanding of the relationship between the establishing shot and the cut to the interior scene. If the child, without hesitation, placed the doll in the correct room (each room in the set had a bed), then we judged that the child had inferred the correct spatial relationship between the shots. Each of the twelve segments incorporated a transition requiring an inference about space, time, implied events, or character point of view. We tested four- and seven-year-olds' reconstruction of the segments.

While seven-year-olds were better than four-year-olds at reconstructing the segments, the four-year-olds did surprisingly well. Averaging across all segments and types of inference required, four-year-olds understood 62 percent of the cinematic transitions and seven-year-olds understood 88 percent. For comparison purposes, we tested a small group of adults; they were 100 percent correct. When we look at the different types of transitions, four-year-olds were correct on 78 percent of implied events, 58.5 percent of spatial inferences, 56 percent of point-of-view transitions, and 48.7 percent of inferences involving time. Overall, the four-year-olds understood basic filmic montage far better than was predicted by Piaget's theory, which predicts essentially zero performance. It is also clear, on the other hand, that failure to comprehend cinematic transitions is common among preschoolers. This research makes it apparent that preschool program design has to take filmic montage very carefully into account and that every transition is a potential occasion for failure of comprehension.

Attentional Inertia

The original magazine format design of *Sesame Street,* with about forty segments per hour, implicitly encouraged its viewers to pay attention to some segments and ignore others. We found that when a segment boundary occurs, the child who is looking at the TV looks away, and the child who has been inattentive looks up at the TV.[25] On the other hand, if the child has been continuously looking for longer than about fifteen seconds prior to the segment boundary, the child is much more likely to keep looking at the next segment.[26] This is part of a phenomenon that we called attentional inertia.[27] Attentional inertia is the deepened engagement with television that begins when a viewer initiates a look at the TV, reaching a state of engagement after about fifteen seconds of continuous looking that further deepens as the look continues. Attentional inertia has been observed in infants as young as three months, in children, and in adults. As the engagement deepens, the viewer shows a decelerated heart rate characteristic of focused attention, reduced distractibility from the TV, and increased memory for the TV content.[28] Continuously engaging a viewer for more than about fifteen seconds, therefore, puts the viewer in a state where he or she is resistant to distraction and is more likely to learn the content. Importantly, attentional inertia is the major mechanism by which a young child will continue to pay attention to the program even when the content is difficult for that child to understand. This notion has important implications for the design of *Blue's Clues*.

Overt Audience Participation

The very first time I deliberately watched preschool children watch television, I saw behavior that contradicted the idea that children are rendered intellectually passive by television. The program was *Mister Rogers' Neighborhood,* and the viewers were three- and five-year-old sisters. Occasionally, Mister Rogers would break the fourth wall, look directly into the camera, and ask the audience a question. Each time, the sisters would answer, sometimes in unison. When siblings watch television together at home, they ask each other questions, judge the plausibility of content, and make predictions about what will happen.[29] In my studies of *Sesame Street* I repeatedly saw that certain segments would elicit audience participation, although most did not.[30] Segments that elicited participation seemed to be those where the audience knew what was about to happen, or where there was an explicit or implicit invitation to participate. For example, if Susan sang the ABC song, the watching children would sing along. If Bill Cosby was trying to count four boys but one boy hid behind him as he was trying to count, the watching children would yell to him that the boy was hiding or would count four boys themselves. When Kermit drew an animated letter K on the screen, the children would draw Ks in the air with their fingers. The producers of *Sesame Street* never adopted audience participation as a consistent goal of the program, but perhaps inadvertently, some of their segments did a great job eliciting it.

Brown Johnson, the executive in charge of Nick Jr., was very much aware of the potential of audience participation in children's programs. I was asked to provide examples of things that would elicit audience participation, and based on my work with *Sesame Street,* I was able to provide numerous examples. She commissioned two pilot programs, "Peter Penguin" and "Play with Me," both of which explicitly invited audience participation. Testing with preschoolers suggested that children would readily answer questions, point to the screen, sing along, and so on. Johnson became very interested in developing a Nick Jr. program that would invite the audience to be interactive. (Her original notion was a preschool game show.) It was clear at that point that audience participation could be part of program design, and Angela Santomero, Todd Kessler, Alice

Wilder (*Blue's Clues* research director), and I eagerly discussed the potential of audience participation in educational programs. Audience participation became a signature of *Blue's Clues,* and later a signature of its companion on Nick Jr., *Dora the Explorer.*

The Blue's Clues *Design*

Before I discuss the creation of *Blue's Clues,* I would like to make the point that after more than thirty years, we now understand something of the positive impact that *Sesame Street* has had on its viewers. In collaborative research we have found that *Sesame Street* viewers had higher grades in English, math, and science, did more book reading, and were less likely to be aggressive as adolescents.[31] It was clear to me that television could have a profound and beneficial impact of long duration on children. Angela Santomero's commitment to a program that would be innovative and would take advantage of what we had already learned about children and television made it easy for me to participate.

An important fundamental decision was that *Blue's Clues* would be educational, and the pilot did not skimp on curriculum. The decision to allow the program to be overtly and clearly educational was a departure for Nickelodeon—indeed, for any commercial television network, for that matter. It should be kept in mind that, as a cable provider, there was no statutory requirement on Nickelodeon to provide educational or informative content. Viacom, Nickelodeon's owner, had not yet acquired CBS, which, as a broadcast network, would eventually face such a requirement. (*Blue's Clues*—which is currently run on CBS on Saturday mornings—helps the network meet its obligations under the Children's Television Act.) The decision to make *Blue's Clues* educational was partly the result of Santomero's passion to produce television that is beneficial to children, and partly the result of Nickelodeon research indicating that parents wanted preschool programs to be educational. For my part, I urged that the program have a curriculum, as I do for all programs I work with. Because the program was going to invite the audience to participate, it was a natural decision to make the core curriculum of *Blue's Clues* focus on social and cognitive problem solving, with the audience actively participating in solving the problems posed by the show.

In addition to my knowledge about child development, my research gave me five basic areas on which to focus advice for the development of

Blue's Clues. These areas are comprehensibility, the role of cues for attention, transitions and montage, attentional inertia, and audience participation. I do not see these areas as being in any sense independent of each other, and I do not believe they provide simple formulas for success. Rather, I believe that they should always be considered in the conception and execution of a program design. In the reality of program production, from casting to initial script ideas to final editing, innumerable decisions have to be made that are constrained by practical factors of time deadlines and cost. Even if considerations of the five areas, plus a general knowledge of child development, suggest particular courses of action, real constraints do not always allow them. The creators of *Blue's Clues* made hundreds of decisions, some with my advice, but usually without my direct input. I cannot take credit for any particular aspect of the design, but I can comment on those aspects of *Blue's Clues* that are consistent with my recommendations.

Before addressing the five principles of design based on my research, I would like to briefly comment on the use of child development knowledge. Understanding the cognitive, emotional, and social capabilities of preschoolers is helpful in every aspect of design. A specific example is the use of the notebook in *Blue's Clues* to record the clues. It is well known among child development specialists that preschoolers have poorly developed memory skills, and that much of memory development is based on learnable skills. One such skill involves the use of external mnemonic aids. I suggested that the notebook be included as a regular feature of the show in order to model the use of lists.

Comprehensibility

The most basic advice I give to producers of preschool programs is to ensure that the content is comprehensible to the audience. Ensuring comprehensibility is not easy. The core audience for *Blue's Clues,* and for most preschool programs, ranges in age from two to six years. Because there are enormous differences in the capacity for comprehension across this age range, great care concerning comprehensibility has to taken during script development, animation preparation, shooting, and postproduction editing. Many things in television that are transparently understandable to an adult can be confusing to young children. Ensuring comprehensibility, along with curriculum issues, is where a background in child development is most valuable.

Because television writers rarely have a background in child development, it is essential that individuals with that background be involved in script development from the earliest stages. Santomero has such a background, as do other members of the research and production staff of *Blue's Clues*. Understanding child development theory and research and having experience with preschool children is exceptionally useful in order to guess whether the audience will understand dialogue, a thinking game, or a recurring program element.

The design of *Blue's Clues* thinking games incorporates a layered approach that takes into account the varying capabilities of the audience. In Angela Santomero's words: "Our philosophy is based on scaffolding and that the layering is inherent in the script and design of each game. We have purposefully taken on this philosophy to go from easier to harder in the problem solving of each episode so that kids do not experience frustration but [rather] . . . will master concepts, feel success, and [be] empowered to try the more challenging concepts."[32] For example, in the pilot episode (which was redone to become the first telecast episode), a chick asked Steve to help him find his friend who was wearing a hat identical to his own. The complication was that the friend was among an array of chicks, all of whom were wearing similar hats. The problem for the audience was one of pattern matching, a challenge for preschoolers. This first problem was within the capabilities of three-year-olds. The second problem (another chick with a different hat looking for a friend) was harder, but within the capabilities of four-year-olds (albeit hard for three-year-olds), and the third problem was challenging but within the capabilities of five-year-olds. Consistent with my recommendation, the chicks modeled a technique for solving the problem. This idea of showing how problems can be solved became the standard for most problems presented in *Blue's Clues*.

If a problem is difficult for a child, one might think that comprehensibility would become an issue. The key is that all the three- to five-year-old viewers should understand the problem, although not necessarily the solution. The child voice-overs provide the solution after giving the preschool audience time to work on it. Consequently, the child is only temporarily frustrated by not having the answer. On the other hand, if the child does provide the answer, he or she feels like part of a larger, knowing, child audience when the voice-over provides the answer too. The layering provides an experience of success for most of the viewers, but also provides a challenge for most of the viewers. In this way, children are rarely frustrated or uncomprehending, and the child voices help keep attention high during these critical educational portions of the program. Moreover, episode repetition, discussed later, provides all viewers the opportunity to try the problems again.

Angela Santomero and I were both impressed by the role of formative research in helping to ensure the long-term success of *Sesame Street*. Such research, among other things, ensures comprehensibility. Rigorous testing with preschoolers of storyboards and animatics (crude video mock-ups of the final product) provides information of unparalleled usefulness concerning places in the script that confuse the audience or simply bore them. Thus, I strongly supported Angela's contention that the production budgets for *Blue's Clues* include funds for formative research. Alice Wilder, an Ed.D. in educational psychology, who also developed the full-fledged curriculum that guides script development, implemented the formative research for the series. Thanks to *Blue's Clues*, today most Nick Jr. original productions, such as *Dora the Explorer*, include formative research as part of the production process.

Cues for Attention

When children watch television, they may look at and away from the TV screen many times in the course of a half hour (about sixty-five times, on average).[33] Even high-attention programs receive many separate episodes of looking; the spaces between looks get shorter, and even while the looks get longer, there are still many looks away from the screen. That means that at any given point in the program, a significant portion of the audience may be inattentive. In a purely entertainment program, the periods of inattention do not matter, as long as the audience is generally attentive and likes the show. In an educational program like *Blue's Clues*, on the other hand, there are points where audience attention is critical to learning and participation. Based in part on my research indicating the importance of auditory cues for attention, the producers of *Blue's Clues* carefully insert auditory signatures and stings to draw audience attention to the program at critical junctures for learning.

Recall that one auditory feature reliably predicts reduced looking at TV: adult male voices. That said, the original host of *Blue's Clues*, Steve, is an adult male (recently replaced by another adult male, Joe). Both Steve and Joe have been extremely popular with their audience, and there is no indication that children attend less to them than to other parts of the program. The creators of *Blue's Clues* auditioned hundreds of actors for these parts and simply chose the best actors for the role, actors who could mime as demanded by the mixed live-action and animated format. They both happened to be adult males.

Three factors help Steve and Joe overcome children's attentional bias against men. One is that they are energetic in a characteristically childlike manner. During the pilot testing, I recall, many children referred to Steve as "that kid"; only a few referred to him as "that man." Second, by breaking the fourth wall and talking directly to the audience, they form a direct relationship with the audience like Mister Rogers, another adult male popular with many young children. Third, they are rarely just talking heads; they are always doing something, even if it is just "actor's business." Children are exceptionally attentive to visual action; talking heads lose attention. Most talking heads on television are men, but the men on *Blue's Clues* are active and form a relationship with the audience. Once that relationship is formed, their voices actually become cues for attention rather than inattention. In other words, it is not qualities inherent to male voices but rather style of presentation that ultimately determines child attention.

Transitions and Montage

Although preschoolers can understand standard video transitions, they may fail to do so, especially when the transitions involve active inferences about time, space, implied events, and character perspective. In addition, the process of working out the nature of a transition presumably places a cognitive burden on the child, occupying intellectual resources that could be devoted to understanding the content. Bearing these facts in mind, any preschool show should be produced with the realization that transitions are likely to confuse at least some in the audience.

Blue's Clues deals with this problem by minimizing the number of transitions that require inference. One way to do this is by placing all the action in a limited number of spaces, with transitions occurring only between these spaces. The primary space is the host's house along with the front and backyards. Transitions within the house are generally done continuously. That is, the host is shown moving (in actuality, miming movement) through different spaces within the house, without the use of cuts. Transitions to the yards may be accompanied by a cut, but done in such a way that the host moves to and through the door, with the shot following the cut showing the movement continuing as the host enters the yard. The biggest transition occurs when the host "skidoos" and jumps into a picture or a book. He does this in a clearly fantastic way with plenty of warning to the audience that the transition is coming. The skidoo continues and ends in the new environment. The *Blue's Clues* audience clearly understands this transition (and loves it). In the mail portion of the program, there is a transition to a live-action sequence in which children talk about a favorite activity connected to the theme of the episode. This transition is accomplished by showing the host holding the letter with the live-action sequence initially limited to the frame of the letter. The camera appears to zoom in on the letter, accompanied by a cut to the live-action sequence itself.

Santomero commented on two other rules developed for the production of *Blue's Clues*: "Two of our Cardinal rules are that we never cut to a place we've never been before in that episode, and if we are going to make a cut we always have dialogue transitions."[34] A dialogue transition involves the host or other character stating clearly, both before and after the transition, "where" or "when" it is to occur. In sum, when a transition requires a major inference requiring a change in frame of reference, *Blue's Clues* gives plenty of cues that the change is coming and gives the audience time and information necessary to process the change.

Attentional Inertia

While attentional inertia was probably not much on the *Blue's Clues* creators' minds, it is frequently on mine when I provide advice on program development. When viewers' attention has been continuously maintained for at least fifteen seconds, they become more deeply engaged, are less likely to be distracted away from the program, and are more likely to remember the content. This works against an apparently natural tendency of child viewers to frequently look away from the TV, perhaps with an unconscious desire to monitor the viewing environment. If, during such a look away, a viewer becomes engaged in an alternative activity, such as playing with toys, even auditory attention is withdrawn from the program, at least at the level of deciphering word and sentence meaning. With an educational program such as *Blue's Clues*, therefore, it is important to keep the audience engaged.

The challenging nature of *Blue's Clues* problem solving demands a deeply engaged audience. If a child fails to understand the problem, the nature of the solution, or the answer to the problem, he or she tends to look away from the TV due to the failure of comprehension. Younger children may look away during varied repetitions of the problem at a more challenging level. If their attention can be kept during these periods, it is likely that the children will expend greater effort in understanding the problem, the modeled solution strategy, and the answer. It is thus important to spend some time building up to the problem with an attention-engaging narrative in which the problem is not only explained, but its solution also becomes emotionally fulfilling, as when viewers help a mildly distressed character (help me find my friend, help me get to my mother, and so on). If attention is sporadic prior to the problem, it may readily be lost during the problem. If attention is engaged prior to the problem, it will likely be maintained during the problem.

Audience Participation

For the most part, the role of audience participation in *Blue's Clues* is designed to get viewers to actively participate in educational problem solving. (Although there are some noneducational, purely fun sequences, as when Blue hides from the host and the audience tells the host where she is or points to the screen.) A key component of preschool audience participation is, first of all, that the children be explicitly invited to participate. The host frequently looks directly into the camera and asks: "Will you help?" A second key component is that the audience needs to know what they are supposed to do to help. The host or another character usually supplies that information, and the child voice-overs explicitly model verbal participation. Finally, and this is crucial, the program must give children sufficient time to respond. This latter point is often difficult for a television director to understand, given the general tendency in the television industry to associate rapid pace with high production value. From an adult perspective, giving children time to respond produces an overly slow program pace. This can confuse parents, as well as TV professionals. During pilot testing, while some parents applauded the pace, others were puzzled and were certain that their children would not like the show because it would be too boring. The children, on the other hand, were wildly enthusiastic. The pilot, incidentally, was called "Blue Prints," but during the testing of the pilot, the children almost universally called the show *Blue's Clues.* Changing the name was a no-brainer.

Other Issues and Later Research

Episode Repetition

Once it became clear that the series would be picked up by Nickelodeon for a late summer premiere, September 9, 1996, the producers had to decide how to schedule the few episodes that would be completed by that time. I had been showing the pilot to my daughter, at about the time of her fourth birthday, as well as to other preschool acquaintances. My daughter enthusiastically watched the show thirteen times over the space of a couple of weeks, and watched it with friends or cousins another four times. Only after seventeen viewings did she stop asking to see it again. The producers had had similar experiences with children of their own acquaintance, although none had actually kept count of viewings. In a quick huddle that occurred during the pilot testing, Angela Santomero and I agreed that it would make sense to repeat the episodes daily for a week at a time. Besides our anecdotal observations that preschoolers would view repeatedly, we also reasoned that comprehension, especially in younger viewers, would be improved, and that problem-solving skills taught in the episodes would be reinforced. Angela also thought that the children would gain a sense of empowerment by knowing the answers to the problems after a week of viewing.

When Nickelodeon agreed to the repetition premiere strategy, there was no published research on repeated viewing of television episodes (Alice Wilder did some preliminary work that suggested the premiere strategy would work), although there was research on repeated reading of storybooks indicating that children's comprehension and appreciation of the books broadens and deepens.[35] Santomero, Wilder, and I argued that we should study the issue, and we convinced Nickelodeon to fund a formal experiment. In the summer of 1996, before *Blue's Clues* premiered, we did a repeated viewing experiment. At preschools, we showed three- to five-year-old children the first episode either one time or on five consecutive days. We videotaped the children as they viewed individually (they had coloring books and blocks to play with), and subsequently tested comprehension and problem solving. We coded the videotapes of the children for looking at the TV and for audience participation.

The results were clear, striking, and to us, very interesting.[36] Looking remained nearly constant across the five repetitions; only five-year-old boys showed a slight drop in attention after about three repetitions. Audience participation, on the other hand, greatly increased with repetition, especially for the problem-solving portions of the episode. As children learned how to solve the problems they would shout out the answers, talk to Steve, point to the screen, jump up with excitement, and so on. Not only did the children become more enthusiastic with repetition, but their comprehension and problem solving greatly improved. After five viewings, the children became adept at solving problems of the same type but which had not actually been shown in the episode.

The repetition strategy clearly worked during the first year of *Blue's Clues*, and it was subsequently adopted for the premiere of Nickelodeon's *Dora the Explorer* in 2000. In an internal and unpublished study of repetition of *Dora*, the Dora research group found almost identical effects of repetition as those we found for *Blue*. Analyses of Nielsen ratings for both shows indicated that there was no systematic change in audience size related to the number of repetitions during the first week an episode appeared.

Experience with the Series and the Nature of Audience Participation

More than any previous television program, *Blue's Clues* was designed to encourage the audience to be active viewers as well as active problem solvers. The most visible aspect of active viewing is audience participation. While it was clear that audience participation increases with episode repetition, we wondered about the impact of experience with the series as a whole. Does *Blue's Clues* change the way children watch television? One question was whether experienced viewers would interact more with a new episode of *Blue's Clues* than would inexperienced viewers. If *Blue's Clues* viewers have learned that they can interact with Steve and the other characters, rather than with a particular episode, then they should be more likely to interact with a new episode than children of the same age who had no prior experience with the program.

As part of research evaluating the cognitive and emotional impact of *Blue's Clues*, Jennings Bryant and his colleagues at the University of Alabama identified preschool children in several towns around the country who had not seen the program. The children lived in towns without cable or in towns where Nickelodeon was not provided as part of basic cable service. We showed an episode of *Blue's Clues* that had not yet been telecast to these children as well as to demographically matched children who were regular viewers of *Blue's Clues*. After videotaping them (in their homes) as they viewed the program, we tested the children for their comprehension of the program. We found that the regular viewers interacted more with the new episode than did the viewers who had never seen the program before. The regular viewers had clearly learned that they could interact with Steve, Blue, and the other characters even when the episode was new.[37]

In a second experiment, we showed experienced and inexperienced viewers an episode of an entirely different series, *Big Bag,* produced by Sesame Workshop, and shown on the Cartoon Network. *Big Bag* is a curriculum-based preschool program that also invites interaction from the audience. In our study, none of the children had ever seen *Big Bag* previously. The question was whether experienced *Blue's Clues* viewers would interact more with *Big Bag* than viewers who had not previously seen *Blue's Clues*. The answer was yes. Experience with *Blue's Clues* not only teaches children that they can interact with particular characters, but it teaches them that they can also interact with television programs more generally. *Blue's Clues* has apparently changed the way preschool children watch television.[38]

From the repetition and experience studies, we have gotten some insights into the nature of preschool audience participation. In the repetition study, we found that the increase in audience participation with episode repetition occurred primarily in the educational problem-solving portions of the show. Our impression was that as the children became more adept at solving the problems, or simply knew the correct answers from earlier viewings, they felt empowered to "help" Steve. This finding was reinforced by the experience study with a new episode of *Blue's Clues*. The experienced viewers were more interactive than inexperienced viewers primarily during recurrent format portions of the program. These are portions of the program that are similar across all episodes (for example, Steve explains the clues game and sings the clues song). From the detailed pattern of results of the studies, we have come to believe that audience participation occurs not only when the audience is invited to participate, but also when the audience clearly knows what it is supposed to do. When children are exposed to new problem-solving content in *Blue's Clues* they look intently and do not interact a great deal; when they have learned how to solve the problems, interaction greatly increases. When children are exposed to familiar content, as in recurrent format portions of the show, they interact a lot. Audience participation reflects what children have learned. It is not part of the learning process itself, but it may well increase preschoolers' motivation to learn.

Closing Comments

Long ago a student asked me a question about children's attention to television. I answered with a guess, a guess that assumed that children's attention was passively controlled by television's formal features. Thirty years later, I know that my answer was mostly wrong. Children are remarkably selective in their attention to television and that selectivity is in the service of their active, curious intellects. Once I realized that children are not passive victims of television, but that they can be active intellectual participants in television, my view of the potential of television to benefit children profoundly changed. The creators of *Blue's Clues* and the creators of Nick Jr. also had that realization. Television for children, and children as viewers of television, will never be the same.

NOTES

1. Marie Winn, *The Plug-In Drug* (New York: Viking Press, 1977).
2. Gerry Mander, *Four Arguments for the Elimination of Television* (New York: William Morrow, 1978).
3. Jane Healy, *Endangered Minds: Why Our Children Can't Think* (New York: Simon & Schuster, 1990), 218–233.
4. Jerome L. Singer, "The Power and Limitations of Television: A Cognitive-Affective Analysis," in Percy H. Tannenbaum and Robert Abeles, eds., *The Entertainment Functions of Television* (Hillsdale, N.J.: Erlbaum, 1980), 31–65.
5. Kate Moody, *Growing Up on Television: The TV Effect* (New York: Times Books, 1980); Thom Hartmann, *Thom Hartmann's Complete Guide to ADHD* (Grass Valley, Calif.: Underwood Books, 2000).
6. Healy, 1990, 219.
7. Robert M. Liebert, John M. Neale, and Emily S. Davidson, *The Early Window: Effects of Television on Children and Youth* (New York: Pergamon Press, 1973.).

8. Daniel R. Anderson and Stephen R. Levin, "Young Children's Attention to *Sesame Street," Child Development,* 47 (1976), 806–811; Linda F. Alwitt, Daniel R. Anderson, Elizabeth P. Lorch, and Stephen R. Levin, "Preschool Children's Visual Attention to Attributes of Television," *Human Communication Research,* 7 (1980), 52–67.

9. Anderson and Levin, 1976, ibid.

10. Alwitt et al., 1980, ibid.

11. Daniel R. Anderson, Elizabeth P. Lorch, Patricia A. Collins, Diane E. Field, and John F. Nathan, "Television Viewing at Home: Age Trends in Visual Attention and Time with TV," *Child Development,* 57 (1986), 1024–1033; Kelly L. Schmitt, Daniel R. Anderson, and Patricia A. Collins, "Form and Content: Looking at Visual Features of Television," *Developmental Psychology,* 35 (1999), 1156–1167.

12. Elizabeth P. Lorch, Daniel R. Anderson, and Stephen R. Levin, "The Relationship of Visual Attention and Comprehension of Television by Preschool Children," *Child Development,* 50 (1979), 722–727.

13. Daniel R. Anderson, Elizabeth P. Lorch, Diane E. Field, and Jeanne Sanders, "The Effect of Television Program Comprehensibility on Preschool Children's Visual Attention to Television," *Child Development,* 52 (1981), 151–157.

14. Ibid.

15. Diane E. Field and Daniel R. Anderson, "Instruction and Modality Effects on Children's Television Comprehension and Attention," *Journal of Educational Psychology,* 77 (1985), 91–100.

16. Lorch et al., 1979, ibid.; Field and Anderson, 1985, ibid.

17. John J. Burns and Daniel R. Anderson, "Attentional Inertia and Recognition Memory in Adult Television Viewing," *Communication Research,* 20 (1993), 777–799.

18. Schmitt et al., 1999, ibid.

19. Anderson and Levin, 1976, ibid.; Alwitt et al., 1980, ibid.; Schmitt et al., 1999, ibid.

20. John E. Richards and K. Cronise, "Extended Visual Fixation in the Early Preschool Years: Look Duration, Heart Rate Changes, and Attentional Inertia," *Child Development,* 68 (2000), 602–620.

21. See, among others, K. L. Schmitt, D. R. Anderson, and P. A. Collins, "Form and Content: Looking at Visual Features of Television," *Developmental Psychology,* 35 (1999), 1156–1167; and D. R. Anderson and R. Smith, "Young Children's Television Viewing: The Problem of Cognitive Continuity," in F. Morrison, C. Lord, and D. Keating, eds., *Advances in Applied Developmental Psychology* (New York: Academic Press, 1984), 116–165.

22. Daniel R. Anderson, Katherine V. Fite, Nicole Petrovich, and Joy Hirsch, "Cortical Activation during Comprehension of Visual Action Sequences: An

fMRI Study," unpublished manuscript, 2000, University of Massachusetts, Amherst, Massachusetts.

23. Robin N. Smith, Daniel R. Anderson, and Catherine Fischer, "Young Children's Comprehension of Montage," *Child Development,* 56 (1985), 962–971.

24. Ibid.

25. Alwitt et al., 1980, ibid.

26. Daniel R. Anderson and Elizabeth P. Lorch, "Looking at Television: Action or Reaction?" In Jennings Bryant and Daniel R. Anderson, eds., *Children's Understanding of TV: Research on Attention and Comprehension* (New York: Academic Press, 1983), 1–34.

27. Daniel R. Anderson, Linda F. Alwitt, Elizabeth P. Lorch, and Stephen R. Levin, "Watching Children Watch Television," in Gordon Hale and Michael Lewis, eds., *Attention and Cognitive Development* (New York: Plenum, 1979), 331–362.

28. John E. Richards and K. Gibson, "Extended Visual Fixation in Young Infants: Fixation Distributions, Heart Rate Changes, and Attention," *Child Development,* 68 (1997), 1041–1056; Daniel R. Anderson, Hyewon P. Choi, and Elizabeth P. Lorch, "Attentional Inertia Reduces Distractibility During Young Children's Television Viewing," *Child Development,* 58 (1987), 798–806; John J. Burns and Daniel R. Anderson, "Attentional Inertia and Recognition Memory in Adult Television Viewing," *Communication Research,* 20 (1993), 777–799.

29. Alison Alexander, Maureen Ryan, and P. Munoz, "Creating a Learning Context: Investigations on the Interactions of Siblings during Television Viewing," *Critical Studies in Mass Communication,* 1 (1984), 345–364.

30. Daniel R. Anderson, Elizabeth P. Lorch, Robin N. Smith, Rex Bradford, and Stephen R. Levin, "The Effects of Peer Presence on Preschool Children's Television Viewing Behavior," *Developmental Psychology,* 17 (1981), 446–453.

31. Daniel R. Anderson, Aletha C. Huston, Kelly L. Schmitt, Deborah L. Linebarger, and John C. Wright, "Early Childhood Television Viewing and Adolescent Behavior," *Monographs of the Society for Research in Child Development,* 68 (1, 2001), Serial No. 264, 1–143.

32. Angela Santomero, personal communication, November 11, 2002.

33. Adults look away from the screen at a similar rate, although they tend to be completely unaware of it. See John J. Burns and Daniel R. Anderson, 1993, ibid.

34. Santomero, 2002, ibid.

35. M. Martinez and N. Roser, "Read It Again: The Value of Repeated Readings during Storytime," *The Reading Teacher,* 38 (1985), 780–786.

36. Alisha M. Crawley, Daniel R. Anderson, Alice Wilder, Marsha Williams, and Angela Santomero, "Effects of Repeated Exposures to a Single Episode of

the Television Program *Blue's Clues* on the Viewing Behaviors and Comprehension of Preschool Children," *Journal of Educational Psychology,* 91 (1999), 630–637.

37. Alisha M. Crawley, Daniel R. Anderson, Angela Santomero, Alice Wilder, Marsha Williams, Marie K. Evans, and Jennings Bryant, "Do Children Learn How to Watch Television? The Impact of Extensive Experience with *Blue's Clues* on Preschool Children's Television Viewing Behavior," *Journal of Communication,* 52 (2002), 264–280.

38. Ibid.

About the Contributors

DANIEL R. ANDERSON is professor of psychology at the University of Massachusetts at Amherst. He has published numerous research articles concerning children's use of television and the impact of television on intellectual and social development. Professor Anderson has consulted extensively with television networks and production companies concerning the development of educational television programs including *Sesame Street, Gullah Gullah Island, Blue's Clues, Bear in the Big Blue House,* and *Dora the Explorer.*

SARAH BANET-WEISER is an assistant professor at the Annenberg School for Communication at the University of Southern California. She is the author of *The Most Beautiful Girl in the World: Beauty Pageants and National Identity,* and is currently working on a manuscript that explores the social history of Nickelodeon.

HEATHER HENDERSHOT is an associate professor of media studies at Queens College, City University of New York. She is the author of *Saturday Morning Censors: Television Regulation before the V-Chip* and *Shaking the World for Jesus: Media and Conservative Evangelical Culture.*

HENRY JENKINS is the director of the comparative media studies program at MIT. He is the author/editor of nine books, including *The Children's Culture Reader, Hop on Pop: The Politics and Pleasures of Popular Culture, Rethinking Media Change: The Aesthetics of Transition,* and *Democracy and New Media.* He is the primary investigator for the Games to Teach Project and writes regularly on the social and cultural impact of media for *Technology Review.*

MARK LANGER is associate professor of film studies in the School for Studies in Art and Culture at Carleton University in Ottawa, and has been a guest curator of animation retrospectives for a number of museums, archives, and festivals. His work has appeared in such journals as *Screen, Cinema Journal, Art History, Animation Journal,* and *Wide Angle.*

VICKI MAYER is assistant professor of communication at Tulane University. She is the author of a book about Mexican American media production, *Producing Dreams, Consuming Youth.*

SUSAN MURRAY is an assistant professor of culture and communication at New York University. Her work has appeared in *Television & New Media* and *Cinema Journal* and in numerous anthologies. She is a coeditor (with Laurie Ouellette) of *Reality TV: Remaking Television Culture.*

NORMA PECORA is associate professor in the School of Telecommunications at Ohio University. She is the author of *The Business of Children's Entertainment* and coeditor, with Sharon Mazzarella, of *Growing Up Girls.* With John Murray and Ellen Wartella, she is currently working on *50 Years of Research on Children and Television.* Pecora is also coeditor of the *Journal of Popular Communications.*

KEVIN S. SANDLER is an assistant professor of media industries at the University of Arizona. He has published widely on popular animation and is the editor of *Reading the Rabbit: Explorations in Warner Bros. Animation* and *Titanic: Anatomy of a Blockbuster.* His forthcoming book is *The Naked Truth: Why Hollywood Does Not Make NC-17 Films.*

ELLEN SEITER is professor of critical studies in the School of Cinema-Television, University of Southern California, where she teaches television studies. She specializes in the study of children and the media and is the author of *Television and New Media Audiences* and *Sold Separately: Children and Parents in Consumer Culture,* and coeditor of *Remote Control: Television, Audiences and Cultural Power.*

LINDA SIMENSKY is senior director of children's programming for PBS. Prior to joining PBS, she was senior vice president of original animation for Cartoon Network. Simensky worked at Nickelodeon from 1986 through 1995. While at Nickelodeon, she served as director of the animation department, where she oversaw animation development for Nick-toons. Simensky is the past president of ASIFA-East (the International Society of Animation) and was the founder of the New York chapter of Women in Animation. She is also on the editorial board of *Animation Journal.*

MIMI SWARTZ is the author of *Power Failure,* a chronicle of the fall of Enron. An executive editor of *Texas Monthly,* she has been a staff writer at the *New Yorker,* and her work has appeared in *Vanity Fair,* the *New York Times, Esquire,* and many other national publications.

Index

ABC (television network), 19, 24, 34, 37, 127
Action for Children's Television, 20, 23, 145
adult actors enacting child characters, 189–90
adult viewers: animation and, 89, 101–2; children's shows popular among, 186; content intended only for, 186–87, 191; Nickelodeon as satisfying, 2–3; and nostalgia for childhood, 81–82; what draws them to kids' shows, 186. *See also* age roles, transgression of; *SpongeBob SquarePants*, intergenerational appeal of
adult-child figures, 188–89. *See also* man-child figures on children's television
adults and children, boundary between the worlds of, 226
Adventures of Jimmy Neutron: Boy Genius, The (TV series and film), 10, 38–39
Adventures of Pete and Pete, The (TV series), 63, 89
Adventures of the Little Koala (TV series), 47, 62
Adventures of the Little Prince (TV series), 31, 47
advertising, 23, 25, 32, 37, 38, 51, 76, 135, 136, 145, 185; fictitious (*Ren & Stimpy*), 169–70
Aeon Flux, 96
African American audience, 126
African American characters, 128. *See also* racial and ethnic diversity
Against the Odds (TV series), 22, 135, 138
age roles, transgression of, 189–93, 204
age-specific dayparts, programming for kids in, 62
Ahlbum, Joey, 91, 95, 96
AIDS special (*Nick News*), 144
All in the Family (TV series), 74
All That (TV series), 54
Amanda Show, The (TV series), 54
America Goes Bananas (TV series), 135
American Express, 21
Anderson, Benedict, 218

Angelica (*Rugrats*), 108–13, 115–19, 190; and "You dumb babies!" trademark line, 109, 115–16
Angelica Knows Best (video), 109
Angelica the Divine (video), 109
Angry Beavers, The (TV series), 58
Angus, Ian, 175n. 11
Animaniacs (TV series), 123, 186
animation, 30–34, 39; history of, 113–14, 157–59, 162–64; and Nickelodeon's success, 51; rising popularity among adults, 89; special appeal of, 11. *See also* Nicktoons
animation production: finances, 93–94; in 1930s–1940s *vs.* 1980s, 92; and original characters, 93; pilot process, 96–106
animatophiles and animatophilia, 50, 159–61, 164–65, 167, 169–71, 174, 176n. 15
Animorphs (TV series), 37
Ansolabehere, Joe, 116
AOL Time Warner, 66n. 21
Archies, The (TV series), 166
Arts Network, 139
As Told by Ginger (TV series), 54
Ascheim, Tom, 62, 67n. 40, 94
attention, cues for, 258–59. *See also* television viewing
attentional bias against men, 259. *See also* male *vs.* female voices
attentional inertia, 253–54
audience participation, overt, 254–55
Austin, Joe, 213
Austin Powers (film), 76
Avery, Tex, 162, 163

Bagge, Peter, 170
Bakshi, Ralph, 90, 114, 166
Banana Splits, The (TV series), 165–66
"Band Geeks" (*SpongeBob SquarePants* episode), 196
Barbera, Joe, 163
Barney and Friends (TV series), 150, 158, 191
Bartlett, Craig, 115, 116
Barzilay, Jonathan, 127

273